The PRO GOLF SCOUTING REPORT

The PRO GOLF SCOUTING REPORT

by

John Gordon

Warwick Publishing
Toronto Los Angeles

ISBN 1-894020-19-7

Published by:
Warwick Publishing Inc., 388 King Street West, Toronto, Ontario M5V 1K2
Warwick Publishing Inc., 1424 N. Highland Avenue, Los Angeles, CA 90027

Distributed by:
Firefly Books Ltd., 3680 Victoria Park Avenue, Willowdale, Ontario M2H 3K1

Front cover photos: Don Vickery
Design: Mercer Digital/Diane Farenick
Editorial Services: Melinda Tate

[redacted]

Printed and bound in Canada

TABLE OF CONTENTS

Acknowledgments

First off the tee should be Jim Williamson and Nick Pitt of Warwick Communications Group, who had the temerity to suggest this project and the good judgment to ask me to do it.

The players themselves should receive substantial credit for their level of expertise at an extremely difficult game and for revealing their human frailties to the public.

The communications departments of the PGA TOUR and Senior PGA TOUR were resourceful. The anonymous authors of the tours' media guides deserve mention for pumping out, under incredible deadline pressure, excellent work. Fellow golf writers at various events around the world gleaned quotes and anecdotes that reappear here.

As always, my family — wife and editor Leslie, son Will and daughters Allie and Maggie — are up for sainthood for putting up with that madman in the attic ... again.

And we salute Jim Fitchette, the late, great Rex Revere who concocted the *Tour de Farce Media Guide* years ago, a talent and a publication to which we can only aspire.

INTRODUCTION

So every professional golfer is a robot, a clone, devoid of personality, programmed to hit a golf ball again and again while never revealing one iota of individuality? We beg to differ.

In the following pages, we've combined official facts and figures with anecdotes, quotes and often-irreverent personal observations. The end result is kind of an illicit union between the official media guides used by every golf writer and *People* magazine. Golf is becoming a global obsession and the best players in the world are household names. The aim of *The 1998 Pro Golf Scouting Report* is to provide pro golf fans with a peek at the person behind the player.

We hope you enjoy this compendium of facts, figures, insight and criticism, not all of it constructive (almost none of it, really). The goal was to humanize the best golfers in the world — young, older, men, women — to enhance your enjoyment of watching them in person or on television.

If you want to find out more about these players and others, you can order official media guides from the respective tours. The PGA TOUR, LPGA and Senior PGA TOUR guides are available by calling 904-285-3700 or check out their Website, www.PGATOUR.com. The LPGA version is available by calling 1-800-766-2781 (www.LPGA.com).

If you have Internet access, you can hit these and dozens of other sites, including those of individual players. The best source for this information is the book, *Golf on the Web,* by John Barton and Hunki Yun (MIS:Press, 1997).

Speaking of the Internet, if you have suggestions for the 1999 edition of *The Pro Golf Scouting Report,* you can contact the author via e-mail at gorgroup@csolve.net.

Statistics, The Suicide Watch and Other Stuff

What you have here, based on 1997 final official earnings, are the players you hear about every day, the ones you want to know more about: the top 70 PGA TOUR money winners, the top 31 exempt players from the Senior PGA TOUR and the leading 30 LPGA players. You will notice two different formats: a detailed description for the higher-profile players and a more general sketch of the less-prominent ones.

Each tour publishes its statistics in a slightly different manner. For you people with the calculators and the six pens in a pocket protector, here's a quick description of the PGA TOUR method:

Driving Leaders (Distance): Divide the total distance off the tee by the number of drives.

Driving Accuracy: The percentage of possible fairways actually hit.

Greens in Regulation (GIR): Hitting the green in one shot on a par 3, two shots on a par 4 or three shots on a par 5. Percentage of greens hit based on number of holes played.

Putting Leaders: Dividing the number of GIR putts by the number of greens hit.

Eagle Leaders: Dividing the number of holes by the number of eagles.

Birdie Leaders: Dividing the number of holes by the number of birdies.

Sand Saves: Percentage of the times a player got up and down out of a bunker; i.e., got out of a greenside bunker and used one putt to finish the hole.

Total Driving: Average rank from Driving Leaders and Driving Accuracy.

All Around: Total rank from all the above.

Money Leaders: What do you think?

Par breakers: Percentage of total holes on which the player broke par.

Putts Per Round: Total number of putts divided by the number of rounds.

Birdie Conversion Percentage: The number of greens hit divided by the number of birdies.

Ball Striking: Total Driving rank plus GIR rank.

Scrambling: Percentage of making par or better after missing the green in regulation.

Bounce Back: Percentage of making birdie or better after posting a bogey or worse.

The Senior TOUR is essentially the same. One major difference between the men's and women's tours is that the LPGA gives you numbers and rankings — no percentages.

The Suicide Watch

We stumbled upon this when we began missing some familiar names. And if you find the game frustrating, how about some sympathy for these descendants of Job.

Mark Brooks: Third on the PGA TOUR money list in 1996

after winning three times that year, including the PGA Championship. In 1997, 108th on the money list.

Steve Stricker: Fourth on the PGA TOUR after 1996 with two victories; 130th after the '97 season.

Corey Pavin: No. 1 on the PGA TOUR list in 1991, fourth in 1995 after winning twice, including the U.S. Open; 169th after '97. (Thank goodness he got a 10-year exemption for winning the Open.)

Not that we're suggesting there's any connection, but these guys all went after the big endorsement deals after their big years. We hope the money was worth the frustration.

And for golf in a nutshell, here's **Chip Beck,** the guy who shot 59 at a PGA TOUR sanctioned event in 1991. He finished 267th on the '97 money list, winning just over 10 grand in 32 tries.

Our 1997 futility award, however, goes to veteran **John Mahaffey,** winner of 10 PGA TOUR events, who was 42nd on the 1990 list. In 1997, he earned $2,850 in 21 starts, an average of about $135 per event, and finishing 333rd.

And you think you have a tough job.

PGA TOUR

Billy Andrade

Don't underestimate Billy Andrade. Here's a guy who, at 5'8", made Rhode Island's all-state high school basketball team. Here's a guy who, ranked 104th in driving, won the long-drive event at the 1997 Skills Competition over guys like John Daly and Paul Stankowski with a 320-yard aberration. (During the season, he spanked one 358 at a tournament.) Speaking of driving, he loves to cruise the nation's highways at warp speed: "I once got a [speeding] ticket on my way to pay a [speeding] ticket." Both he and buddy Brad Faxon (also from Rhode Island) appeared in Woody Harrelson's bowling movie *Kingpin* ... we bet it seemed like a good idea at the time.

Despite his light-hearted persona, he's not play-acting at being a pro golfer. He set the TOUR on its ear in 1991, when he won the Kemper Open and the Buick Classic back to back. Last season's solid play included a fifth at The Players Championship, which helped move him up 15 spots on the final money list to No. 31. We think '98 could be a breakthrough year for wee Billy.

The Man

William Thomas Andrade, 5'8", 155 lbs. Born Jan. 25, 1964, in Fall River, MA. Resides Bristol, RI, and Atlanta, GA. Wife, Jody; son, Cameron James; daughter, Lelia Grace. Attended Wake Forest University. Enjoys all sports. Turned pro in 1987 and joined the TOUR in 1988.

Off the Tee

Not much to write home about here: 104th in driving distance with a 266.5 yard average and 143rd in accuracy. He birdied 63 of the 405 par-3 holes he played, ranking him 22nd, and birdied 40% of the par-5s (38th). The par 4s hurt him: making only 163 birds out of 1,042 holes left him 67th.

Hitting the Green.

Although Andrade hit exactly two out of every three greens he aimed at, that still left him 54th among his peers.

In Trouble

Andrade managed to get up and down out of the sand 88 times out of 158 tries, 70th best on TOUR with a 55.7% average.

Flatstick Facts

Almost 29 putts per round translate into 58th-best on TOUR, but his 1.755 average of putts per green hit in regulation ranked him 14th overall.

The Scorer's Tent

Tough little competitor who shows flashes of brilliance but lacks the closing punch. His round-by-round scoring stats: 23rd before the cut, 11th after the third round, but a nauseating 153rd in the final round. Thank God those aren't reversed or he'd be trying out for extra parts in all of Woody's movies. He can make lots of birdies despite his lack of length, but consistency eludes him.

Stuart Appleby

Let's call this kid the "Big Cohuna." No, our spelling isn't off; that's the name of the town where he was born Down Under. That's also where he hit golf shots from one field to another as he was doing chores on his parents' dairy farm and where he risked life and limb as an Australian Rules Football player. (That's right up there with "javelin catcher" as far as risky sports go, in our humble opinion.)

After winning four events on the Australian PGA Tour's Foundation Tour in 1994, Appleby made the leap to the NIKE TOUR in '95, finishing fifth on the money list. That qualified him for the big TOUR in '96, but he couldn't crack the top 125 and returned to Q School. He didn't make the same mistake in '97, becoming the first Q School grad to earn more than $1 million the following year ($1,003,356, 18th). He won the Honda Classic and posted four other top-10 finishes, including runner-up honors behind Phil Mickelson at both Bay Hill and the Sprint International. That financial windfall meant a lifestyle change, we're sure, not the least of which is that his wife no longer caddies for him.

The Man

Stuart Appleby, 6'1", 185 lbs. Born Cohuna, Australia, May 1, 1971. Resides Orlando, FL. Wife, Renay. Enjoys action sports and motor racing. Turned pro in 1992 and joined TOUR in 1996.

Off the Tee

A strapping lad who can hammer a tee shot — his longest drive was 361 yards, 11th longest of the season on TOUR. His average was 278.4 and he hit 68.5% of fairways (98th).

Hitting the Green

They must have bigger greens in Oz: Appleby ranked 127th in GIR (63.6%). His scoring average was 70.37 (33rd) and he ranked fifth in par-5 birdie leaders (46.5%).

In Trouble

Only 53rd in the scrambling category (60.7%), he was a wizard out of bunkers, getting up and down 64.2% of the time, fifth best on TOUR.

Flatstick Facts

A little more time spent on the practice green would make Appleby "Oz-some." The rest of his game is good and getting better, but he was 131st in putting on greens hit in regulation (1.797) and needed 29.15 total putts per average round (81st).

The Scorer's Tent

As a former Aussie Rules footballer, Appleby heads the unofficial committee pushing for full body contact during all TOUR events. Seriously, he has been a winner at every level at which he's competed, body contact or not. He got a taste of the TOUR winner's circle in '97 and all that entails. He's hungry for more and he should get it, providing he can buff up the suspect aspects of his overall game: iron play and putting. Turns 27 this season and will not be making a return trip to the minors, guaranteed.

Phil Blackmar

No matter where Phil Blackmar finishes on the money list, he will always be a big man on the PGA TOUR. Make that the biggest man on the PGA TOUR. At 6'7" and 245 pounds, Blackmar looks more like an NFL offensive lineman or NBA power forward than a pro golfer. Or maybe he looks like just who he is ... a down-to-earth good old boy who used to drive a Coke truck. As a matter of fact, he also used to audit banks and repair golf clubs and sprinklers prior to making it on TOUR.

After an abysmal 1994 season (missed 25 of 30 cuts, 213th on the money list with $28,159), he was considering a return to one of those jobs. "But," he says with the resigned attitude of a father with four kids to put through college, "I couldn't come up with anything that would get me the money I need." So he returned to Qualifying School and rededicated himself.

It worked. In 1995 he had five top 25s and finished with $154,801 (121st) and in 1996 he edged up to $229,274 (96th). Last season ($642,400, 32nd) was his best finish since 1985 when he was 28th. Not surprisingly, he posted victories in both years — the '97 Shell Houston Open and the 1985 Greater Hartford Open. But it had been a long dry spell since his last win, the 1988 Provident Classic. All three came in playoffs.

The Man

Philip Arnold Blackmar, 6'7", 245 lbs. Born San Diego, CA, Sept. 22, 1957. Resides Corpus Christi, TX, plays out of Kings College CC. Wife, Carol; daughters, Kristin Ashley and Kelli Michele; sons, Philip James and Mark Fredrik. Attended University of Texas. Enjoys fishing. Turned pro in 1980; Q School in 1984 and 1994.

Off the Tee

Not surprisingly, Blackmar was among the longer drivers on TOUR at 274.3 yards (40th) but 192nd in accuracy (57.9%).

Hitting the Green

He found the green in regulation a paltry 62.2% of the time (158th) but was third overall in birdie conversions (33.1%). He averaged 3.65 birdies per round (29th) and was especially effective on par 4s (16.7%, 28th) and par 5s (39.6%, 34th).

In Trouble

Good touch around the greens, with a 59.9% scrambling average and a 21.1% bounce-back rating. His sand-save average was 58.4%, 38th on TOUR.

Flatstick Facts

How about eighth on TOUR with 1.747 putts per GIR? His 28.38 average putts per round was sixth best in '97.

The Scorer's Tent

With the powerful motivation of four college tuitions facing him, Blackmar may just keep hanging around the top 30 to 40 money winners for the next few years. Since his youngest son is six years old, Daddy will no doubt be heading for the Senior TOUR, too. Nothing has come easy for him and he doesn't help his own cause sometimes: Leading by two shots on 71st hole of the '97 Shell Houston Open, he chipped across the green and into the water. He ended up having to win a playoff to post his first win in nine years. (Look for a playoff at this year's event, too. There have been 10 since 1980!) Although he turns 41 this year, Blackmar's potential matches his height. This former Coke truck driver will be the real thing again in '98.

Jay Don Blake

A flashy player who would rather be drag racing than golfing, Jay Don Blake is the guy whose bag used to display the Hooters' restaurant logo. But it's as unfair to call him "Jay Don Flake" as it is to call Scott Hoch "Scott Choke." He's been grinding it out on TOUR since 1981, winning just once (1991 Shearson Lehman Brothers Open) and compiling some runner-up performances. He's the only TOUR pro we're aware of who had a professional drag racer (Bob Vandergriff, Jr.) caddy for him ('97 Bell Canadian Open). We wonder who caddied when Hooters sponsored him...? Just wondering, dear. Last season was typical: Made 18 cuts in 28 events (one WD) with three top 10s and 10 top 25s. Blake earned $378,484 (65th).

The Man

Jay Don Blake, 6'2", 180 lbs. Born St. George, UT, Oct. 28, 1958. Resides St. George, UT. Wife, Marci; daughters, Jamie Dawn and Bridgette; son, Patrick. Attended Utah State University. Enjoys drag racing, all sports, hunting and fishing. Turned pro in 1981; Q School 1986.

The Stats

Blake led the TOUR in putting in 1991 (1.733/GIR) and was third in 1992 but was 61st in 1997 (1.77). Going the wrong direction, Jay Don. However, he was 27th in average putts per round (28.71). He still pokes the odd tee shot pretty good, averaging 268 yards (81st).

The Skinny

Blake turns 40 this year and seems content to tread water in the middle of the pack, biding his time until he can next drive his hot rod in competition. We don't think he'll have to worry about preparing any trophy acceptance speeches — at least not on TOUR.

Michael Bradley

Michael Bradley can play. We mean really, really play. A few years back, he won two events on the chronically under-appreciated Canadian Tour and shot 59 during a pro-am at a tough golf course. After making it to the big TOUR, he hasn't dropped out of the top 125. Even after missing a month in 1994 due to an elbow injury in a pickup basketball game, he managed a 104th-place finish. In 1996, he had six straight top-20 finishes in the spring and won the Buick Challenge in the fall. Last season didn't feature any wins and Bradley wound up 47th ($465,887).

The Man

Michael John Bradley, 6'0", 190 lbs. Born Largo, FL, July 17, 1966. Resides Valrico, FL. Wife, Jennifer; daughter, Brooke Kathryn. Attended Oklahoma State University. Enjoys sports. Turned pro in 1988; Q School in 1992.

The Stats

The long ball is the foundation of Bradley's game. His average in '97 was 273.8 yards, but he hit the longest measured drive of the TOUR season — 381 yards — during the second round of the Walt Disney World/Oldsmobile Classic.

The Skinny

If you're drafting for a golf pool, we think Bradley is undervalued. He'll turn 32 this summer and is starting to realize the woods are full of long hitters. Once he hones the remainder of his game — and notices he was 177th on TOUR in driving accuracy — he will win again, maybe on an annual basis.

MIKE BRISKY

Another journeyman who has flip-flopped between the big TOUR and the NIKE loop, but who appears to be inching up the ladder. In 1994, Mike Brisky was 200th on the money list. He rocketed to 92nd in 1995 and 84th in '96. Last season, he finished 67th with $367,112. He pounded through 30 tournaments, making 20 cuts (seven straight from February through April) and posting six top-10 finishes, including a solo third at the Deposit Guaranty Golf Classic. He came close to winning the '95 Buick Open, but lost in a playoff to Woody Austin, who would go on to be that season's rookie of the year. (Austin would also be playing the NIKE TOUR this year, but that's another story ... and small consolation to Brisky.)

The Man

Michael Charles Brisky, 6'1", 185 lbs. Born Brownsville, TX, May 26, 1965. Resides Winter Garden, FL. Wife, Judy; sons, Jacob and Joel. Attended Pan American University. Enjoys fishing, movies and Bible study. Turned pro in 1987; Q School in 1993 and 1994.

The Stats

Some pretty good numbers here: seventh among putting leaders (1.745/GIR), 24th among birdie leaders (average 3.7 birdies per round) and 13th in overall birdie conversion (32.1%).

The Skinny

Brisky hits 33 this year and is motivated to continue his climb up the money list. He comes from a family of 10 children, so he's got to be used to going after what he wants. If he can shake the affliction of a third-round scoring average of 72 (148th), he just might move up another dozen places by the end of this season. If you're the last guy to pick in the golf pool and you feel lucky ...

Tom Byrum

What are the odds that Onida, SD (population 850), would produce not one, but two PGA TOUR pros? We aren't sure, but we know it's unlikely. Granted, Tom Byrum and his brother Curt have performed a tag-team act for most of their careers — a couple of years on together, one on, one off, but still ... In 1989, each brother won an event (the Kemper Open for Tom and the Hardee's Golf Classic for Curt), matching a similar feat by Dave and Mike Hill in 1972.

In 1997, after elbow surgery, Curt finished 219th on the TOUR money list and is toiling on the NIKE TOUR. Tom, on the other hand, earned more money on the big loop in '97 than he had in the previous four seasons combined — $525,161 (42nd). He made 15 cuts out of 21 with 11 top-25 finishes and five top 10s. He even had back-to-back seconds at the Canon Greater Hartford Open and the Buick Open. He finished ninth at the PGA Championship. He ranked second in the TOUR's vital all-around statistical category. And this is the guy who couldn't crack the top 125 list from 1991 through 1996? Whew. What a stupid game.

The Man

Thomas Elliott Byrum, 5'10", 175 lbs. Born Onida, SD, Sept. 28, 1960. Resides Sugar Land, TX. Wife, Dana; daughters, Brittni Rene and Corinne. Attended New Mexico State University. Enjoys hunting, fishing and all sports. Turned pro in 1984; Q School in 1985, '91, '92 and '96.

Off the Tee

Straight hitter (76.8%, 12th) but not overly long (269.1 yards, 73rd). He ranked fifth in total driving (combined accuracy and distance).

Hitting the Green

Byrum hit 67% of greens in regulation (48th) and his overall birdie conversion rate was 30.7% (33rd). He was 12th in total eagles with nine and 15th in total birdies with 362.

In Trouble

He was 19th in scrambling, making par or better 62.6% of the time he missed the green in regulation, and 24th in bounce back.

Flatstick Facts

Bit of a lapse in this all-too-important category. Byrum was 46th among putting leaders (1.771) and needed 29.03 putts per round on average (69th).

The Scorer's Tent

Maybe Tom Byrum finally figured out that life on TOUR beats pumping gas in Onida, SD. Or maybe he decided that four trips to Q School was enough. Perhaps he's reached that age — 38 — where he's out of options. Could be 1997 was just one of those X-Files things. (Remember: Even a blind pig finds the odd acorn.) Whatever the case, he's got a volatile game that we wouldn't want to bet our retirement savings on. Might make another half-mil in '98 or might be down the road. Roll them dice, Tom.

Mark Calcavecchia

The 1997 season proved that the rumors of Mark Calcavecchia's demise were greatly exaggerated. All he did was win the Greater Vancouver Open, post a runner-up finish at the Bob Hope Chrysler Classic and fourths at three other events. Combine those with a fifth at the Canon Greater Hartford Open and a T10 at the British Open (the first time he'd been back at Royal Troon since his win there in '89) and you've got a player who wins $1,117,365 (14th) to move into 11th spot on the all-time list ($7,612,931). Calc has eight TOUR wins, five more offshore and went wire to wire to win the unofficial Subaru Sarazen World Open in November.

While he dominated several TOUR statistical categories, he spoke for many of his peers when he said, "It gets harder and harder out here every week to win with the 20-somethings." He might not have won the Greater Vancouver Open had he not broken his putter in anger during the second round. Stealing a replacement from Jeff Maggert's locker, he went on to shoot 65 (just Maggert's luck). Ironically, his win at the GVO means he won't be defending his title there this year, since the victory made him eligible for the NEC World Series of Golf which is held at the same time.

The Man

Mark John Calcavecchia, 6'0", 200 lbs. Born Laurel, NE, June 12, 1960. Resides West Palm Beach, FL, plays out of Old Marsh GC. Wife, Sheryl; daughter, Britney Jo; son, Eric Jordan. Attended University of Florida. Enjoys bowling and music. Turned pro in 1981; graduated Qualifying School in 1981, 1982, and 1983.

Off the Tee

Fourteenth in driving distance (279.1 yards) and 86th in accuracy (69.1%).

Hitting the Green

Attention 20-somethings: Calcavecchia was sixth on TOUR in greens in regulation (70.1%), birdies per round (3.91) and eagle frequency (one every 116.4 holes). He was third in total eagles (15), seventh in total birdies (379) and fifth in the all-around category. So there.

In Trouble

Although he won't be putting on any bunker clinics (his sand-save average was 53%, 111th on TOUR), he managed to maintain a scoring average of 70.0 (16th).

Flatstick Facts

The numbers can't tell the story better than a Calc quote: "How can I expect to win a golf tournament if I can't make a 12-inch putt?" In fact, he missed two of that length at the '97 British. For the record, he needed 29.47 putts per round (131st).

The Scorer's Tent

The son of a bowling alley owner, Calcavecchia has always had a workingman's aura, which makes him a fan favorite. His wife caddies for him occasionally. He would have a roomful of trophies if not for his putting ("You fight the demons," he says). He hasn't finished out of the top 50 on TOUR since 1986. He fought back from cartilage and ACL damage after a skiing accident. He wears his emotions on his sleeve. He would make the All-Madden Golf Team (if there were such a thing). What's not to like? He's going to kick some 20-something butt this year and for years to come.

Brandel Chamblee

"Ah, yes. The '97 Brandel Chamblee. Often smooth, occasionally sparkling, with a hint of insouciance. Definitely the finest Chamblee we've seen in this country this decade." It's not a wine, you pretentious twit. It's a golfer. Having said that, the preceding oenological description fits this player pretty well. Chamblee had his best year on TOUR in '97, finishing 70th ($334,664). He had a pretty good year at home, too, welcoming his first child into this world — Brandel Jr. (we're not kidding). Back on TOUR, he made 15 out of 25 cuts and posted three top 10s, including two T2s (Quad City Classic, Canon Greater Hartford Open).

The Man

Brandel Eugene Chamblee, 5'10", 155 lbs. Born St. Louis, MO, July 2, 1962. Resides Phoenix, AZ. Wife, Karen; son, Brandel, Jr. Attended University of Texas. Enjoys tennis and horses. Turned pro in 1985; Q School 1987, '90, '91 and '92.

The Stats

Umm...Was 30th in putting ... Umm... Was 12th in third-round scoring average ... Umm...

The Skinny

Chamblee has been in the cellar (now stop that!) often enough that he doesn't want to try TOUR school again in his late 30s. The competition is way too tough. The motivation of another mouth to feed may be enough to stabilize his career. Put him away for another year and see if he matures. (We said stop that!)

Stewart Cink

The word "rookie" has a whole different meaning when it's followed by the phrase "...of the year." And that's just what Stewart Cink was on TOUR last season. Of course, that's what happens when you win the Canon Greater Hartford Open, post four top-10 finishes and earn $809,580 in official money (29th) in your first year on TOUR. Cink is no stranger to prominence: he set a NIKE TOUR record for single-season earnings in 1996 with $251,699, posting 14 top-10 finishes in 21 starts. Although he was already a husband and father while still in college, he managed to garner all-American honors three times.

The Man

Stewart Ernest Cink, 6'4", 205 lbs. Born Huntsville, AL, May 21, 1973. Resides Atlanta, GA; plays out of White Columns GC. Wife, Lisa; sons Connor and Reagan Braswell. Attended Georgia Tech. Enjoys family and computers. Turned pro in 1995 and joined TOUR in 1997.

Off the Tee

Still improving: his 269.8-yard average was 68th on TOUR while his 68.6% accuracy rating was 96th.

Hitting the Green

Hit only 64.8% of GIR (95th), but his final-round scoring average was a stellar 70.06 (seventh).

In Trouble

Cink is already one of the best bunker players around. His 62.2% sand-save average was 11th best on TOUR. In addition, he was 35th in scrambling — making par or better after a bogey or worse.

Flatstick Facts

Ranked 99th in putts per GIR (1.787) but 49th in average putts per round (28.93).

The Scorer's Tent

Talk about your new breed. Cink has the physical size, all-round game, mature attitude and mental toughness to do just about anything he wants. He missed 12 of 31 cuts in '97, but once he hits his TOUR rhythm, he'll be scary. He has the potential to top the money list sooner than later. Tiger Woods and his like hold no mystique for Cink, who defeated Tiger in a college match. The sky's the limit.

Russ Cochran

What does Russ Cochran have in common with Bob Charles, Sam Adams, Ernie Gonzalez and Phil Mickelson? They are the only lefthanded golfers to win on TOUR. Quite a mixed bag, no? Cochran's first and only win came in the 1991 Centel Western Open when Greg Norman — stop us if you've heard this before — crashed and burned. Norman went from Lear Jet to ValuJet as only he can, jettisoning a five-shot lead with eight holes to go. ("Thanks a lot, Greg." "You're welcome, Russ.") Cochran ended up 10th on the money list that year but stumbled in subsequent seasons. The worst was 1995 when recurring disk problems in his neck contributed to him dropping to 131st. In 1996, he crawled back to 62nd and in 1997, he rode eight top-25s and five top-10s to 46th place ($470,929).

The Man

Russell Earl Cochran, 6'0", 160 lbs. Born Paducah, KY, Oct. 31, 1958. Resides Paducah, KY. Wife, Jackie; sons, Ryan, Reed and Case; daughter, Kelly Marie. Attended University of Kentucky. Enjoys basketball. Turned pro in 1979; Q School in 1982.

Off the Tee

Cochran's average drive in 1997 went 270.5 yards, which sounds pretty darn good to us mortals, but that was only 62nd among his colleagues. He hit 66.9% of fairways (125th). Damn, these guys are good.

Hitting the Green

At 69.2%, his GIR stat was 14th on TOUR. He birdied 17.3% of the par 4s (16th) and was ninth in total birdies (373).

In Trouble

Average at best: 54% in sand saves (98th) and 60th in scrambling.

Flatstick Facts

Only 84th among putting leaders (1.783/GIR) and 138th in average putts per round (29.5).

The Scorer's Tent

This is a tough way to make a living. In 1991, Cochran was sniffing a win at the TOUR Championship but couldn't shake co-leader Craig Stadler, losing to the Walrus on the second playoff hole. Would that have propelled Cochran to a more illustrious career? Who knows. As it is, he's found his level and will stay there.

John Cook

Both John Cook's TOUR career and his golf game can be characterized as streaky. He won events in 1981, 1983, and 1987 and then won three times in 1992, finishing third on the money list. Three years later, he was 97th. After missing six of the first eight cuts in 1996, he took a hiatus, spending time with Ken Venturi.

Although we assume Venturi did more than replace Cook's Golf Pride grips, the results were impressive. Cook won the CVS Charity Classic and the FedEx St. Jude Classic, tying the TOUR record with opening rounds of 16-under 126 (64-62). He finished the season in 19th position ($831,260). He started the '97 campaign with a bang: five shots behind after three rounds of the Bob Hope Chrysler Classic, he shot 62-63 to win by one. He missed the cut in seven of the 28 events he entered in '97, posting 11 top-25 finishes and six top 10s. Cook earned $815,903 (28th) last season.

The Man

John Neuman Cook, 6'0", 175 lbs. Born Toledo, OH, Oct. 2, 1957. Resides Rancho Mirage, CA. Wife, Kristin; daughter, Courtney; son, Jason. Attended Ohio State University. Enjoys auto racing, skiing and all sports. Turned pro in 1979; Q School 1979.

Off the Tee

Not bad in the accuracy department (71.8%, 52nd), but losing distance over the years (263.9 yards, 132nd).

Hitting the Green

Cook excels here: his 71.1% average hitting greens in regulation was second on TOUR in '97. He was 23rd in total birdies (346).

In Trouble

Unremarkable ability in challenging situations, apparently. Sand-save average of 49.3% was 144th on TOUR and his scrambling stat of 61.1% was 49th.

Flatstick Facts

Another typically streaky facet of Cook's game. He was 99th among putting leaders, with 1.787 per GIR, and needed 29.71 on average per round (159th).

The Scorer's Tent

Tough call. Cook is a youthful 40-year-old, but his roller-coaster career — and game —make any prediction dicey. If Venturi would caddy for him, it would make this call a lot easier ... Let's say he will have another top-40 year, based on the fact that he plays a lot of events and has the potential to fire some incredibly low numbers. Too bad his putting is so sloppy; with his GIR numbers he could be awesome.

Fred Couples

Try as we might, we can't figure out what goes on in that pretty little head of Freddy Couples. We think we know what makes him tick, write it all down, and then we have to pull this book off the press to add the fact that he beat Bruce Lietzke in a playoff to win the 1998 Bob Hope Chrysler Classic. After the event, Couples alluded to the fact that his father died from cancer last November and a close female friend was also diagnosed with the disease. He implied those situations inspired him to put forth more effort. "I love to play golf. I love to compete. I know I don't always show it. But winning again is important because I know I have what it takes. ... I hope to be more of a battler."

The TOUR's leading couch potato and poster child for somnolence (look it up) has posed a puzzle for fellow competitors and fans alike for the almost two decades he's been on TOUR. "When Freddy wants to play, he's the best," Tom Kite said just before picking Couples as a captain's choice for the '97 Ryder Cup. There's no question about that. He's claimed 13 TOUR victories including the 1992 Masters and The Players Championship in 1984 and 1996. Five international victories include two Johnnie Walker World Championships and the low individual honors at the World Cup. But in 1997, the tragic plight of his father and friend dragged him down to the point where golf mattered less than it ever had. As a result, he finished outside the top 30 for only the second time in the last 11 years. He played in only 15 events, preferring to remain close to his family and friends, but posted seven top 10s. He dusted Ian Woosnam 8&7 at the Ryder Cup on his way to a 2-2 record. Hey, Fred, we're glad you're back. But there's a whole bunch of your fellow players who just decided to stay a little longer on the practice tee.

The Man

Frederick Steven Couples, 5'11", 185 lbs. Born Seattle, WA, Oct. 3, 1959. Resides Dallas, TX. Single. Attended University of Houston. Enjoys all sports, tennis, antiques, bicycling and antique cars. Turned pro in 1980; Q School in 1980.

Off the Tee

There are few things more enjoyable than watching Couples' loopy, lazy, lashing swing propel a golf ball down the fairway. While the cruel fates have inflicted an arthritic back on this future

Hall of Famer, he still managed to rank eighth in driving distance in 1997, but 131st in accuracy (66.6%). However, he was 30th in total driving.

Hitting The Green

He ranked 18th in GIR (68.7%), was fourth among eagle leaders (one every 114 holes), 10th among birdie leaders (one every 3.86 holes), 22nd among scoring leaders (70.13), seventh in par-5 birdies (45.5%), 18th in ball striking,12th in total eagles, 11th in top-10 finishes, sixth among par breakers ... and he's single (again), good-looking and rich (third among career money winners with $8.9 million at the end of '97).

In Trouble

Finesse is not Couples' strong suit: he was 158th in sand saves (47.4%) and 177th in scrambling (54.2%) but 14th in bounce back.

Flatstick Facts

Didn't play all that much, but the putter betrayed him frequently. He was 84th among putting leaders (1.783) and used the flatstick an average of 29.89 times per round (182nd).

The Scorer's Tent

Despite his painful personal life, Couples has retained the boyish charm that has made him a fan favorite for nigh on 20 years now. He played in 15 events, made $448,385 (55th) and had some outstanding statistics. One sore point: he ranked 14th in scoring average prior to the cut, 37th in the third round and 150th on Sunday. This could reflect the increasing strain on his bothersome back. If, as he says, he's rededicated himself to the game and his spine cooperates, we may well see a return to his heyday. Pick him. Pick him now.

Robert Damron

In all the hoopla surrounding Stewart Cink, most people forgot there was another pretty good rookie on TOUR in '97: Robert Damron. There's something a little Trevino-esque about this stocky, good-natured mini-tour refugee and college dropout. We're not sure why. Contrary to popular belief his father was not a Kentucky coal miner. His dad was in the coal business, sure enough, but made enough money by his mid-30s to retire to a spot overlooking the 10th green at Arnold Palmer's Bay Hill Club. Not quite the same thing as swinging a pick-ax underground. After Damron knocked around for a while, including a stint on the developmental Canadian Tour ("I didn't play great," he said after earning a total of $16,000, "but I came back feeling like a better player, more experienced."), he survived Q School and made the first two cuts on the '97 TOUR campaign. Although he missed 15 of 32 cuts, he managed four top-10 finishes, including two T3s (Buick Classic, FedEx St. Jude Classic), making $455,604 (53rd).

The Man

Robert Douglas Damron, 5'8", 185 lbs. Born Pikeville, KY, Oct. 27, 1972. Resides Orlando, FL. Single. Attended University of Central Florida. Enjoys all sports. Turned pro in 1994; Q School in 1996.

The Stats

Damron has a pretty solid game. He was 27th in total driving, 24th in total eagles and 36th in total birdies. His scrambling stat of 61.3% was 42nd on TOUR and he was 37th in bounce back.

The Skinny

No wonder this kid ran out of steam in mid-season. He signed up for 32 events — a far cry from the cushy all-American life at college or the more relaxed Canadian Tour schedule. Don't forget he only turned 25 at the end of the '97 season. Much has been made of his close association with Arnold Palmer. If this kid is as canny as we think he is, he will consult with The King at every opportunity. If the TOUR high life doesn't trip him up, Damron will take his place in the top 25 money winners in '98.

David Duval

OK, so we're impressed this guy hit the weights last season, dropped 40 pounds, developed muscles and went from looking like a well-padded yet cheery collegian to resembling a well-toned, but menacing, mid-level coke dealer/Porsche salesman. (The wraparound sunglasses help avoid allergies, wind and glare, but what's with that facial hair?) What we're really impressed with is that Duval went from being Rodney Dangerfield ("can't get no respect") with seven runner-up finishes in his two-year career to Reggie Jackson ("Mr. October") with three wins in that lovely autumn month. Another one of those "can't miss" college prospects (whoops ... it took him 93 PGA TOUR events to notch his first win), Duval went from 32nd to 17th to ninth to second on the money list as a result of his stunning surge.

An eclectic enigma, Duval's private persona holds very little resemblance to the intense, occasionally churlish impression he gives golf fans. Friends say he likes to read (everything from Tom Robbins to Ayn Rand), mountain bike, surf, shoot pool, drink beer, savor fine wines, fish and, of course, exercise. Tragically, he lost his older brother Brent to aplastic anemia when he was nine. No wonder he said prior to his breakthrough: "If not winning a golf tournament is the worst thing that happens to me, I'll be all right." All we can say is that Seve and his European squad were lucky David Duval wasn't picked for the 1997 Ryder Cup team by that knucklehead Kite.

The Man

David Robert Duval, 6'0", 160 lbs. Born Nov. 9, 1971, in Jacksonville, FL. Resides Ponte Vedra Beach, FL. Single. Attended Georgia Tech. Turned pro in 1993 and joined the TOUR in 1995.

Off the Tee

Duval smokes the driver pretty good, averaging just over 280 yards, good for 12th spot. However, he was 89th in accuracy.

Hitting the Green

He hit almost 70% of greens in regulation (24th). In 393 par-3 holes, he made 69 birdies (17.6%), tops on TOUR. Overall, his birdie conversion rate was 33.4% (second on TOUR to Tiger Woods). His nine eagles were good for 12th place.

In Trouble

When it comes to operating out of the sand, Operation Desert Storm this guy is not. His 45.7% success rate in getting up and down from bunkers left him in the dust of 167 other players.

Flatstick Facts

Duval steered the ball around the green an average of almost 29 times per round in 1997, 59th best on TOUR.

The Scorer's Tent

Late in the season, when the retro-rockets finally kicked in, Duval blasted to second place on the TOUR and world money lists with $1,885,308. This came after he set a record for second-year TOUR players with $977,079 (10th place) in 1996. This could be his Tiger-beating year, if ... his rigorous exercising doesn't lead to another flare-up of his shoulder tendinitis, he becomes more comfortable with being a star and he becomes more consistent, losing his troublesome habit of missing a bunch of cuts (eight out of 21 starts in 1997). He almost made it four wins in a row at the Mercedes Championships in January this year — Ben Hogan in 1953 was the last to win four in a row — but after being just one shot back after Saturday, he posted a one-over 73 to finish tied for sixth.

STEVE ELKINGTON

If Ernie Els, coincidentally right next to Elkington in this book and on the 1997 money list, is known as "The Big Easy," then we can't resist labeling Elk "The Big Lazy." This transplanted Aussie should have won everything in sight by now, but he needs serious motivating. His eight TOUR wins in a dozen years include two Players Championships, a Mercedes and a PGA title — how can someone who is so dominant against stellar fields doze off in lesser events? Ironically, he lists "caricature drawing" as one of his interests; here's hoping that after his career is finished he isn't viewed as a caricature of the great player he could have been. He blew away the field at the '97 Players, posting rounds of 66-69-68-69-272 for a wire-to-wire, seven-shot win, becoming only the third player to win two of those prestigious titles. The other two were Jack Nicklaus and Fred Couples. It will be interesting to see which of those two Elkington will emulate: Couples, the talented underachiever, or Nicklaus, who was satisfied only with a victory.

The Man

Stephen John Elkington, 6'2", 190 lbs. Born Dec. 8, 1962, in Inverell, Australia. Resides Sydney, Australia, and Houston, TX. Plays out of Champions GC. Wife, Lisa; daughter, Annie Elizabeth; son, Samuel Ross. Turned pro in 1985 and joined the TOUR in 1986.

Off the Tee

Like all of Elkington's stats, his driving figures are mediocre. He averaged 268.1 yards (79th) off the tee and was 81st in accuracy. Not what you would expect from a big, strong guy with a textbook swing.

Hitting the Green

Despite his lackluster tee game, Elk recovered nicely, hitting 69% of greens in regulation, leading to his 70.09 scoring average (19th).

In Trouble

Again, nothing striking here, with a 56.5% success rate out of the sand (65th).

Flatstick Facts

After Elkington finishes with a sports psychologist to figure out his motivational problems, maybe he should head over to Dave Pelz or some other putting priest: he was 156th in putting last year (29.65 per round).

The Scorer's Tent

In 1997, the big lug won two tournaments before the end of March (both in Florida), then pushed cruise control. Nonetheless, he won over $1 million for the second straight year and, when pushed, can put on some awesome displays of talent. Trailing Els by six going into the final round of the '95 PGA, he shot 64 and beat Colin Montgomerie with a 25-foot putt on the first playoff hole. The number of events he plays (17 in '97) decreases in direct proportion to the size of his bank account. A fascinating, frustrating player with potential you know will never be realized.

Ernie Els

"The Big Easy." Cool nickname. But this bruiser who looks more like a linebacker than a pro golfer hails from South Africa, not New Orleans, and — if we hadn't already used it on Steve Elkington — we could dub Els "The Big Lazy." And, like Elk, he appears to need a cattle prod at times to get him moving. The ever-quotable Brad Faxon says Els' heart rate "is 35 or something. He'll never die." Adjectives like easy, smooth, calm, nerveless, serene and their like are used ad nauseum to describe both the man and his swing. He's a young powerful lion straight from the veldt who, having feasted on his prey by winning a tournament, pauses a few weeks to allow for digestion.

But we digress ... Els claimed his second U.S. Open in four years at Congressional in '97, becoming the first foreigner in 87 years to do so (attention, trivia buffs: Scotsman Alex Smith did it in 1906 and 1910). And that was just one highlight of a fabulous 1997 season. He was the first player since Tom Watson in 1980 to successfully defend a title wire to wire when he won the Buick Classic the week after the Open. That got him to No. 1 on the world rankings for a week. He led countrymen David Frost and Retief Goosen to South Africa's first Alfred Dunhill Cup title. He lost the chance to win his fourth straight Toyota World Match Play Championship when Vijay Singh bested him. He won the MasterCard Grand Slam of Golf with a record total of 133, defeating Masters champ Tiger Woods (136), PGA winner Davis Love III (138) and British Open victor Justin Leonard (149). Enough already.

The Man

Theodore Ernest Els, 6'3", 210 lbs. Born Johannesburg, South Africa, Oct. 17, 1969. Resides in Fancourt, South Africa, and Orlando, FL. Single. Enjoys movies, reading and sports. Turned pro in 1989 and joined the TOUR in 1994.

Off the Tee

Curiously, this strapping lad ranked 52nd on TOUR in driving distance (271.6 yards) and 125th in accuracy (66.9%).

Hitting the Green

Barely made the top 100 on TOUR in greens in regulation (64.7%, 97th), doesn't make a lot of birdies (213, 154th on TOUR) or eagles (6, 55th) and rarely converts his birdie chances (29.2%, 76th). All he does is win. So much for statistics.

In Trouble

And Els is in trouble a lot, if you believe the previous stats. He was 114th in sand saves (52.9%) and 100th in scrambling (58.7%).

Flatstick Facts

Like the rest of his stats (except for victories and earnings), his putting numbers are unremarkable — he averages just over 29 putts per round (67th).

The Scorer's Tent

In 1994, the first time he shows his face on these shores, he has the gall to win the U.S. Open. Since then, he's won five times on TOUR (should be more, we say), but boasts 20 more titles internationally. Big fish, small pond syndrome? If he persists in his globetrotting, his game on this continent will suffer. However, if he dedicates himself, no one can stop him. That's right, Tiger — no one. He entered 19 events, made 15 cuts and had 11 top-25 finishes, including two wins and a tie for second at the Buick Open. His $1,243,008 in official TOUR winnings was ninth best in '97, but he was third worldwide with $1,814,029. Maybe there is something to this globetrotting stuff...

Bob Estes

Which of the following statements is correct? (1) Bob Estes won the 1994 Texas Open and finished 14th on the money list, or (2) Bob Estes didn't come close to winning anything in 1996 and finished 149th on the money list. All of the above? Correct. We have it on good authority that aliens abducted the real Bob Estes and left behind a clone with the golfing ability of Cosmo Kramer in '95 and '96. Another, less credible, theory suggests that Estes was suffering a tinge of burnout. "Playing the TOUR and finding a golf game is one big puzzle," he said at one low point. "Golf was not fun. I definitely had thoughts of doing something else." He had some elbow problems and tinkered incessantly with his equipment; at some events, the specs of his clubs changed from round to round. But we like the X-Files idea better. In any case, Special Agents Mulder and Scully have confirmed that the authentic Bob Estes returned to the TOUR in '97, making the cut in 15 of the 19 events he entered (10 in a row from May through September). He had the second-longest string of rounds at par or better (25) and three top-10 finishes. Welcome back, Bob. "Trust no one. The truth is out there."

The Man

Bob Alan Estes, 6'1", 175 lbs. Born Graham, TX, Feb. 2, 1966. Resides Austin, TX; plays out of The Hills at Lakeway. Single. Attended University of Texas. Enjoys music and hunting. Turned pro in 1988; Q School in 1988.

The Stats

We quote from no less an authority than the official *PGA TOUR Media Guide:* "PGA TOUR statistics confirm return to form — first in sand saves (TOUR record 70.3%), first in scrambling (68.8% par or better after missed GIR), second in total putts (28.19 per round), fifth in bounce back (24.4% birdies or better after bogey or worse), ninth in scoring before cut (70.0) and fifth in final-round scoring average (69.8)."

The Skinny

You can't have him. We already picked him.

Brad Fabel

Once you get to the 66th guy on the '97 money list, chances are you're in deep grinder country. It took Brad Fabel 13 seasons to vault to 66th place on the money list ($375,122). Hey, it's a living! He's taken the revolving-door approach to the TOUR, ducking out now and again for a refresher course with the NIKE TOUR boys. He dropped out of college because he was "burned out on golf." Hard to imagine how he feels now.

The Man

Bradley Scott Fabel, 6'0", 185 lbs. Born Louisville, KY, Nov. 30, 1955. Resides Nashville, TN. Wife, Beth; sons Austin and Morgan Scott. Attended Western Kentucky University. Enjoys fishing, hunting and University of Kentucky basketball. Turned pro in 1982; Q School in 1984.

The Stats

What can we say? He managed to survive the season without injuring any spectators that we're aware of.

The Skinny

Some cause for optimism in the four top-10 finishes Fabel posted in '97. He made 18 of 29 cuts (one WD) and had 10 top 25s. Will he win a tournament in '98? No way. This is a Fabel, not a fairy tale. (Sorry. We couldn't resist.)

Nick Faldo

That's Nicholas Alexander Faldo, MBE, to you, bub. In addition to the extraordinary list of kudos Faldo has received for golf, the Queen has also anointed him with the honorific "Member of the British Empire." What did he do to deserve that? For starters, he notched 33 international victories, including the Open championships of Britain, France, Spain, Switzerland and Ireland — then he won the European Open just to make a clean sweep of the continent.

After accomplishing all there was to do across the pond, he moved to the U.S. in 1995 to make a full commitment to the PGA TOUR. (Are you listening, Colin Montgomerie?) He won the first event he played in that year, edging Greg Norman by a shot at the Doral-Ryder Open. He had won three times over here previously — two of those being the 1989 and '90 Masters. He won his third Masters title in 1996. That was when the hapless Norman, doing a great impression of a deer caught in the headlights of a transport truck, blew a six-shot lead on Sunday to lose by five strokes. (That's not a misprint.)

Overall, Faldo has six PGA TOUR victories, including the '97 Nissan Open. His six major titles — he won the British Open in 1987, '90 and '92 in addition to his three Masters — are second only to Tom Watson's eight among active players. He came close to adding a U.S. Open to the list in 1988, but lost a playoff to Curtis Strange. Ranked the top player in the world for 81 weeks in 1993-94, Faldo was the first international player to be named PGA of America Player of the Year. His 11th appearance at the Ryder Cup set a record and the two points he collected set another record for total points (25).

The Man

Nicholas Alexander Faldo, 6'3", 195 lbs. Born Welwyn Garden City, England, July 18, 1957. Resides Orlando, FL, and Weybridge, England. Daughters, Natalie and Georgia; son, Matthew. Enjoys fly-fishing and flying helicopters. Turned pro in 1976; Joined TOUR in 1981 and 1995.

The Stats

A rather forgettable year for Faldo, whose stolid exterior belies a mercurial nature. He won the Nissan Open in March and then imploded, apparently. His T3 at the Kemper Open in June was his only other top-10 finish out of 15 events in '97. He made 11 cuts and had one WD. Not only did he miss two consecutive cuts for the first time since '94, he missed the cut in two majors — the PGA and The Masters — for the first time in his career. He was the defending Masters champ so he had to hang around until Sunday to drape the green jacket around Tiger Woods. Talk about adding insult to injury.

As far as his statistics go, he was sixth in driving accuracy. As for the rest — yada, yada, yada. It was an atypical year. The one troubling aspect of his performance, as far as we are concerned, is his putting. He was 156th among putting leaders (1.806/GIR) and needed 29.64 per round (153rd). He putted 69 times (!) during the first two rounds of the '97 Masters on his way to shooting 75-81-MC. Too bad he can't have his caddie, Fanny Sunesson, stroke the putts as well as line them up.

The Skinny

In Faldo's case, MBE also stands for "Must Be Enigmatic." We think we like Faldo, but we aren't sure. Is he the robotic, mechanical, agonizingly slow player we see on many occasions, or is he the gregarious goofball featured in those Mizuno commercials? Is he the shy recluse who purchased a 400-acre island off Ireland, accessible only by boat, so he could hide out from the world? Or is he a fun-loving guy who's dating a coed half his age? Like the rest of us, he's an amalgam of a whole bunch of things. Unlike the rest of us, he's one of the best golfers of this century. If his personal life settles down and he is allowed to do what he does best, then Faldo will certainly rank higher on the '98 money list than the 58th position he held at the end of 1997. However, as he celebrates his 41st birthday this July, he must realize that the downhill slide has begun.

Brad Faxon

The ever-youthful, always quotable refugee from *Leave It To Beaver* (look at that face: he must have been Beaver, Peter Jacobsen could be Eddie Haskell and Tim Herron, of course, is Lumpy) needs a shot of self-confidence. For some reason, he doesn't seem to think he belongs in the TOUR's upper echelon. Perhaps his 10th-place finish on the money list (his second consecutive million-dollar season) and his first win since 1992 will give him a shot in the arm. He appeared to believe in himself after winning the '97 Freeport McDermott Classic in April (although he missed the cut the next week at The Masters), when he tied for second at the MCI Classic and finished solo second at the Greater Greensboro Chrysler Classic. He had as many top-10 finishes (six) as missed cuts out of the 23 events he entered. He finished third in the Toyota World Match Play (that's good) and then, horror of horrors, lost to Bernhard Langer on Valderrama's 17th green to ensure Europe kept the Ryder Cup (that's bad). Devastated by a divorce, he tinkered with his equipment and swing, hoping to find the magic combination: he added a Great Big Bertha driver, an old Ping putter, a better attitude, a flatter swing plane and tossed his 60-degree wedge.

The Man

Bradford John Faxon, Jr., 6'1", 170 lbs. Born Oceanport, NJ, Aug. 1, 1961. Resides Barrington, RI. Daughters Melanie, Emily and Sophie Lee. Enjoys all sports except hunting and fishing. Turned pro and joined the TOUR in 1983.

Off the Tee

The new Great Big Bertha bumped him all the way to 165th in driving (260.1 yards) and 166th in accuracy. Yippee. That accuracy stat is surprising considering Fax drilled his own caddie in the back off the tee at the Canon Greater Hartford Open — tack on two strokes please, Mr. Faxon. Anyone watching the '97 Skills Challenge on TV will realize that calling his long game "erratic" is an understatement.

Hitting the Green

Enough said about his long game: Faxon hit only 62.6% of greens in regulation (146th). Thank God he can putt.

In Trouble

He was 35th in both sand saves and scrambling (making par or better after missing the green in regulation).

Flatstick Facts

That heading should read "Flatstick Fax." This guy led the TOUR in putting, averaging 28.17 per round. So for those of us who want a tip — just what goes through your head, Brad, when you're putting? "I'm not really thinking about anything when I'm putting." Gee, thanks.

The Scorer's Tent

Nagged by self-doubt and a rotten playoff record (1-5), the likeable Faxon will have to overcome personal problems in order to repeat his success of the past two seasons. He turns 37 in August and this will be a pivotal season in his career. His Ryder Cup performance (1-2, didn't make a birdie until his 45th hole, and you already know about Langer) was blown out of proportion but took its toll on him. If he gets the momentum, look out. Not only can he putt, but this streaky ball-striker can flat-out play; he shot 28 on the front nine during the '95 PGA Championship.

Dan Forsman

Dan Forsman is a nice guy but he may be a bit frayed at the edges. Working with Mac O'Grady will do that to a man. Perhaps he's just a little too devout, too fragile — who else would put "truth" under "Special Interests" in the *PGA TOUR Media Guide*? Who else would attend a clinic put on by Joey O — a unique combination of inspirational speaker and trick shot artist? Lighten up, Dan. In 1992, he celebrated his 10th anniversary on TOUR by finishing 10th on the money list on the strength of a win and three seconds. Since then he's swooped up and down the list, coming dangerously close (123rd) to dropping off the exempt list in 1996. Last season he finished 56th on the money list with $443,034 with four top 10s. He might have added his fifth TOUR title had he not stubbed a chip and made bogey on the first playoff hole at the Walt Disney World/Oldsmobile Classic. Que sera sera, right, Mac?

The Man

Daniel Bruce Forsman, 6'4", 205 lbs. Born Rhinelander, WI, July 15, 1958. Resides Provo, UT. Wife, Trudy; sons, Ricky and Thomas. Attended Arizona State University. Enjoys snow skiing, reading, fly-fishing, all sports, the arts, church activities, truth (we told you so). Turned pro in 1982; Q School 1982.

The Stats

Forsman won the MCI Long Distance Driving Competition ... OK, so that was in 1987. But he still smokes that high, sweeping hook. His average drive traveled 271.1 yards (56th) and he nailed one 352 (23rd) at one event. He was 51st in GIR, but his putting is abysmal (1.805, 154th). Makes an eagle every 189 holes (31st) but that is small consolation when your scoring average is 71.10 (80th).

The Scorer's Tent

Who knows? If O'Grady gets Forsman's ions all facing in the same direction, or whatever that knucklehead does, then Forsman might keep it going in 1998. A return to his 1992 form is too much to ask of this 40-year-old, but chances are good he will match his '97 season. We like those top 10s.

David Frost

David Frost is on the comeback trail. Don't get the wrong idea. He wasn't down and out on Skid Row, drinking muscatel. (That's for sure — he owns Frost Vineyards in South Africa, a 300-acre estate that will produce its first crop this year.) But after winning nine events from 1988 through 1994, he all but disappeared from our radar screen. But he won the '97 MasterCard Colonial in convincing fashion (66-63-69-67-265) and, although he missed 11 cuts in 23 events, he managed five top-25 finishes. Earnings of $458,700 got him to 50th place on the list, about level with his '95 and '96 ranking. OK, so maybe we're going easy on him because he's a decent guy with a sense of humor. After edging Fred Couples at the '93 Canadian Open, he chose a Toronto restaurant called "Fred's Not Here" in which to celebrate his win. In the '90 USF&G Classic, he joined a not-so-exclusive club when he holed out from a bunker on the 72nd hole to beat — you guessed it — Greg Norman.

The Man

David Laurence Frost, 5'11", 172 lbs. Born Cape Town, South Africa, Sept. 11, 1959. Resides Dallas, TX; plays out of Preston Trail GC. Wife, Corrie; sons, Andre, Jacques, Nicholas and Sean; daughter, Noelle. Enjoys all sports, rugby. Turned pro in 1981; Q School in 1984.

The Stats

Try as we might, we can find few bright spots in Frosty's '97 stats. The one relative highlight was his third-round scoring average of 70.45 (35th). But that only stuck out because the rest of his numbers are so bad.

The Skinny

We suspect that personal distractions were the root of Frost's nosedive between '94 and '97. Nobody hits the skids that quickly after being fifth on the money list in '93. If things are calm on the business and home fronts, we foresee a return to his former greatness. He'd better get it in gear, though. His window of opportunity is shrinking as he moves in on 40. He won't do it for the money, that's for sure. He stands 18th on the TOUR career money list with $6.3 million and that doesn't count earnings from his eight international victories, including three Million Dollar Challenges (1989, '90 and '92).

Fred Funk

Grinder, iron man, one of the hardest workers on TOUR ... Fred Funk is those things, but much more. Here's a guy who worked as a newspaper circulation supervisor, assistant pro and college golf coach (University of Maryland 1982-1988) before joining the TOUR in 1989 as a 32-year-old rookie. Although he went without a win last year for the first time since 1994, he posted two thirds and a fourth on his way to winning $544,419 (38th). No one has played in more TOUR events this decade than Funk — 220 as of the end of the '97 season. And, due to his fanatical fitness regime, he appears pretty durable, despite suffering a torn rotator cuff in his shoulder in 1986. He reinjured it in 1991 in a boogie board accident. (We call that kind of recreational decision the "Steve Jones Syndrome.")

The Man

Frederick Funk, 5'8", 165 lbs. Born Takoma Park, MD, June 14, 1956. Resides Ponte Vedra Beach, FL. Wife, Sharon; sons, Eric and Taylor Christian. Attended University of Maryland. Enjoys water and snow skiing. Turned pro in 1981; Q Schools in 1988 and 1989.

Off the Tee

Funk plummeted in the accuracy department in 1997 — all the way to second after leading the TOUR in that statistic the two previous seasons. Last year, he hit 79.8% of the fairways, which was two percentage points higher than his average in 1996. However, in a familiar scenario, he was near the bottom in distance — a 260.2-yard average was162nd best.

Hitting the Green

Those 7,000-plus-yard TOUR courses pose problems for short hitters like Funk. He hit 66.2% of GIR (67th) and when he missed the green, he still made par or better 63.1% of the time (14th in scrambling). He was fifth on TOUR in total birdies with 382.

In Trouble

We know he can scramble and he's OK out of the sand, getting up and down out of the bunker 56.4% of the time (67th). His bounce-back rating was 54th (20.6%).

Flatstick Facts

Funk was 113th among putting leaders (1.791 putts per GIR) and needed an average of 29.25 putts per round (97th). Maybe he should putt with his driver.

The Scorer's Tent

Durable, dedicated and down the middle ... those words describe Funk, too. He plays a mind-boggling number of events, but makes a lot of cuts (25/33 in '97). Even though he'll turn 42 this year, we don't think he'll wander too far away from the top 30 money winners. An even-money bet to win again in '98 if he can avoid a bothersome tendency to shoot a big number in the third round.

Jim Furyk

"An octopus falling out of a tree." That's how TV commentator David Feherty described Furyk's swing. Indeed, even Furyk was moved to near nausea the first time he saw his roller-coaster move on video. To hell with them, Jimmy. It's the end, not the means (viz. Arnold Palmer, Lee Trevino, Miller Barber, et al). The end result in 1997 was that he finished fourth on the money list ($1,619,480) but without a single victory, unless you count the Argentine Open (and we don't). He calls his swing his "trademark [but] I can't really work on mechanics. It looks complicated but it really isn't." Yeah, right. If that swing had a designer label, it would read "Rube Goldberg." He practices doggedly — and good thing, too. As a result, his steady play belies the nutty swing; the pretzel-like route always seems to deliver the clubhead in the ideal position at impact. What more do you want? Thirteen top-10 finishes, including eight in a row, in 27 starts, tied him with Davis Love III for top spot on TOUR.

The Man

James Michael Furyk, 6'2", 200 lbs. Born May 12, 1970, in West Chester, PA. Resides Ponte Vedra Beach, FL. Single. Attended University of Arizona. Enjoys all sports. Turned pro in 1992 and joined the TOUR in 1993.

Off the Tee

Apparently Furyk expends so much energy getting the driver back on line that there's nothing left at impact: He was 144th on TOUR in driving distance (262.9 yards) but fifth in accuracy, hitting almost four out of every five fairways. How come those two stats never match up?

Hitting the Green

Nothing exceptional here. Furyk hit two-thirds of the greens in regulation and converted 31% of his birdie opportunities (24th on TOUR). Par 3s weren't overly friendly to him, as he birdied only 54 of 393 for a 13.7% success rate. Par 4s were better, but he shone on the three-shot holes (139/333, 41.7%, 18th).

In Trouble

Decent enough short game, but bunker shots can pose a problem. He cashed in on only 78 of 142 sand-save chances in 1997. Thank goodness he can putt.

Flatstick Facts

What can we say? He led the TOUR in putting in 1995, had a hiccup in '96 (T37) and rebounded to sixth in '97.

The Scorer's Tent

So Furyk can't hit it out of his shadow (relatively speaking). All together now: "Drive for show and putt for dough." We pick him to win a major in '98. He's mature and confident enough and — unlike the rest of us who sit back and criticize it — trusts his swing implicitly. He played well against tough fields in 1997: T2 at The Memorial, T5 at the U.S. Open, fourth at the British Open, T6 at the PGA Championship and second at The TOUR Championship. This year's Open at San Francisco's Olympic Club might just be this octopus's playground.

Brent Geiberger

Brent Geiberger has a hefty load to carry, being the son of Al Geiberger — nicknamed "Mr. 59" after setting the PGA TOUR 18-hole scoring record of 59 in the 1977 Danny Thomas Memphis Classic. Thank goodness his brawny son has big shoulders. And he demonstrated that he's up to the task of carrying on the family name on the regular TOUR in his rookie year of 1997 when he finished 62nd on the money list. He shot 65 (just six shots away...) to finish T2 at the LaCantera Texas Open on his way to being nominated rookie of the year (Stewart Cink won). He made 19 of 29 cuts with one WD, posting 11 top 25s and one top 10. Had some success on the NIKE TOUR in '95 and '96, finishing 11th on the money list in '96 to miss his PGA TOUR card by $132. A pretty impressive golfing family: his brother John is the coach of the NCAA-champion Pepperdine University golf team.

The Man

Brent Andrew Geiberger, 6'4", 200 lbs. Born Santa Barbara, CA, May 22, 1968. Resides Palm Desert, CA. Single. Attended Pepperdine University. Enjoys hockey, basketball and his computer. Turned pro in 1993; Q School in 1996.

The Stats

Gotta like the looks of this from a rookie: 24th in driving distance, 84th in accuracy, 15th in total driving; 27th in greens in regulation, 42nd in among birdie leaders; 41st in sand saves, 33rd in par-4 birdie leaders, 26th in scrambling.

The Skinny

The champion bloodline will tell out. Geiberger the Younger will not only match, he just might surpass Geiberger the Elder. He may never shoot 59, but if we had a mid-round pick, this would be it. Brent has stats that many TOUR stalwarts would kill for, as listed above; he also was 15th in ball striking and 13th in third-round scoring. He got a little tired midseason, but is a strapping lad who turns 30 this year. He's got the game, he's getting used to life on TOUR and he'll have more stamina this season. Look out!

Bill Glasson

How do you go from almost filing for permanent disability in 1991 to finishing 22nd on the PGA TOUR money list ($926,552) six years later? You can find out by asking Bill Glasson — you know, that blond guy who looks like a cross between a California lifeguard and a serial killer. As recently as 1996, Glasson recorded only eight starts and finished 198th on the list with just over $50,000. Not his choice, to say the least. Blame his "bad genes," he says, without a smile. Four knee operations, four sinus operations, a lip operation (don't ask), elbow surgery, a lower back problem and an operation to reattach his right forearm muscle ... and then he gets sued by the company that supplied him with his personal plane. He was facing the possibility of bankruptcy. "The TOUR needs more animation, more lively personalities," Glasson observes. "I just don't happen to be one of them." Gee, why not? At 38, he's 45th on the career money list with $4,206,807. A couple of million dollars and a few more operations and he'll be the real Six Million Dollar Man. (Is Woody Austin any relation to Steve?)

The Man

William Lee Glasson, 5'11", 165 lbs. Born Fresno, CA, April 29, 1960. Resides Stillwater, OK. Wife, Courtney; son, Maxwell Alexander; daughter, Dakota Jade. Attended Oral Roberts University. Enjoys flying his own plane (well, he used to anyhow). Turned pro in 1983; Q Schools in 1983, 1984.

Off the Tee

Glasson may be semi-Frankensteinian medically but he's anything but a stiff with a driver in his hands. At 287.5 yards, his average drive was third best on TOUR and, unlike most long hitters, his accuracy rating wasn't all that bad: 69.1% (86th). His longest measured drive in '97 traveled 360 yards — but there were 12 other players who hit it farther!

Hitting the Green

How about fourth in GIR with a 70.3% average? Glasson was second among birdie leaders (4.18 average per round). While par 3s weren't his favorite (he birdied 14.9%, 45th best on TOUR), he fared better on the par 4s (17.9%, sixth) and par 5s (47.6%, fourth). He was second in the par

breaking stat (number of birdies/eagles vs. total number of holes played; 289/1,224; 23.6%).

In Trouble

Trouble? You think this guy doesn't know trouble? What's a bad lie when you've had every operation except Desert Storm? He was 40th in sand saves (58.3%) and — how appropriate is this? — led the TOUR's bounce-back category at 27.9%. That stat evaluates how frequently a player posts a birdie or better after a bogey or worse.

Flatstick Facts

Glasson ranked 48th at 1.772 putts per green hit in regulation but needed 29.53 putts per round average (145th).

The Scorer's Tent

Nobody was more surprised than Glasson when he won the '97 Las Vegas Invitational, his seventh TOUR title. "Where are we playing?" he asked when advised that, due to his victory, he had qualified for the TOUR Championship the following week. After he found out where it was, he finished T4. In 19 events, he managed six top 10s, withdrew twice and missed one cut. He led the TOUR's all-around category, which evaluates — you guessed it! — overall performance ranging from driving to putting and scoring. Definitely our PGA TOUR comeback player of the year ... maybe the decade. Despite his sullen mien, we respect RoboGolfer's game and are rooting for him to have a couple more good years. Anything more than that would be asking too much. His birth certificate may have been issued in 1960, but the body is 1930s vintage.

PAUL GOYDOS

"Sunshine" is what some of the other players call Paul Goydos, in a sarcastic reference to his grim outlook. Not that he hasn't had some cause for feeling down in the dumps. This former substitute teacher has bumped up and down the list, heading back to the minor leagues a time or two. But his win at the '96 Bay Hill Invitational was cause for hope. He ended up 44th on TOUR that year, with four top 10s in 29 events. He posted some good rounds in '97, especially 31-35-66 in the final round of the Walt Disney World/Oldsmobile Classic to clinch fifth place. He dropped to 61st spot in '97 while making 21 of 30 cuts and posting five top 10s and nine top 25s.

The Man

Paul David Goydos, 5'9", 190 lbs. Born Long Beach, CA, June 20, 1964. ResidesLong Beach, CA; plays out of Virginia CC. Wife, Wendy; daughters, Chelsea and Courtney. Attended Long Beach State University. Enjoys sports. Turned pro in 1989; Q School in 1992 and 1993.

The Stats

Better than you'd imagine. Hammers the ball more than 268 yards off the tee and hits almost 74% of the fairways (31st), ending up 15th in total driving. He's a pretty decent putter (1.773, 51st) and excellent in sand saves (61.3%, 16th) and scrambling (62.2%, 29th). All-around, he ranked 22nd.

The Skinny

Goydos made 15 of 29 cuts in 1996, winning once. In '97, he made 21 of 30. Are we sensing a trend here? If he doesn't let his disposition get in his way, he's got the tools to be a real sleeper for someone with a late pick in your golf pool. If he plays a lot this year, makes most of the cuts and posts half-a-dozen top 10s, you got a bargain. If he ever gets over his habit of stumbling in the third round (113th in scoring average on Saturdays), he might even win one for you.

Jay Haas

Jay Haas has been a TOUR mainstay for years; that's why he's 16th among career money leaders. He's won nine times in his 21-year career, but not since 1993. Last season was a disappointment, but maybe he thought he was headed for an acting career after appearing in that Hootie and the Blowfish music video. *Not.* Back to reality, Jay. Not a great year for someone who has finished as high as 13th (1982), but he still had four top 10s (T5 at the U.S. Open) and 11 top 25s in his 24 starts, making the first seven cuts in a row. Maybe he's been talking to his uncle, 1968 Masters champ Bob Goalby.

The Man

Jay Dean Haas, 5'10", 180 lbs. Born St. Louis, MO, Dec. 2, 1953. Resides Greenville, SC; plays out of Thornblade GC. Wife, Janice; sons, Jay Jr. and William Harlan; daughters, Winona Haley, Emily Frances and Georgia Ann. Attended Wake Forest University. Enjoys all sports. Turned pro in 1976; Q School in 1976.

The Stats

Nothing at all wrong with Haas' stats that a little consistency wouldn't cure. He was 23rd in total driving, 27th in GIR, 30th among putting leaders, fourth in sand saves and eighth all-around.

The Skinny

If he can keep it going for four rounds, Haas will win this season. At the very least, we foresee a handful of top 10s and a big jump up the money list from his 57th position in '97 ($437,895). That was his worst season since 1991 and we consider it an aberration despite the fact that the last time he plunged into the 50s in money won, he followed that with placings of 89th and 84th. That trend won't repeat itself. Haas is a great, dark-horse pick who will improve at least 20 spots in '98. Has had great success in the Southwest, so watch him there.

Dudley Hart

Maybe Larry Mize was just trying to help. Mize dinged Dudley Hart on the wrist with a practice ball at the '97 Phoenix Open, forcing Hart to withdraw. You see, Hart began the '96 season — his best so far on TOUR — recuperating from surgery to repair three wrist ligaments torn when he hit a root at the '95 Canon Greater Hartford Open. He even won an event — the Bell Canadian Open — that year, finishing 47th on the money list. Well, whatever Mize's thoughts were — assuming he had some at the time — Hart failed to hold his spot on the money list in '97, dropping to 60th. He came close to winning the FedEx St. Jude Classic, but witnessed Greg Norman do what had been done to him so often — birdie the last three holes to edge Hart by a shot. Three top 10s and six top 25s came in the 14 events in which he made the cut. He missed 13 others and, of course, there was the WD. Doesn't Mize know Hart's nickname is "Mini-Volcano" due to his incendiary temper? Big NHL fan. Lucky there's no penalty box in golf.

The Man

Howard Dudley Hart, 5'10", 170 lbs. Born Rochester, NY, Aug. 4, 1966. Resides West Palm Beach, FL. Single. Attended University of Florida. Enjoys hockey, football, basketball and baseball. Turned pro in 1990; Q School 1990.

The Stats

What's to say? Leads the TOUR in torn wrist ligaments? Hart hits it fine off the tee, averaging almost 270 yards and hitting two-thirds of the fairways. Most of the stats are mediocre, with the exception of sand saves, where he was 31st (59.3%).

The Skinny

Won't turn 32 until August and, with that temper (he says it's under control), he may need more maturing than most. We wouldn't take a chance on him this season, but it's too soon to write him off altogether.

Tim Herron

We aren't sure who Tim Herron's agent is, but we are positive he relies greatly on the counsel of Drew Carey Image Consultants. His co-workers labeled him "Lumpy" when he showed up for his first day of work at the golf course in Wayzata, MN, and the tag has stuck. "I have a lumpy image," he admits. "I have grass in my shirt, my shirttail is out ... that's the way I am."

He is a conundrum in many ways. He couldn't do better than 25th on the NIKE TOUR money list in 1995 (his best finish was a third) after an all-American collegiate career and stints on the Canadian and Australian tours. Then he blasts through the PGA TOUR Qualifying School and beats some of the best players in the world to win the '96 Honda Classic. He finishes 39th on the money list in his first full year on TOUR. Last season started out with him making eight of the first nine cuts and winning the LaCantera Texas Open in September. So he ends up 33rd on the list with $640,997. He loves to win and cash the big checks so "I can sleep in when I want, do what I want," says the fun-loving bachelor whose vices include cigarettes and having the odd wobbly pop.

The Man

Timothy Daniel Herron, 5'10", 210 lbs. Born Minneapolis, MN, Feb. 16, 1970. Resides Scottsdale, AZ; plays out of Rush Creek CC. Single. Attended University of New Mexico. Enjoys fishing, pool and snow skiing. Turned pro in 1993; Q School in 1995.

Off the Tee

When Herron gets that low center of gravity and the sizable "power pod" that droops over his belt heading down the fairway, the results can be awesome. While his average drive traveled 279.7 yards (13th), he powdered one 376 (third longest on TOUR in '97). Accuracy, schmaccuracy ... so he only hit 65.5% of the fairways. It's fun to watch him whale on the ball.

Hitting the Green

Not bad in this department, hitting 66.4% of greens in regulation (62nd). He was third among eagle leaders, notching one every 113.6 holes. He was second in total eagles with 16 and 19th in total birdies with 356.

In Trouble

With that mischievous smile and sense of humor, this guy's probably been in trouble since he was wearing diapers. Oh, you mean on the golf course? He could use a little work in the bunkers, getting up and down only 54.3% of the time (96th) and he ranked 119th in scrambling.

Flatstick Facts

Herron ranked 75th among putting leaders, needing 1.780 putts per GIR. He used the putter an average of 29.31 times per round (112th).

The Scorer's Tent

Oodles of talent here and the positive impact of winning in his rookie and sophomore years can't be overemphasized. He tied the course record at TPC at Eagle Trace with a 10-under 62 on his way to the '96 Honda Classic title. His victory over Tiger Woods at the 1992 U.S. Amateur was one of only two losses Woods registered in 23 U.S. Amateur matches. He may lack the killer instinct, turning on the jets only at the last minute. Very impressive in third round, leading the TOUR with a 68.90 stroke average. If he doesn't become complacent, he will be a force in '98 and beyond. And there's no question the TOUR can use his unique presence. He can play in our foursome anytime.

Scott Hoch

Hoch. Hmm ... rhymes with ... Now stop that! Labeled "Scott Choke" after gargling the peanut butter over a two-foot putt to lose the 1989 Masters to Nick Faldo, Hoch admittedly has done little to help his own cause since. He self-destructed at the 1995 Shell Houston Open, handing the title to Payne Stewart after leading by five shots heading into the last nine holes.

Then, in another apparent attempt to slash his professional wrists, Hoch (rhymes with "duh") invoked an embargo on the golf media. ("Paging Dr. Kevorkian...") Too bad the vastly underrated Hoch, who by all accounts is a decent enough sort, can't seem to remake his personal image. "That seems to be my M.O. — to screw up or give a tournament away and then battle back later to prove myself," he observes. Don't be too quick to write off a guy who has won eight times in his 18 years on TOUR (OK, so two of them were Quad Cities Opens) and finished sixth on the '97 money list ($1,393,788). Remember he was a 41-year-old Ryder Cup rookie last year and went undefeated (2-0-1) at Valderrama. And did you realize Hoch trailed only Vijay Singh in number of consecutive cuts made at the start of this season (24)? He is extremely consistent on the golf course and a decent enough person off it: when he won the 1989 Las Vegas Invitational, he donated $100,000 to the Arnold Palmer Children's Hospital in Orlando, FL.

He's got the game, but unfortunately he's also got a name. Even his quotes are lame: "If you can't enjoy it, it won't be any fun." Jeez, he's his own worst enemy.

The Man

Scott Mabon Hoch, 5'11", 170 lbs. Born Nov. 24, 1955, in Raleigh, NC. Resides Orlando, FL. Wife, Sally; son. Cameron; daughter, Katie. Enjoys all sports (his father was an all-American in baseball at Wake Forest and his brother was a pro bowler). Turned professional and joined the TOUR in 1979.

Off the Tee

Not nearly long enough to have accomplished as much as he has thus far, if you believe the experts! Averaged a smidgen over 260 yards in 1997 (161st) but hit 75.9% of the fairways, good for 17th on TOUR.

Hitting the Green

Now this is where that distinctive upright swing comes in handy, resulting in crisp, accurate iron shots. Hoch was 13th on TOUR in greens in regulation (69.3%) and eighth among scoring leaders (69.70).

In Trouble

Hoch was third in scrambling (66.4%) in 1997. The scrambling stat calculates how often a player makes par or better after missing the green in regulation. You may recall Hoch nailed a 60-foot chip for eagle on the 72nd hole to steal the '97 Greater Milwaukee Open from Loren Roberts by one shot. He got up and down out of the sand about 60% of the time (28th).

Flatstick Facts

We assume the 24 inches of brain cramp at the '89 Masters was an aberration, although Hoch still doesn't dazzle anyone with his putting prowess: 28.94 putts per round left him 50th on TOUR.

The Scorer's Tent

A solid, super-consistent player who has missed being in the top 40 money winners only once since 1982 (when he had shoulder surgery), Hoch is a terribly underrated player. You just don't win eight PGA TOUR events and six international titles if you're as bad as most people say he is. Eleven top-10 finishes, no missed cuts and a 70.03 scoring average equaled almost $1.4 million in '97 and moved him into 10th place on the career list ($7,899,250). We'd take him on our team any day as long as nagging injuries (shoulder, back) don't slow him down.

Lee Janzen

In 1991, Lee Janzen was just another TOUR journeyman. After an all-American college career, he was 72nd on the money list and didn't appear to have a clue about how to win. Two years later, he had won the U.S. Open, beating Payne Stewart by tying Nicklaus's Open scoring record (67-67-69-69-272). Another two years down the road, Janzen was third in earnings ($1,348,966) after a three-win season.

At the start of 1997, it looked like he would just keep on winning. But golf is such a cruel game: he managed seven top-10 finishes, including two runner-up spots and a solo fourth in the PGA Championship, but no victories. Still on the "cruel game" theme: In the final round at the Colonial, Janzen, a former Little Leaguer, tried to flip his ball to his caddie. Instead, it sailed past the caddie and landed right in his golf bag, nestled among several other identical balls. Had Janzen not been able to identify it by a grass stain, he would have been penalized for a lost ball.

In addition to his throwing arm, we must question the quality of his decision making, particularly after being picked as a captain's choice for the '97 Ryder Cup team (he also played in '93). He chose to play the LaCantera Texas Open immediately prior to the event because he loves the Mexican food in San Antonio and someone (probably a European) told him the course was similar to Valderrama, the Ryder Cup site in Spain. Nevertheless, he posted a 2-1 record. Shows you what we know.

The Man

Lee MacLeod Janzen, 6'0", 175 lbs. Born Austin, MN, Aug. 28, 1964. Resides Orlando, FL. Wife, Beverly; son, Connor MacLeod. Attended Florida Southern College. Enjoys music, movies, snow skiing, all sports. Turned pro in 1986 and joined TOUR in 1989.

Off the Tee

Generally touted as a straight hitter, but ranked 81st in accuracy in '97 (69.6%). His average drive traveled just over 270 yards (59th) and he was 31st in total driving (average rank from distance and accuracy).

Hitting the Green

Janzen hits only two-thirds of greens in regulation (62nd) but makes the most of his opportunities. He was eighth among birdie leaders, making an average of 3.88 per round and ninth among par breakers (number of birdies and eagles per round). Overall, his 32.6% birdie conversion rate was seventh last season. And don't write him off if he's a few strokes back heading into Sunday. His final-round scoring average of 69.7 was fourth on TOUR.

In Trouble

Terrible out of the bunkers, with a sand-save average of 53.2% (109th) but his scrambling ability isn't bad. He made par or better 61.7% of the times he missed a green in regulation.

Flatstick Facts

The key to his birdies and eagles: Janzen was second on TOUR, averaging 1.726 putts per GIR. Overall, he needed 28.45 putts per average round (ninth).

The Scorer's Tent

He earned a 10-year exemption with his 1993 U.S. Open win, but Janzen isn't one to rest on his laurels. If he can knock some of those pushy 20-something players off the leaderboards this season, he is a good bet to restart his winning ways. He remains a solid, durable player, making the cut in 24 of the 27 events he entered in 1997, earning $877,832 (24th). Fifteen top-25 finishes and seven top-10s make him a good addition to any golf pool. It's unlikely he will drop off the face of the earth ... unless some agent talks him into switching equipment. (See Suicide Watch, page 12).

STEVE JONES

Without being sacrilegious, the career of born-again Christian Steve Jones has been resurrected more often than you know who. A second-team all-American at Colorado, Jones put himself through the agony of the TOUR's Qualifying School in 1981, '84 and '86. Once on TOUR, he demonstrated consistency and occasional brilliance, winning the AT&T Pebble Beach Pro-Am in '88 and then claiming three titles and three-quarters of a million dollars the next year.

So what happened to Mr. Jones between 1990 and his U.S. Open win in 1996? A dirt bike just about ripped his left ring finger off, that's what happened. To compensate for the resulting chronic problems, he invented a sort of reverse overlap grip for full shots that he uses to this day. "I probably should do a video on that grip and sell it ... It would mess up a lot of people!" (We recall a prominent golf magazine doing an instructional article on that grip a while ago. Thanks a lot!)

The '96 Open was a blessing and a curse: it rejuvenated his career, but the demands placed on the winner burned him out in a hurry. Outside distractions and the pressure to make the '97 Ryder Cup team, which intensified after his quick start in the first three events of '97 (T6 Mercedes Championships, T9 Bob Hope Chrysler Classic, won Phoenix Open), sucked all the fun out of Jones. Aside from placing second at the Tucson Chrysler Classic (he's tough to beat in Arizona), he missed the cut in eight of the next fifteen events. Once his Ryder Cup chance disappeared, Jones reappeared, winning his second Bell Canadian Open in September. At that event, he was jocular and entertaining — "I felt like Trevino." "I've learned a big lesson," he said later, vowing never to lose his focus again.

Off the Tee

Jones deserves full marks for creating that unique grip and making it work to his advantage, at least in length. He powders the ball 278.2 yards on average, but with only a 65.7% accuracy rating (139th).

Hitting the Green

Hits about two-thirds of the greens in regulation (67th) and converts 30.5% of his birdie chances overall (34th). He would be murder on a par-3 course, since he boasts a 16.3% birdie average on the one-shotters (11th).

In Trouble

Not his strong suit: 68th in scrambling (60.1%) and a lowly 108th in sand saves (53.3%).

Flatstick Facts

Yuck. He was 137th in putting (1.799) and needed 29.49 putts per round overall.

The Scorer's Tent

There's no "quit" in Jones. He had to make par on the last hole of the sectional qualifier for the '96 Open and then went on to win the whole enchilada, posting the lowest winning score ever in an Open at Oakland Hills (two-under 278). He's a long-time competitor, having been an all-state basketball player in high school. If he looks in the mirror, realizes he's 40 years old and stays off dirt bikes, he'll be cashing checks all the way to the Senior TOUR. Those three years off might have extended his career on the regular TOUR as well. Don't bet against Steve Jones appearing at a check presentation near you in '98. Of course, the real reason we like him is that he is a two-time Colorado sand greens champ, which means he's good with both a golf club and a rake. (If you haven't played a sand greens course, don't even ask...)

Tom Kite

We realize that this is totally subjective, unfair, immature and juvenile, ... but we just don't like Tom Kite. There's something peculiar about the man. It could be that he looks like the geeky kid we all liked to beat up in grade school.

Now that we've got that off our chest, here's why you should like him — and why you should pick him in the golf pool draft. Although he will turn 49 just after this TOUR season ends, Kite's résumé is Hall of Fame material, and he showed little sign of faltering in 1997. He has 19 TOUR victories and we are still dumbfounded when we recall his unbelievable performance winning the '92 U.S. Open when the flagsticks were bending 90 degrees on windswept Pebble Beach. Although he hasn't won since 1993 (Bob Hope Chrysler Classic, Nissan Los Angeles Open), he posted five top-10 finishes last season, three of which were in majors. Maybe being Ryder Cup captain inspired him to his best position on the money list since 1994 ($631,252, 35th), but we think it's because Kite is one tough competitor who would rather poke his eyes out with a tee than give up. He won a tournament every year from 1981 through 1993, except for 1988 when he had three runner-up finishes, on his way to becoming the first player to bank career earnings of $6 million, $7 million, $8 million and $9 million. (Greg Norman beat him to $10 million.)

The Man

Thomas Oliver Kite, Jr., 5'8", 163 lbs. Born Austin, TX, Dec. 9, 1949. Resides Austin, TX. Wife, Christy; daughter, Stephanie Lee; sons, David Thomas and Paul Christopher. Attended University of Texas. Enjoys landscaping. Turned pro in 1972; Q School in 1972.

Off the Tee

We're impressed. Although Kite's average drive was 269.3 yards (72nd), he poked one 360 at a TOUR event, the 13th longest measured drive in '97. His accuracy is enviable, too — 72.5% (45th). In total driving, which combines distance and accuracy ratings, he was 19th overall.

Hitting the Green

Again, he's got better-than-average accuracy with his irons, hitting 67% of greens in regulation. He was ranked 30th in the ball-striking category, which combines his rank in total driving with his GIR rank.

In Trouble

We're not impressed. He was 143rd in sand saves (49.5%), 75th in scrambling and 139th in bounce back.

Flatstick Facts

The putter is not Tom Kite's best ally: he ranked 154th among putting leaders, averaging 1.805 putts per GIR, and needed an average of 29.64 putts per round (153rd).

The Scorer's Tent

He won the Vardon Trophy for low stroke average on TOUR in 1981 and 1982 and retains that solid, albeit mechanical, repeating swing. In a couple of years, he will be living large, kicking some round-belly butt on the Senior TOUR, but he is one proud Texan who is committed to doing his best right now. He took a licking for both his Ryder Cup team's performance and his approach to the team captaincy (were we the only ones who didn't ride around Valderrama in his cart?), and he will try to make those critics eat their words by winning on TOUR this year. And he will. It might even be at a major. Now that would be a lovely swan song to the TOUR. (But we still don't like him.)

Tom Lehman

If it weren't for two mis-hit 7-irons during the '97 U.S. Open, it would have been another fabulous year for one of the most likeable players on TOUR. Perhaps one of the most memorable and heart-felt quotes from the 1997 season was his, "I'd give anything for a mulligan right now," as his hopes sank along with his golf ball into the water at the 71st hole at Congressional.

That event marked the third consecutive Open in which Lehman held the 54-hole lead, a feat accomplished previously only by Bobby Jones. He was PGA TOUR player of the year in '96 after winning the British Open and the TOUR Championship and posting a then-record money total of $1,780,159. For a week in April '96, he was the No. 1-ranked player in the world, joining Fred Couples as the only Americans to hold that vaunted position. Not bad for a grinder who tried nine times to get through qualifying school, played 11 different tours around the world and seriously considered becoming the golf coach at his alma mater. If nothing else, the years of scrabbling made him mentally tough and determined to make the most of his opportunity when it finally came.

The Man

Thomas Edward Lehman, 6'2", 190 lbs. Born Austin, MN, March 7, 1959. Resides Scottsdale, AZ. Wife, Melissa; daughters Rachael and Holly; son, Thomas Andrew. Attended University of Minnesota. Enjoys hunting and church activities. Turned pro in 1982 and joined TOUR in 1983.

Off the Tee

Consistent. His 271.4-yard average was 55th on TOUR and his 72.8% accuracy rating was 38th. Second in ball striking, which combines total driving (average of driving distance and accuracy) with the greens in regulation stat.

Hitting the Green

First on TOUR with a 72.7% average. Did you see him at the '97 Skins Game? What more can we say?

In Trouble

Lehman was fifth in scoring (69.62) and fourth in the all-round stat. He wasn't awesome out of the sand, getting up and down about 55% of the time.

Flatstick Facts

The flaw in an otherwise bulletproof game: he was 84th among putting leaders, requiring 29.96 whacks per round.

The Scorer's Tent

Lehman, a devout Christian and family man, no doubt abides by the dictum: "It matters not whether you win or lose, but how you play the game." After all, it was he who quoted Joshua 1:9 to fellow competitor Steve Jones during the final round of the '96 U.S. Open ("Be courageous and strong, for that is the will of the Lord."). Jones must have listened, because he won the tournament.

Lehman is used to working hard for results and will be motivated, not discouraged, by last season. He was close, real close, to a super year in '97 but didn't get the breaks. He played well against strong fields: second in the Mercedes Championships, third in the U.S. Open, sixth in The Players Championship and T10 in the PGA Championship. In November, he kicked everybody's butt in the Skins Game, winning 10 skins and $300,000, over O'Meara, Woods and Duval. He'll return to the winner's circle again this year, guaranteed.

Justin Leonard

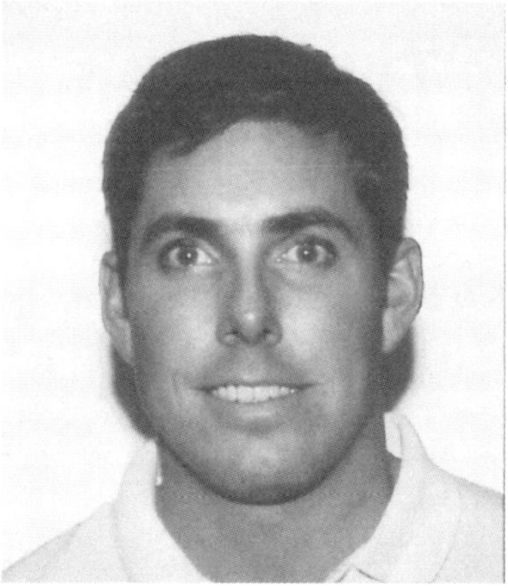

What you see is what you get: A clean-cut Texas kid with a bad lid who will be winning TOUR events for the next couple of decades. Hey, Jasper: Give your little brother his cap back. (Jasper is his nickname — ironic that Jesper Parnevik was the guy he gutted in the final round of the British Open, isn't it?)

Calling Leonard a grinder at the start of his young career might have been a touch shortsighted. While he averages 30 events a year on TOUR, he's no journeyman, winning the '96 Buick Open prior to his breakthrough '97 season where he added the Kemper Open and the British Open. His final money stats show that he's headed for the top: 126th in 1994, 22nd in '95, 11th in '96 and fifth last season. He's composed, likeable, looks just fine in the Polo gear he endorses and, it seems, no one has a bad word to say about him. No wonder *Cosmopolitan* magazine has named him one of the 25 most eligible bachelors in the world. His feet are firmly on the ground (appropriate for a guy who has great balance in his swing); when he entered the media center at the 1997 NEC World Series of Golf, he said: "If you ever hear me complain about coming in here or, you know, signing autographs or anything, just hit me!"

The Man

Justin Charles Garret Leonard, 5'9", 160 lbs. Born June 15, 1972, in Dallas, TX. Resides Dallas, TX, plays out of Kiawah Island, SC. Single. Enjoys fishing. Turned pro and joined the TOUR in 1994.

Off the Tee

Leonard traded in his steel-shafted persimmon driver for a 45-inch, 7.5-degree metal driver with a graphite shaft last season, adding 15 to 20 yards and allowing him to shape tee shots better. (How's that for an advertisement for technology?) Nonetheless, he ranked 172nd on TOUR in driving distance (259.2 yards) and 48th in accuracy.

Hitting the Green

He may not be a grinder, but Leonard certainly defines "scrambler." He was second on TOUR in the "scrambling" stats category, making par or better 67.1% of the time after missing the green in regulation. For the record, he hit less than two-thirds of the greens in regulation. He was third in par-3 birdies at 17.3% (70/405 holes).

In Trouble

We think the "scrambling" stat explains what happens when he's in trouble. In addition, he was 26th on TOUR in sand saves (59.8%).

Flatstick Facts

Looks like Leonard can get up and down from just about anywhere. Combine his scrambling ability with his 28.28 putts per round (third on TOUR) and that sums up the situation. He drained putts from anywhere on his way to winning the British, especially during his final-round 65.

The Scorer's Tent

Justin Leonard is the real deal. He's one of the few whose psychological strength and mental toughness match his physical ability. He will never hit it farther or straighter than everyone else on TOUR, but he will always find a way to win. Even as an amateur, he made the cut in five of the eight TOUR events he played in. He is consistent: his scoring average through all four rounds of all events in 1997 never wavered more than .19 (from 70.46 in first two rounds to 70.65 in final round). There's no doubt that this guy has the character not to let the inevitable off-course distractions and immense wealth ($1,587,531 in 1997 TOUR earnings) derail his career as so many others have. (See Corey Pavin, Steve Stricker and others on the "Suicide Watch" on page 12).

Davis Love III

Even if you thought this guy was Opie with a 1-iron, you had to cheer when Davis Love III won the 1997 PGA Championship under the rainbow at Winged Foot. Everybody hugged him — his caddie/brother, his wife and his mother — as the aura of his late father hovered above them.

Too bad it had taken Love — "the best player who hasn't won a major" — 10 years and 30-odd kicks at the can to win a big one. And although he had 10 TOUR wins coming into the 1997 season, nobody was more disappointed than Love. In his own words, "I came out here as a 20-year-old kid thinking that majors would be my best chance." He was relying on a combination of length and pedigree (his father was a renowned instructor who died in a 1988 plane crash at 53); what he didn't realize was that putting was the secret ingredient. Kidney stones (that may explain the pained, tight-lipped expression he often has) and a wonky wrist in 1997 signaled that Love is no longer one of the TOUR's resilient young guns.

His dad's favorite line was, "Follow your dream and enjoy the trip." Love has adhered to that philosophy thus far, but we'll wait to see if his PGA win makes him complacent. He enjoys the occasional cigar (some of them Cuban, rumors say ... hoo, what a rebel), stock car racing, fishing, hunting and his family. Dabbles in course architecture. Should have no trouble staying focused to avoid being tagged "the best player who won only one major."

The Man

Davis Milton Love III, 6'3", 175 lbs. Born April 13, 1954, in Charlotte, NC. Resides in Sea Island, GA. Wife, Robin; daughter, Alexia; son, Davis IV. Attended University of North Carolina. Turned pro and joined TOUR in 1985.

Off the Tee

Don't be deceived: this narrow-shouldered, apparently unathletic beanpole can smoke it! His 285.8-yard average was fourth best on TOUR last year, but he averaged 307-plus on his way to winning the PGA Championship. It's taken him years to learn how to throttle back, but the results are evident. He ranked sixth in converting birdies on par 5s (46.4%) and notched 11 eagles (8th) on his way to third place on the TOUR money list ($1,635,953).

Hitting the Green

Only eight players hit more greens in regulation than Love (70%). His length gives him an advantage on the par 4s and par 5s, but he struggles on the par 3s. In 1997, he birdied only 11% of the par 3s, 158th best on TOUR.

Flatstick Facts

Despite professing that putting is the key to major success, Love ranked 150th on TOUR in that category (29.58 putts per round).

In Trouble

Like many players who hit it a ton, Love probably could stand a few more hours working on his short game. Suspect putting, combined with a sand game that sucks (he ranked 100th in sand saves), are glaring deficiencies.

The Scorer's Tent

Just how good were those three 66s at Winged Foot? Especially the last round with the weather and that little bulldog Justin Leonard nipping at his heels? This guy has done more than justify his dad's faith in him. He was 4-0 in Ryder Cup singles matches until his brain cramp at Valderrama in '97 (0-4 overall), but he came back from Spain to win the Buick Challenge. Two wins in a season aren't unusual, but the major was significant. He's TKO'd the naysayers forever. He was tied with Jim Furyk for most top-10 finishes in 1997 (13). And he's nowhere near done inching up that career money list (he's sixth at $8,470,982). Get ready to light up another stogie or two, Davis.

Steve Lowery

If we had bet you last Oct. 5 that Steve Lowery would come within a hair's breadth of tying Al Geiberger's TOUR record of 59, you would have lost some money. Lowery, whose previous claim to fame was winning the '94 Sprint Invitational, made the turn at 29 — "I wasn't going to be happy with that" — was 10 under after 13 that day and needed to birdie three of the last five holes to shoot 59. He made three pars and then birdied 17 and 18 to post a 60. Since he started the final round 13 shots back of leader Davis Love III, who shot 68, Lowery didn't win the Buick Challenge, finishing third. He ended the season in 44th spot on the money list.

The Man

Stephen Brent Lowery, 6'2", 225 lbs. Born Birmingham, AL, Oct. 12, 1960. Resides Orlando, FL. Wife, Kathryn; daughters, Kristen Branch and Lauren Elizabeth. Attended University of Alabama. Enjoys sports. Turned pro in 1983; Q School in 1987.

Off the Tee

Lowery's a big, powerful player whose average drive last season went 277.8 yards (20th) and found the fairway 65.5% of the time (142nd).

Hitting the Green

Skilful shotmaker, hitting 67.6% of GIR, and ranked 14th among par breakers. He was second among eagle leaders, making one every 104.8 holes, and had 17 in total — more than anyone else on TOUR. He was 26th among birdie leaders (3.68).

In Trouble

Nothing exceptional in sand saves — 56.6%, 62nd — or scrambling — 59.3%, 80th — but he was 11th in the bounce back category, making birdie or better 23.4% of the time following a bogey or worse.

Flatstick Facts

A weak spot. Lowery was 78th among putting leaders (1.781/GIR) and 105th in putts per round (29.29).

The Scorer's Tent

Despite a hiccup in 1996, when he dropped to 80th, Lowery appears poised to become a fixture in the top 50 money winners. Unlike some of his peers near the middle of the top 125, however, he possesses the all-round game to add two or three more titles to the one he garnered in '94. He ranked 18th in the TOUR's all-around stat in '97 and was second in final-round scoring average (69.6). Of course, that 60 at the Buick Challenge helped.

Andrew Magee

There's something just a little off center about Andrew Magee. He lists "whistling" as one of his favored pastimes in the *PGA TOUR Media Guide*, was born in Paris, France (his dad worked there at the time), and conducts a charity pro-am called the Santa Claus Open at TPC of Scottsdale with — aha! — Gary McCord. That explains a lot. Magee, who has quietly stayed on the top 125 list since his sophomore TOUR year of 1985, had an exceptional season in '97. He threatened to win the Greater Vancouver Open and the B.C. Open before finishing second in both, and posted five other top-10 finishes on his way to earning $750,007 (30th). That wasn't his best year though. That would have been 1991 when the three-time all-American won two events, had seven top 10s and finished fifth on the money list.

The Man

Andrew Donald Magee, 6'0", 180 lbs. Born Paris, France, May 22, 1962. Resides Paradise Valley, AZ. Wife, Susan; daughter, Lindsey Ellenberg; sons, Campbell Joseph and Oliver Andrew. Attended University of Oklahoma. Enjoys travel, swimming, fishing and whistling. Turned pro in 1984; Q School 1984.

Off the Tee

Magee is no slouch, driving the ball an average of 274.1 yards (41st) and hitting 67.9% of fairways (108th).

Hitting the Green

He was 45th in hitting greens in regulation in '97 (45th), 11th among eagle leaders and 29th in birdies. He especially likes par 5s, where his birdie conversion rate of 42% was 15th on TOUR.

In Trouble

Decent out of the sand with a 57.5% save percentage (48th). He was 34th in scrambling (34th) and seventh in bounce back.

Flatstick Facts

Like the rest of Magee's stats, there's little to complain about here. His 1.767 putts per GIR were good for 35th place, while he needed an average of 29.01 putts per round (63rd).

The Scorer's Tent

We like Magee's all-round game (he finished ninth in that significant statistical category in 1997) and think he is a player to watch in '98. However, he hasn't shown much consistency from year to year, hopping up and down the top-125 list. If he gets off to a quick start, he may keep building on that momentum. Definitely a keeper in any golf pool, especially if he can get motivated.

Jeff Maggert

Without casting any aspersions on Jeff Maggert's sexual orientation, we think his post-golf career should be modeling bridesmaids' dresses. Talk about not knowing how to win — he's posted 10 runner-up finishes in his seven years on TOUR. And he seems to be getting better and better at figuring out how to cough up a sure victory. He led the '97 U.S. Open by a shot after 54 holes and then went four over on the last three holes, finishing fourth. Tied for the lead on the 72nd hole of the Canon Greater Hartford Open, he makes bogey to finish — you guessed it — second. ("Paging Dr. Heimlich...Dr. Heimlich to the 18th tee, please.") He lost the '96 Shell Houston Open in a playoff after leading going into Sunday and had two other bridesmaid results that season. Somebody up there hates Maggert: when he led the '96 AT&T Pebble Beach National Pro-Am after 36 holes, they cancelled the event due to weather. Of course, that decision relieved Maggert of the opportunity to blow another sure thing. "If I can win as many tournaments as I've finished second in, I'm going to have one hell of a career," he said last year. You should live so long, Jeff. He went 2-1 in the '97 Ryder Cup matches but we all know the U.S. ended up second.

The Man

Jeffrey Allan Maggert, 5'9", 175 lbs. Born Columbia, MO, Feb. 20, 1964. Resides The Woodlands, TX. Wife, Kelli. Attended Texas A&M. Enjoys fishing, hunting and camping. Turned pro in 1986 and joined TOUR in 1991.

Off the Tee

Maggert's not a big man and doesn't hit it far (264.3-yard average, 125th) but he makes up for it with accuracy, hitting 75.3% of fairways (19th).

Hitting the Green

Hitting 67.9% of greens in regulation placed Maggert 32nd on TOUR in '97, but his putting meant only a 28.2% birdie conversion average (109th).

In Trouble

He's lucky he hits all those greens, because his scrambling sucks: 160th on TOUR (he made par or better 55.6% of the time he missed a green in regulation). His bunker play is abominable: a sand-save average of 45.7% was 168th on TOUR.

Flatstick Facts

Maggert was 68th in putting on GIR (1.778) and required an average of 29.65 putts per round (156th).

The Scorer's Tent

We like Maggert, but we just can't figure out when the planets will be in the proper alignment for him to win a tournament. He's gotta be mentally tough to weather this plague of near-biblical proportions. "This game will discourage you to death if you let it," he admits. Don't let it, Jeff. In '97, he made $835,884 on TOUR (26th) and played well at the Ryder Cup. He's finished no lower than 38th on the money list since 1992, and is a good bet to maintain that trend. "He's one of those players who could explode and become a great player," says Brad Faxon. If he doesn't get a win this year, he might just explode.

Doug Martin

Doug Martin's a nice guy who didn't finish last in '97. Au contraire, he had his best season in six TOUR campaigns, finishing 64th on the money list ($383,593). He played 30 events, making 22 cuts, posting 10 top-25 finishes and three top 10s. His best performance was T5 at the Honda Classic. He's a three-time all-American and lives for Notre Dame football, even spending time on the sidelines with former coach Lou Holtz.

The Man

Douglas Allan Martin, 6'0", 190 lbs. Born Bluffton, OH, Dec. 6, 1966. Resides Edgewood, KY. Wife, Gaylynn; sons, Cody Alan and Macy. Attended University of Oklahoma. Enjoys family, sports and Notre Dame football. Turned pro in 1989; Q School in 1991.

The Stats

Eleventh on TOUR in driving accuracy (77%) but 187th in distance (255.6 yards). Martin hits 67.2% of GIR (45th) and was 20th in scrambling. Unfortunately, his stroke average on Saturday explodes to 71.36 (95th) before settling to an impressive 70.29 (11th) on Sunday.

The Scorer's Tent

Nice guy, solid stats, grinding. If he had a little more length, he'd be a regular winner. He's only 31 and if he keeps improving at the rate he did from '96 to '97 — cutting almost half a stroke off his scoring average — he'll vault up the money list in short order. Maybe he's playing on Saturday while listening to the Notre Dame game on his Walkman? If you've got last pick, throw him a Hail Mary.

Scott McCarron

What a bag of toys this guy is. Which means he's the kind of person we would like to play golf with ... and party with after. A good all-round athlete at UCLA, he graduated with a major in history and a double minor in barhopping and goofing off. Then he wandered among the developmental tours for a while, winning the Canadian Tour's 1993 Q School along the way. He admits to really liking the Hooters Tour because of the wings and beer at the sponsor's restaurants. Now there's a man with his priorities straight.

Putrid putting made him give up golf for four years, so he worked for his dad's clothing business. While watching a Senior TOUR event, he was inspired to try a longer putter. He constructed one himself and nearly won the U.S. Mid-Amateur a few months later. He's used a version of that contraption to win his two TOUR titles ('96 Freeport-McDermott Classic, '97 BellSouth Classic).

Another factor adding to his success was his vastly improved third- and fourth-round scoring average. He attributes that to getting married: "My wife is making me stay in on Friday nights." This is the same guy who won the BellSouth Classic after pulling a hamstring while trying to outrun Dicky Pride during a second-round rain delay (don't ask). McCarron credits the injury with making him shorten his swing, improving his ball striking. (Now there's a concept David Leadbetter hasn't even considered.) He's a licensed pilot and loves sky diving, but we trust having a two-year-old daughter will temper his thrill seeking.

The Man

Scott Michael McCarron, 5'10", 170 lbs. Born Sacramento, CA, July 10, 1965. Resides Rancho Murieta, CA. Wife, Jennifer; daughter, Courtney. Attended UCLA. Enjoys flying, skiing, mountain biking, sky diving. Turned pro in 1992; Q School in 1994.

Off the Tee

Pound for pound, one of the longest hitters on TOUR, averaging almost 284 yards (seventh). Now for the familiar refrain — "The woods are full of long hitters" — McCarron was 155th in accuracy (64.5%).

Hitting the Green

He was 95th in GIR (64.8%) and 64th in birdie average but 15th among eagle leaders, averaging one every 162 holes and notching nine in total (12th). He made birdie on 42.5% of the par 5s he played (13th). As mentioned, his scoring average is exceptional on Saturday (69.75, eighth) and Sunday (70.07, eighth).

In Trouble

Not a great scrambler, making par or better only 58.8% of the times he missed a green in regulation, and his sand play could stand some work: he got up and down from greenside bunkers only 54.1% of the time (97th).

Flatstick Facts

Mediocre — he ranked 55th among putting leaders, needing 1.774 putts when he hit a green in regulation; overall, he used his elongated putter 28.94 times per round.

The Scorer's Tent

That time spent wandering in the non-TOUR wilderness did this former wild thing a lot of good. He matured, got married and honed his game to the point that in 1997, his third season, he was 25th among money winners with $852,459. (That's a pile of wings and beer at Hooters.) He had seven top-10 finishes, including T10 at both the U.S. Open and the PGA Championship which matched his finish at the '96 Masters. Another win in '98 is certainly within his grasp and a major is definitely not out of the question. We would feel more comfortable if he could lose that nasty habit of missing cuts — nine of 26 (with one WD) in 1997.

Phil Mickelson

Phil Mickelson has more than one reason to feel left out: Not only is he one of only a couple of lefties on TOUR (Russ Cochran and 1997 Q-School grad Mike Weir are the others), but he is getting lapped by his 20-something peers. "David Duval wins the last three tournaments of the year. Justin Leonard wins a major. Ernie Els wins the U.S. Open — again," Mickelson observed after winning the Mercedes Championships, the first TOUR event of 1998. "I felt like in college I had a pretty good record against these guys, and for me not to be playing at that level was disappointing." Hey, Phil, the Mercedes may have had a good field, but it's no major. You're still on the outside looking in. Mickelson is supertalented; his wedge player is legendary (have you seen him hit the ball backwards over his head?), but he has yet to elevate his entire game to the highest level.

Granted, expectations were heightened when he won the 1991 Northern Telecom Open as an amateur. He won twice in '97. In addition to the Bay Hill Invitational, he won the Sprint International, posting 48 points and breaking his own record of 43 set in 1993. But they are far from majors, too. "The best player who hasn't won a major" label now is the object of a game of tug-of-war between Mickelson and Colin Montgomerie. (Don't blame us — blame Davis Love III.) We like Montgomerie's chances.

The Man

Philip Alfred Mickelson, 6'2", 190 lbs. Born San Diego, CA, June 16, 1970. Resides Scottsdale, AZ. Wife, Amy. Attended Arizona State University. Enjoys all sports, especially football, and flying. Joined TOUR in 1992.

Off the Tee

Murders the ball (284.1 yards, fifth on TOUR) but — and stop us if you've heard this before — doesn't find a lot of fairways (67.3%, 120th). "Drive for show and putt for ... majors?"

Hitting the Green

Mickelson is a Seve-like shotmaker, which accounts for the fact that he hit 67.5% of greens in regulation despite hitting his tee shots into various area codes.

In Trouble

Shotmaking genius whose creativity is often tested by the situations he puts himself in. Surprisingly, he was only 63rd in scrambling and got up and down out of bunkers just over half the time (55.6%, 72nd).

Flatstick Facts

Middle of the pack here: 35th on TOUR, needing an average of 29.96 putts per round.

The Scorer's Tent

Despite his blasé, oftentimes robotic appearance, friends say he can be fiery and cocky, bordering on arrogant. You have to like his chances when he takes the lead going into the final round — he has won six of seven times when he's been in that situation. His win in January marked his sixth straight year with a TOUR win, tying him with Greg Norman. Like Norman, he is a pilot, qualified for jets. He'd better strap on some booster rockets in the next couple of years if he's going to prove the cynics (like us) wrong. We hope he does, but he may be too complacent with his gorgeous former-cheerleader wife and millions in the bank. (OK, so we're jealous.) Anybody who hits rockets off the tee and creates shots that no one else has ever considered should have more to show than a handful of mid-level titles.

Colin Montgomerie

Is Colin Montgomerie the "jerk of the world," as Fred Funk advises? Should his first name be pronounced, as one observer suggested, "Colon" because he is such a ... sphincter? Should his surname be spelled, as a British tabloid said during the '97 British Open, "Montglumerie"? Is it just us, or is it really obvious that no photo of him looks complete until you squint and imagine a giant baby pacifier sticking out of his mouth? But the line we like best, from the ever-quotable "Anon.," is: "Thank God he's such an idiot. If he ever grew up, he'd win everything in sight."

The other quote we like is from Monty himself: "I am a bad loser; I have always been a bad loser." He apologized publicly and privately to the U.S. Ryder Cup squads after some inappropriate comments were exaggerated by the U.S. media. That was after he won 3 ½ of a possible five points at Valderrama. "It's getting me down, this major business," he said tearfully last summer after losing his second U.S. Open to Ernie Els. (He also lost to Els in an 18-hole playoff at Oakmont in '94.) The U.S. Open "is the world championship of golf," he said last year. He might as well have had a sticker across his mouth that read, "Insert Own Foot Here." His father, James, is the secretary of Royal Troon, where the British Open was played last year. OK, so the guy is his own worst enemy. Let's hope the golf media pick a moving target for a change this year and focus on what Monty can do on the course.

The Man

Colin Montgomerie, 6'1", 210 lbs. Born Glasgow, Scotland, June 23, 1963. Resides Oxshott, Surrey, England. Wife, Eimear; daughters, Olivia and Venetia Grace. Attended Houston Baptist University. Enjoys music, cars and films. Turned pro in 1987.

The Stats

Since Monty did not play the required minimum number of rounds on the PGA TOUR, we can offer you only this: He played in nine events and finished 37th on the money list

($578,991.) One other note from '97: He — not Tiger — was the No. 1 money winner worldwide with $3.366 million after claiming the $1-million first prize in the Andersen Consulting World Championship of Golf. (For the record, Tiger was fifth with $2.38 million. Ernie Els was second, Davis Love III was — appropriately enough — third and Nick Price was fourth after winning the $1 Million Challenge in South Africa.) In addition to the World Championship, he won the World Cup of Golf, the Murphy's Irish Open and the Compaq European Grand Prix to bump his career victory total to 20.

The Skinny

(Somehow, that heading seems inappropriate...How about: The Full Monty?).

Although Montgomerie now is vying with Phil Mickelson for the unenviable title of "the best player not to win a major," we like the big Scot's chances. He's coming off his record fifth straight European Order of Merit title and a 2-up win over '97 PGA champion Davis Love III in the final of the Andersen Consulting World Championship of Golf. (He dusted U.S. Open winner Els in the semis.) He did recant his promise to play over here fulltime if he won his fifth money title in Europe, which puzzled us until we noticed that he and his wife are expecting another baby this spring. Will he win a major this year? Yes. You read it here first.

Frank Nobilo

Compiling the *PGA TOUR Media Guide* can't be a whole lot of fun (they can't get away with the stuff we can). But you have to give them credit for a great line in Frank Nobilo's bio: "Ancestors were Italian pirates who, after running out of things to pillage on the Adriatic, resettled in New Zealand in the early 1900s." You could write a novel based on that line!

But we digress again. After turning pro in 1979, Nobilo sailed among the offshore tours, doing a bit of plundering himself. He scored 10 victories, including the '95 and '96 Subaru Sarazen World Open Championships — a non-TOUR event played in the U.S. In his second full year on TOUR, he pirated the '97 Greater Greensboro Chrysler Classic title from Brad Faxon in a playoff. He entered 19 events, missed four cuts and withdrew once. Four top 10s and nine top 25s helped boost his '97 season earnings to $891,315 (23rd). Now 38, Nobilo is fighting various physical ailments ranging from a mysterious, arthritis-like condition in his wrists to back problems that stem from — take your choice — hitting his head on the bottom of a swimming pool when he was a teenager, or being born with right leg shorter than his left. (Har, matey, are ye sure that's not a peg leg?)

The Man

Frank Ivan Joseph Nobilo, 6'0", 190 lbs. Born Auckland, New Zealand, May 14, 1960. Resides London, England. Daughter, Bianca. Enjoys squash and motor racing. Turned pro in 1979 and joined the TOUR in 1997.

Off the Tee

Middle of the pack in both distance (270.7 yards, 59th) and accuracy (70.4%), but 25th in total driving (the average rank from the driving distance and accuracy stats).

Hitting the Green

Nobilo was 54th in GIR (66.7%) but 167th in birdie conversions (26.3%). A good iron player, he made birdies on 15.2% of the par 3s (31st).

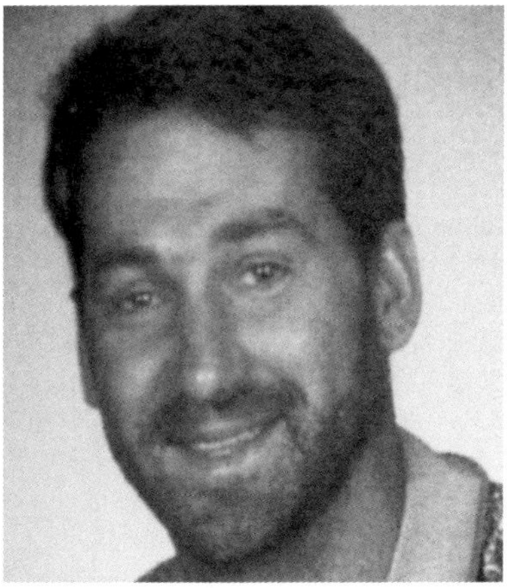

In Trouble

He was 168th in scrambling (making par or better after missing the green in regulation). Fortunately he is a wedge wizard, getting up and down out of the sand 64.6% of the time (third best on TOUR).

Flatstick Facts

Nobilo no doubt wishes, as Hogan once suggested, that all greens be funnel-shaped and have a tube attached leading to the next tee. He was 162nd in putting on GIR (1.808) and required almost 30 putts per average round (29.88, 181st).

The Scorer's Tent

"It was difficult coming to America," Nobilo said last season. "Nothing seemed to be easy ... but I thought my best golf was ahead of me." With that fundamentally sound swing, the bearded Nobilo (is that that pirate thing again?) may be right. And he's not after merchant vessels like the Buick, Chrysler and Mercedes. He wants the behemoths, the men o' war — the majors. Look at his record: T10 in the '97 British (he shot 68-68 on the weekend at Troon), T4 in the '96 Masters, T8 at the '96 PGA and T13 in the '96 U.S. Open. Now that it appears the doctors have that wrist thing figured out, the Good Ship Nobilo is poised for a broadside on TOUR in '98.

Greg Norman

Most sharks are renowned for inflicting pain, but Greg Norman, who carries the nickname "Great White Shark," is becoming the poster child for the golfing gods' cruel jests, more used to absorbing pain than dealing it out. For instance, he is the only golfer ever to lose all four major championships in a playoff. Every highlight film offers him up as a sacrificial lamb, usually at the hands of some journeyman, although his monumental collapse at the 1996 Masters (allowing Nick Faldo to make up a six-shot deficit in the final round for the win) won him some sympathy.

Sympathy was about the only thing Norman didn't have: how about 18 career wins on the PGA TOUR, the first player to hit $10 million in career earnings, not missing a single cut in four different years, PGA TOUR player of the year in 1995, two British Opens, perennially the top-ranked player world wide... After his pathetic loss to Faldo, he said it didn't matter because "I still have $40 million." False bravado, say those who know the man: winning, not whining, is his trademark. While other business interests and global travel have taken their toll on his on-course performance, the Great White Shark will make a vengeful return in 1998. Hard to believe he turned 43 this year, isn't it?

The Man

Gregory John Norman, 6'0", 180 lbs. Born Feb. 10, 1955, in Queensland, Australia. Resides Hobe Sound, FL. Enjoys fishing, hunting, scuba diving. Turned pro in 1976 and joined the PGA TOUR in 1983.

Off the Tee

You may find this hard to believe, looking at Norman's vicious swipe at every tee shot, but he ranked 75th on TOUR last year, with a 268.8-yard average. However, that was compensated for by hitting almost 75% of the fairways he aimed at. He was 17th in total driving.

Hitting the Green

What he's lost in length in his 20-plus years as a pro, Norman has made up for in accuracy. He hit seven out of ten greens in regulation, leading to his eighth-place ranking in average birdies per round (3.88, or 198 in 51 rounds). Astoundingly, he made only two eagles.

In Trouble

For a player with awesome power, Norman demonstrates magical finesse occasionally. He has chipped in to win events (a 66-foot chip in 1995 won him the NEC World Series of Golf in a playoff) and his sand play is admirable (11th on TOUR in 1997 with a 62% average).

Flatstick Facts

Norman's putting can most charitably be described as "streaky." Unfortunately, it's usually "streaky bad." He averaged almost 30 putts per round last year, good for 131st spot on TOUR. Yecch.

The Scorer's Tent

OK, so the guy chokes, he can't putt and he's getting older. All he did was win two TOUR events last season (FedEx St. Jude Classic and NEC World Series of Golf) and post $1,345,856 in TOUR earnings ($1,793,649 worldwide). That petty cash kept him atop the worldwide career money list with 1997 official deposits of $11,910,518. Of course, he'll need that as a down payment on his personal $38-million, 63-passenger Boeing 737 when it's delivered next year. Hold the Great White Shark Telethon plans, please.

David Ogrin

The only guy on TOUR who admits he dreamed of being a switch-hitter. Whoops ... that should read "switch-hitting catcher" as in baseball. Ogrin loves the Chicago Cubs so much (there's no accounting for taste) that he named his son Clark Addison after an intersection near Wrigley Field. (Thank goodness gambling wasn't his avocation. "Crap Table" is no name for a kid.) After finishing 34th on the money list in '96, helped along by winning the LaCantera Texas Open, Ogrin dropped two spots last year, but still earned $593,683. He entered 27 events, made 21 cuts, withdrew once and was disqualified once. The DQ came when Ogrin impersonated a one-car pileup at the Mercedes Championships, signing an incorrect scorecard after the first round. What can we say — he's a Cubs fan.

The Man

David Allen Ogrin, 6'0", 220 lbs. Born Waukegan, IL, Dec. 31, 1957. Resides Garden Ridge, TX. Wife, Sharon; daughters, Amy, Jessica and Dana; son, Clark Addison. Attended Texas A&M. Special Interests: Christianity, children, Chicago Cubs. Turned pro in 1980; Q School in 1982 and 1992.

Off the Tee

Doesn't hit it as far as you might think for a big man — his 263.3-yard average was 141st on TOUR. Better in the accuracy department, though, hitting 70.5% of the fairways (69th). Ranked 122nd in total driving (combined distance and accuracy rating).

Hitting the Green

Not his strong suit, either. He ranked a lowly 132nd in GIR (63.4%), but 17th in scoring (70.06).

In Trouble

Good scrambler, making par or better 64.9% when he missed the green in regulation (seventh on TOUR). He was 14th in the bounce-back category, making birdie or better 22.8% following a bogey or worse.

Flatstick Facts

Ogrin ranked 25th among putting leaders at 1.762 putts per GIR. He was ninth in average putts per round — 28.45. Sure helps offset that GIR stat, doesn't it?

The Scorer's Tent

A solid citizen who can shoot some really low numbers. After three rounds of the '97 MasterCard Colonial, he had a tournament-record total of 195 (66-67-62) and a one-shot lead over Tiger Woods. A brain cramp on Sunday produced a 72 and a tie for second. The inconsistency demons have plagued him throughout his career. What will happen in '98? Ogrin is 40 years old and, we assume, has given up his dream of playing for the Cubs. Now is the time to settle down and grind out a comfortable life on TOUR. He will win again, maybe not this year, but we foresee another top-40 money list ranking in '98.

Mark O'Meara

Is Mark O'Meara destined to be the answer to a trivia question: Which player won just about every pro-am format TOUR event each year he played but couldn't win a major? What's with a guy who, in 18 years on TOUR, has won six pro-am events: the AT&T Pebble Beach National Pro-Am (formerly the Bing Crosby) a record five times and the 1991 Walt Disney/Oldsmobile Classic. And he lost two others in playoffs! And they call Jesper Parnevik weird...

This is not to say O'Meara is a one-trick pony. He has 14 TOUR wins, including the '95 Bell Canadian Open and the '96 Mercedes Championships, and six international triumphs including the 1997 Trophee Lancome. His two wins over here in '97 were the AT&T (of course) and the Buick Invitational; they and four other top 10s helped him bank $1,124,560 (13th) in TOUR winnings, bumping him to fifth spot on the career money list ($8,506,774). He may have been getting complacent until Tiger Woods joined the TOUR and moved into the same Orlando neighborhood. He beat the young phenom by a shot at last year's AT&T and matched Tiger's final-round 64 as the two friends finished T2 at the '98 Mercedes Championships.

The Man

Mark Francis O'Meara, 6'0", 180 lbs. Born Goldsboro, NC, Jan. 13, 1957. Resides Windermere, FL. Wife, Alicia; daughter, Michelle; son, Shaun Robert. Attended Long Beach State. Enjoys golf course consulting, hunting and fishing. Turned pro and joined the TOUR in 1980.

Off the Tee

Never renowned for length (261.7 yards, 153rd) or accuracy (63.2%, 168th), and not improving with age.

Hitting the Green

Unremarkable 66.4% of greens hit in regulation (62nd).

In Trouble

Workmanlike around the green, but excellent out of greenside bunkers: a 61.8% sand-save average was 15th best on TOUR.

Flatstick Facts

Now you're talking! O'Meara was fifth among putting leaders at 1.742.

The Scorer's Tent

Some say O'Meara is self-absorbed, maybe self-centered, but we want him on our team, no matter what the sport. "I've always thrived on the fact that when I've had a chance to win, I've got the job done." Was 2-2 at Valderrama in the U.S. Ryder Cup loss. Mentally tough and has a good all-round game that can ignite into excellence. Uses his friendship with Tiger to give young Mr. Woods an occasional reality check. When Tiger thrust his arm into the air to celebrate a great shot, O'Meara snapped at him: "Don't be giving me that fist deal. I'm going to bury you." Especially tough on the West Coast and don't even talk to us about pro-ams.

Jesper Parnevik

Where do we start? Jesper/Yesper (whatever!) may be in the running for slowest player on TOUR (that's a non sequitur, isn't it?) but he's definitely lapped the field when it comes to the "loonies in regulation" statistical category. Nice guy, but ... there's something about him reminiscent of Seinfeld's Kramer — maybe it's the pegged pants, the hair or the suspicion that he's receiving channels that aren't on cable. Did we mention he believes in reincarnation? "I've been taken back before to a previous life. In fact, I've been back a few times. I wasn't a golfer in those times." Oh brother. We know he stole the turned-up brim hat from Will Smith (check out the opening sequence of a *Fresh Prince of Bel Air* rerun if you think we're kidding). That would be appropriate for this son of Sweden's most famous comedian. (In the words of former PGA TOUR regular Dan Halldorson: "Is that like being the tallest midget?") He eats volcanic dust to cleanse his system: "I bring it back from Sweden. It's really expensive. It tastes just like regular dirt." Couple of problems with that statement: First, how does he know what regular dirt tastes like? And, second, wouldn't it be cheaper and easier just to gnaw on the lava rocks in the bottom of his barbecue?

Parnevik hasn't won on TOUR but has six international victories to his credit. He finished 12th on the '97 money list with $1,217,587, made 19 starts, missed three cuts, had nine top-10 finishes and 11 top 25s.

The Man

Jesper Bo Parnevik, 6'0", 175 lbs. Born Stockholm, Sweden, March 7, 1965. Resides South Palm Beach, FL. Wife, Mia; daughters Josetin Peg and Penny. Attended Palm Beach Junior College. Enjoys tennis. Turned pro in 1986 and joined the TOUR in 1993.

Off the Tee

Not stellar in this department: only 108th in driving distance (266.1 yards average) and 98th in accuracy.

Hitting the Green

Hit just over two-thirds of greens in regulation (48th), but can this guy cash in on par-5s: he birdied 114 of the 239 three-shotters he played, for a 47.7% success rate (third on TOUR).

In Trouble

Parnevik was 32nd in the scrambling category, making par or better 62.1% of the times he missed the green in regulation. He ranked 10th on TOUR in sand saves, getting up and down 62.4% of the time.

Flatstick Facts

Mediocre numbers here: 28.92 putts per round was 47th best on TOUR in '97.

The Scorer's Tent

The Swedish goofball contrasts a solid game with a sideshow brain. The TOUR needs more like him. If Justin Leonard hadn't shot one of the great rounds of all time on Sunday at Troon last July, Parnevik would likely be the 1997 British Open champ. Of course, if he had looked at the scoreboard coming up 18 at the '94 British and known all he needed with his two-shot lead was a par, he could have won that year as well. He had five runner-up finishes in '97. If he masters his gag reflex in the final round of tournaments, he'll surprise a lot of people. "He's not as weird as everyone seems to think," attests wife Mia. We agree; nobody could be. He will break through in '98 with at least one win.

Craig Parry

How good is Craig Parry? We will never know. And that's just fine with Parry, who splits his time between the PGA TOUR and the rest of the world. He maintains homes in Australia and the U.S. and is making quite a nice living, thank you very much. He's notched 16 tournament wins worldwide, but never on the PGA TOUR. He has several runner-up finishes, including two solo seconds in '96, his best year over here with earnings of $454,203 in 24 events. Last year, he played 20 times, making 16 cuts (four top 10s), and earning $387,603 (63rd). Call him "Popeye." Most of his mates do, because of his muscular forearms. Ironically, he was tied for the lead after two rounds of the 1992 Masters with none other than Ian Woosnam, whose nickname is — you guessed it — "Popeye."

The Man

Craig David Parry, 5'6", 170 lbs. Born Sunshine, Victoria, Australia, Jan. 12, 1966. Resides Sydney, Australia, and Orlando, FL. Wife, Jenny; daughter, April; sons, Ryan and Brendan. Enjoys sailing, water sports, cricket, rugby, computers and Australian Rules Football. Turned pro in 1985; joined TOUR in 1992.

The Stats

Nothing outstanding, just consistent enough to make a nice income. Hits his average drive 264 yards and finds 71.2% of the fairways (59th). He was ranked 40th all-around by the TOUR. Trips himself up in the third round, ballooning to a 71.94 scoring average (147th). He was 25th overall among scoring leaders (70.17).

The Scorer's Tent

"No worries, mate." Parry will stroll through his 20 or so events on TOUR this year, just as he has for the past half-dozen years, making his usual quarter-mil-plus and enjoying life. We envy him. Hard to say what he could do if he spent an entire season here. He's played well in a couple of majors (T3 in the '93 U.S. Open), but still a wild card.

Chris Perry

If pedigree and past performance count for anything, then Chris Perry may be the all-time TOUR underachiever. His father was major-league pitcher Jim Perry and his uncle Gaylord Perry is the Hall of Fame pitcher. Chris played baseball and hockey growing up before developing into an all-American golfer. What happened when he hit the TOUR? Until his 48th-place finish on the '97 money list ($460,984), his best had been 56th in 1987. A trip to the NIKE TOUR in '94 may have recharged his batteries: he was player of the year, topped the money list and didn't miss a cut in 24 events, winning once.

The Man

James Christopher Perry, 6'1", 195 lbs. Born Edenton, NC, Sept. 27, 1961. Resides Powell, OH. Wife, Katharine; son, Andrew Christopher; daughter, Emily Ann. Attended Ohio State University. Enjoys all sports, college football, snow skiing and family. Turned pro in 1984; Q School in 1984.

The Stats

Perry is kind of like a control pitcher in baseball. He is more concerned with where the ball ends up than how fast it gets where it's going. His average drive went 263 yards (143rd) but it found the fairway 69% of the time (89th). His strength is hitting greens, however: his 67.6% average was 36th on TOUR. His 381 birdies were good for sixth best in '97.

The Skinny

Last season was the first time Perry cracked the top 50. He came awful close to winning on two occasions: T2 at the B.C Open one shot back of Gabriel Hjertstedt (the first Swede to win on the PGA Tour) and T5 at the GTE Byron Nelson Classic. Making the cut in 22 of 32 events added up to 11 top-25 finishes. He's got the ability and the competitive genes. Maybe he's just a late bloomer.

Nick Price

We really like this guy, but someone, somewhere, with a lot more influence than us, really has it in for Nick Price. Having endured widely publicized health problems recently (sinuses, shoulder, ribcage muscles), he scripted a recipe for disaster: changing equipment, focusing on off-course business distractions and writing an instruction book. The most tragic blow came when longtime caddie and dear friend Jeff "Squeeky" Medlin died from leukemia in June 1997. The pair were together for 6 ½ years, winning 21 times worldwide, including six majors.

Drawing on his indomitable inner strength, Price rededicated himself to becoming the dominant player he was in the mid-'90s. Remember when he won six times, including the British Open and the PGA Championship, in 1994, after winning four in 1993? We think he's back and rarin' for a fight. In response to an off-hand comment by Tiger Woods, Price said: "Us 40-somethings, we're not washed up yet. ... It's not like experience is just going to shrivel up and crawl away."

The Man

Nicholas Raymond Leige Price, 6'0", 190 lbs. Born Durban, South Africa, Jan. 28, 1957. Resides Hobe Sound, FL; plays out of The Medalist. Wife, Sue; son, Gregory; daughters, Robyn Frances, Kimberly Rae. Enjoys water skiing, tennis, fishing, flying. Turned pro 1977 and joined the TOUR 1982.

Off the Tee

How does someone with a blur-like swing finish fourth on TOUR in driving accuracy (79.3%)? Maybe we should have read his book after all. His length is less remarkable (267.3 yards), but it obviously wasn't a huge handicap, based on his $1,053,845 in winnings in 1997 (17th on TOUR). He was ninth in total driving, which combines length and accuracy.

Hitting the Green

He was 21st in GIR (68.4%) and 15th in birdies (3.78 per round). He killed the par 4s; making birdie on 18% (114/634). Most notably, his 68.98 scoring average led all players, earning him the Vardon Trophy and the TOUR's Byron Nelson Award.

In Trouble

Price hit a lot of greens and, even when he didn't he managed to make par or better as evidenced by his 65.8% scrambling stat (fourth overall). Being in a bunker obviously goes against his grain: he got up and down only 55.7% of the time (70th).

Flatstick Facts

Remember that "Fat Lady Swings," or whatever that abomination was called, that Price used when he was on his tear a few years back? Whether it was the design or simply a psychological edge, it boosted his erratic putting to new heights. Maybe Bobby Grace could develop a "Daughter of Fat Lady" or something to rekindle that ability in '98. In 1997, Price was 39th in putting at 1.768 (putts per GIR) and needed an even 29 putts per average round.

The Scorer's Tent

Heeee's baaaack! Price won five times worldwide in 1997, including the MCI Classic on the PGA TOUR and the Million Dollar Challenge in South Africa. He led all players in scoring average, meaning his ball striking is superb and his putting is acceptable. In 1997, he played in 16 TOUR events, posting 14 top-25 finishes and reaching the top 20 in money winners for the first time since his unbelievable '94 season. When, not if, Price wins his first event in '98, watch out for him in the majors. He may be 41 years old, but he's got that killer instinct back.

LEE RINKER

All Lee Rinker needs is motivation. After his first futile effort on TOUR, it was no less a deity than Jack Nicklaus who encouraged him to take another shot at the brass ring. That wore off after a while and Rinker found himself on the NIKE TOUR. We're not saying that this is any more than coincidence, but as soon as he found out he and his wife were going to have a baby, Rinker started to play better. Not great. Better. Lee Jr. was born in July 1995 and Abigail Rose was born in April 1997. Ain't it interesting that Rinker seems to have been reborn himself in the past couple of years? He's managed to stay in the top 125, winning about $185,000 in official money in '95 and '96. In 1997, he had the best year of his career. So good, in fact, that his earnings of $415,442 (59th) exceeded his career earnings to that point. Rinker was solo second at the GTE Byron Nelson Classic and T2 at the B.C. Open. He was T5 at the Greater Milwaukee Classic as well to round out his top 10s. He made 17 of 31 cuts. Brother Larry has been a TOUR member since 1981 and sister Laurie Rinker-Graham has two LPGA Tour wins.

The Man

Lee Cross Rinker, 6'0", 185 lbs. Born Stuart, FL, Nov. 10, 1960. Resides Beavercreek, OH. Wife, Molly; son, Lee Jr.; daughter, Abigail Rose. Attended University of Alabama. Enjoys music and sports. Turned pro in 1983; Q School in 1994.

The Stats

Nothing outstanding, but was 36th among par-3 birdie leaders. He doesn't hit the driver long, averaging 261.4 yards, but hits exactly 70% of the fairways. He's OK in greens in regulation, finding almost two out of three (64.4%).

The Skinny

Suddenly, at the age of 37, Lee Rinker is firing rounds of 65-63 to tie Tiger Woods after two rounds of the GTE Byron Nelson Classic. He finished up 69-68, alone in second. He managed quite a few rounds in the 60s in '97, unfamiliar territory for him. Either our "family" theory is right on, or this guy is just another late bloomer. Worth taking a flyer on in either case.

Loren Roberts

If you're talking about late bloomers, how about Loren Roberts? His victory at the '97 CVS Charity Classic was his fifth title, all since his 38th birthday and, in general, he peaks in the latter part of the season. He looked to be a shoo-in at the Greater Milwaukee Open but Scott Hoch spoiled the party by chipping in a 60-footer to nudge Roberts into a tie for second.

Roberts, who has been a pro for almost 25 years, goes about his business in a quiet, purposeful way. You may not have noticed that he has won a TOUR event in each of the past four years and has been in the top 30 money winners for the same period. He is the model of dogged determination, rivaling Tom Lehman for return trips to Q School before hanging on for good. Regardless of what we said, watch out for him in March at Bay Hill; his first two TOUR wins came at that event ('94 and '95). He is the epitome of a solid citizen, but we're still trying to figure out why a guy who's born and raised in California now chooses to live in Tennessee.

The Man

Loren Lloyd Roberts, 6'2", 190 lbs. Born San Luis Obispo, CA, June 24, 1955. Resides Germantown, TN. Wife, Kimberly; daughter, Alexandria; son, Addison. Attended Cal Poly San Luis Obispo. Enjoys clubmaking, hunting and all sports. Turned pro 1975 and graduated Qualifying School 1980, 1982, 1983, 1986 and 1987.

Off the Tee

Bunts it down the fairway, relatively speaking. His 251.4-yard average was 191st on TOUR but check out that 77.7% accuracy stat, good for eighth spot.

Hitting the Green

Maybe because he's hitting two or three clubs more into greens, his GIR average was 65.1% (89th). But look out on the par 3s: he was second on TOUR with a 17.4% birdie average on the one-shot holes.

In Trouble

Fabulous out of the sand. He was 11th among his colleagues with a 62.2% save average. He was also 11th in scoring, with a 69.88 average, but No. 1 in final-round scoring (69.41). You know he's not going to run and hide if he's in the hunt on Sunday. He can recover from adversity, too. His scrambling stat of 62.5% was 20th.

Flatstick Facts

David Ogrin coined the moniker, "Boss of the Moss," for Roberts to honor his putting prowess. He was third on TOUR at 1.734. He credits the fact that the practice green was just outside the pro shop door when he was an assistant pro in the '70s; he would stroke putts for hours while keeping one ear tuned to the phone. According to him, "Dead straight putts are the hardest to make."

The Scorer's Tent

The only things that seem consistent about Roberts are his putting and the adage, "you're not getting older, you're getting better." He missed five of the first nine cuts in '97, but posted a T6 at Bay Hill and a solo third at The Players Championship in that span. He ended the season with nine top 10s, fourth best on TOUR. His record in the majors is spotty.

Those who say The Masters has turned into a putting contest will be surprised to learn he missed the cut (85-77) there in '97 and at the British Open. He was T13 at the U.S. Open but T49 at the PGA. And this was the guy whom Ernie Els needed 20 playoff holes to dispose of at the '94 U.S. Open. We'd like to say Roberts will win again this year, but at 43, we don't like his chances. Nevertheless, he will make it to the top 30 again, based on his consistency and putting.

Vijay Singh

His player bio in the *PGA TOUR Media Guide* looks relatively normal ... until you get to Birthplace (Fiji) and Special Interests (snooker, cricket, rugby, soccer). Then you notice where he has won events: Malaysia, France, Nigeria, Ivory Coast, Morocco, Zimbabwe, Spain, Germany, England, South Africa, Sweden and the U.S. It's got to be Vijay Singh, the late bloomer who claimed the '93 PGA TOUR rookie of the year award when he was 31 after winning his first of two Buick Classics (he won again in '95). He added the Buick Open last year, along with the Memorial, to bring his TOUR total to five and his "Buick total" to three. (Heaven help the rest of the TOUR players if he ever wins a Mercedes event.)

Don't ignore his 18 international victories; they prove Singh knows how to win and obviously enjoys the feeling. Along with his two TOUR wins in '97, he won the South African Open and the Toyota World Match Play Championship. That last one is significant. He defeated three-time defending champ Ernie Els1-up, ending Els' string of 11 straight match victories. It was a measure of revenge for Singh, who lost to Els 3&2 in 1996. In what is perhaps the most outrageous stat from the TOUR, Singh had made a record 47 straight cuts dating back to the '95 PGA Championship (golf poolsters, take note!). He posted nine top 25s and four top 10s, earning $1,059,236 (16th).

The Man

Vijay Singh, 6'2", 198 lbs. Born Lautoka, Fiji, Feb. 22, 1963. Resides Ponte Vedra Beach, FL. Wife, Ardena Seth; child Qass Seth. Enjoys snooker, cricket, rugby, soccer. Turned pro 1982 and joined TOUR 1993.

Off the Tee

He's big and he hits it appropriately, smoking an average drive 280.9 yards, but finding the fairway less than two-thirds of the time (64.2%). Nobody's perfect.

Hitting the Green

His 65.8% GIR average isn't up to expectations, but he manages a 28.2% birdie conver-

sion rate (37.7% on par 5s due to his length off the tee). He was eighth on TOUR in total eagles with 11, but 95th in birdies (277).

In Trouble

Singh was 78th in sand saves with a 55.3% average and 80th in scrambling (making par or better after missing a green in regulation).

Flatstick Facts

As a lady of the evening in New Orleans once murmured to us, "It ain't the wand, cher, it's the magician." That's good advice for Singh, too. In an effort to cure his putting woes, he has had more putters than President Clinton has had scandals. (We'd rather play with Bobby Jones than Paula Jones, anyhow.) Whatever the cause, he was 171st in putting at 1.817 putts per green hit in regulation and needed an average of 29.54 putts per round.

The Scorer's Tent

Vijay Singh (his first name means "victory" in Hindi) will win again in '98. Let's see: he won a Buick-sponsored event in '93, '95 and '97; that means he's not due for another until 1999. But the big guy could be a factor anywhere else, and especially at a major — how about the British? Despite neck and back problems a few years ago, he appears to be durable and is working with a personal fitness trainer. "I am only 34 and I have a long way to go before I give up," he told reporters after the '97 season. His late arrival on the PGA TOUR may work to his advantage. He's not worn down by the rat race and has maturity on his side. At 35, he's just reaching his prime.

JEFF SLUMAN

Quick! What do pro golfers Orville Moody and Jeff Sluman have in common? Prior to Feb. 23, 1997, the answer would have been: They are the only two pros who won only one tournament in their PGA TOUR careers and that was a major. In Sluman's case, it was the 1988 PGA Championship. But last season, he edged Steve Jones by a shot to win the Tucson Chrysler Classic. "Maybe the monkey's off my back now," said Sluman, who up until that point also held the dubious distinction of earning the most money on TOUR in the 1990s without a win ($3,252,950). He had to endure nine years and 241 TOUR events between victories. (Sluman may be short on some things — he's 5'7" — but not on patience, obviously.) During those years, he posted eight runner-up finishes, including three playoff losses. He played in 29 events in '97 (making 20 cuts and withdrawing once), posting nine top 25s and three top 10s, and made $634,203 (34th).

The Man

Jeffrey George Sluman, 5'7", 140 lbs. Born Rochester, NY, Sept. 11, 1957. Resides Chicago, IL. Wife, Linda. Attended Florida State University. Enjoys old cars, the stock market, Akita dogs and wine. Turned pro in 1984; Q School in 1982 and 1984.

Off the Tee

For a small man, Sluman pokes it pretty good, averaging 266.6 yards (103rd). Somewhat surprisingly, he ranked only 70th in accuracy (70.4%).

Hitting the Green

He was 59th in GIR (66.6% — Get back, Satan!) Nothing remarkable about his birdie stats (26.3% overall, 167th) but explain to us how he ranked 37th in total eagles with seven.

In Trouble

Nine years without a win — he could give seminars on trouble. Still, he ranked 91st in sand saves (54.7%) and 52nd in scrambling (making par or better after missing the green in regulation.)

Flatstick Facts

Probably the underlying cause of Sluman's dry spell. He was 126th among putting leaders, averaging 1.795 putts on greens hit in regulation, and required an average of 29.45 putts per round (126th).

The Scorer's Tent

Despite his stunning ascent to stardom in '88, Sluman is a grinder. He will show the odd flash of brilliance but they are very rare — like when he shot 65 in the final round of the '88 PGA to win by three after trailing by five after Saturday. He's a great guy and a solid TOUR citizen. It may be another nine years before he wins again. Sheesh, he'll be on the Senior TOUR by then! Having said that, he seems to elevate his game for the majors on occasion. Could lightning strike twice?

Craig Stadler

Shaq. Michael. Elvis. ... Walrus. OK, so maybe Craig Stadler isn't as instantly recognizable as those other one-namers, but in the more than two decades since he came to the TOUR, even casual golf fans have identified with him. He has always been more than a professional golfer — not that there's anything wrong with that. He has been a living, breathing (sometimes fire-breathing), swearing, sweating human being, just like the rest of us. He never shrank from displaying his emotion on the course (judging from his physical appearance, he never shrank, period) and it worked for him. His enormous moustache led to the predicable nickname, but he was anything but ponderous with a golf club in his hand. He's registered 12 TOUR wins thus far, the last in 1996 (Nissan LA Open), and in '97 finished in the top 50 money winners for the 15th time ($525,304, 41st). His string of 28 rounds at par or better was the best on TOUR last season. In 21 events, he made 16 cuts (one WD) and posted nine top 25s and six top 10s, including seconds at the Nissan Open and the Buick Invitational. A pretty good average.

The Man

Craig Robert Stadler, 5'10", 220 lbs. Born San Diego, CA, June 2, 1953. Resides Denver, CO. Wife, Sue; sons, Kevin and Chris. Attended University of Southern California. Enjoys snow skiing and hunting. Turned pro in 1975; Q School in 1976.

Off the Tee

An even 100th in driving distance (266.9 yards), Stadler soared to 44th in accuracy (72.4%). He was 32nd in total driving.

Hitting the Green

Hit a smooth 68.2% of greens in regulation (22nd). He was 20th among birdie leaders (3.71) and had a 44.6% birdie rate on par 5s (eighth). Still has the ability to post more than his share of birdies and eagles each round (22nd in par breaking).

In Trouble

This Walrus does not like the sand: he got up and down out of greenside bunkers only 52.9% of the time (114th). His bounce-back ranking was excellent — he made birdie or better 24.9% of the times following a bogey or worse (third).

Flatstick Facts

Stadler was 73rd among putting leaders (1.779 putts per GIR) and required 29.12 putts on average for each round (77th).

The Scorer's Tent

The 20-somethings on TOUR must think that dinosaurs roamed the earth when Stadler was born. Unlike the dinosaurs, however, the Walrus is not extinct and still possesses that fearsome killer instinct. Although he's turning 45 this summer, he has the potential to win again. At the very least, he will post some top 10s this year and stay in the top 50 earners for the 16th time. Don't ignore the fact that he was 26th in the vital all-around statistic in '97. Pay no attention to those critics who say he's miserable and washed up. We have it on good authority that he's neither.

PAUL STANKOWSKI

Picture this: Paul Stankowski is 10 shots back of Tiger Woods heading into the final round of the '97 Masters, but tells the media he still isn't out of it. "If I can shoot five, six, seven birdies early — like in the first three holes — I can definitely put some heat on him." We know Stanko is a devout Christian, but come on ... We like to think the gregarious Stankowski had his tongue slightly in his cheek, but you never know. This is the player who surreptitiously tucked some Augusta National bunker sand into a Masters souvenir glass and took it home because he wasn't sure he would ever make it back. Good luck keeping him out. He's headed for stardom, and soon. Although he grew up near a golf course in California, he didn't take up the game until Easter Sunday 1978; 18 years later to the day, he's holding the Bell South Classic trophy. That made him the first player ever to win on the NIKE and PGA tours in consecutive weeks. In fact, the Bell South was his fifth win in 12 months worldwide.

The Man

Paul Francis Stankowski, 6'1", 195 lbs. Born Oxnard, CA, Dec. 2, 1969. Resides Flower Mound, TX. Wife, Regina. Attended University of Texas-El Paso. Enjoys all sports. Turned pro in 1991; Q School in 1993 and 1995.

Off the Tee

Stankowski was 21st in driving average (21st) but only 125th in accuracy. When the spirit moves him, he can take it deep, although his longest on the TOUR's measured holes was "only" 329 yards (124th).

Hitting the Green

Only 88th in GIR (65.2%), but 16th among eagle leaders (averaging one every 165.3 holes, 11 total) and 19th in birdies (one every 3.72 holes, 376).

In Trouble

Only 56th in scrambling (60.6%) and 90th in sand saves (54.8%).

Flatstick Facts

The switch to contacts from spectacles helped immensely, says the man who has his caddie line up every putt. Even so, he was 42nd in putting (1.770 on greens hit in regulation), and required 28.92 per average round.

The Scorer's Tent

Stankowski may look like a good time waiting to happen, but a close call in college smartened him up. He's married, mature and mighty talented. Playoffs don't scare him — he won both his TOUR titles in extra holes. He should improve on his 21st spot on the 1997 money list ($929,405). He and actor Andy Garcia, a mid-handicapper, shot a record 43-under at the AT&T Pebble Beach National Pro-Am. 43-under? Come on. Maybe he should get some sand from Garcia to go along with the stuff from Augusta ...

Payne Stewart

Hard to believe the owner of that lovely, languid swing is 41 years old. Granted, first-time observers have a problem focusing on the swing since Payne Stewart insists on wearing those knauseating knickers at every tournament. (There's gotta be some good reason. Maybe a man in long pants frightened his mother when she was pregnant with Payne?)

Despite our feelings about his sartorial smorgasbord, we do respect the player inside: his nine wins on TOUR include the 1989 PGA and the 1991 U.S. Open. He is seventh on the all-time money list with $8,465,062. Some of his wins might deserve an asterisk: Who can forget — try as you might — that Bataan Death March of an 18-hole playoff at Hazeltine with Scott Simpson for the '91 Open? And weren't you hoping the earth would open up and swallow Scott Hoch as he barfed up the '95 Shell Houston Open to Stewart after leading by seven shots on Sunday?

But overall, Stewart has delivered good value to golf fans in the past 17 years. While he may not be able to hold back the hands of time, Stewart is still doing all right for a 40-something. In 1997, he won more than $500,000 for the ninth time and posted seven top 10s in 23 events, finishing 40th on TOUR. Not like the old days, when he was second (1989) and third (1990), but still respectable.

The Man

William Payne Stewart, 6'1", 180 lbs. Born Springfield, MO, Jan. 30, 1957. Resides Orlando, FL. Wife, Tracey Ferguson; daughter, Chelsea; son, Aaron. Attended Southern Methodist University. Enjoys hunting, fishing and cooking. Turned pro in 1979; Q School in 1981.

Off the Tee

The old boy still has some pop in the big stick. Stewart's average drive in '97 traveled 270.9 yards (57th) and he hit 67.3% of the fairways (120th.).

Hitting the Green

Needs improvement: 65.5% GIR stat was 83rd on TOUR. However, he was 18th among scoring leaders with 70.07. He was 12th in total eagles with nine.

In Trouble

Great scrambler, posting par or better 63.3% of the times he missed the green in regulation (11th). Bunker play was another story — he was 100th in sand saves (53.8%).

Flatstick Facts

Saves a lot of strokes here: he ranked 28th among putting leaders (1.764) and needed 28.73 putts on average per round (30th).

The Scorer's Tent

Maybe because he's so noticeable (those damn plus fours), handsome and personable, we've always had this nagging feeling that Stewart could have done more. (Hmm, maybe he shares more with Fred Couples than a languorous swing motion.) Advancing age has brought some physical complaints: bone chips in his elbow had to be removed in 1996 and he had a nerve problem in his neck a few years back. Nevertheless, he ranked third in the important all-around statistical category in 1996 and, although he dropped to 28th in 1997, he retains the ability to end up in the winner's circle at least once more before he goes to the Happy Hunting Ground of the Senior TOUR. Could be this year if he rectifies one problem: his scoring average before the cut was 70.17 (16th), then he pushed the snooze button. His final-round scoring average was 107th (71.6).

Kevin Sutherland

One of two Sutherland brothers on TOUR, David being the other one. Kevin has been on and off the TOUR more than once, hitting the mini-tours and NIKE TOUR during one hiatus or another. In 1997, he played in 27 events, had four top 10s, six top 25s and made $455,860 (52nd). He came awfully close to winning the Shell Houston Open when Phil Blackmar scalded a chip into the water to fall back into a tie with Kevin. Although Kevin lost when Blackmar birdied the first playoff hole, his second-place check of $172,800 was more than his previous career earnings.

The Man

Kevin John Sutherland, 6'1", 185 lbs. Born Sacramento, CA, July 4, 1964. Resides Sacramento, CA. Wife, Mary. Attended Fresno State University. Enjoys basketball and baseball. Turn pro in 1987; Q School in 1993, '95 and '96.

The Stats

The Sutherland boys are often seen practice putting together at TOUR stops. Kevin might want to reconsider that idea, since he ranked 99th in putting last year. He's even worse off the tee with a 135th rating in total driving. His strength appears to be hitting greens (66.7%, 54th), sand saves (63.8%, sixth) and scrambling (61.2%, 45th).

The Skinny

Kevin turns 34 this year and, like many journeymen before him, may hit his stride in the next couple of years. He's got the physical game — his final-round scoring average of 70.5 was 20th on TOUR last year — but he has yet to demonstrate the mental toughness and determination that separates the men from the boys. Not a bad pool pick based on his four top-10 finishes in '97 if his fear of yet another Q School motivates him sufficiently.

HAL SUTTON

Few players arrived on TOUR with more fanfare than Hal Sutton did, and even fewer lived up to those expectations. In 1982, his rookie season, Sutton posted three seconds, a third and then won the final event of the season. He topped the money list the next season, winning the Tournament Players Championship (now The Players Championship) and the PGA Championship. He won two events in 1985 and '86. But, as is often the case, the fall from grace was fast and ruthless. The positive attention turned to rumor mongering and the focus was on his failed marriages. Although Sutton would not win again until 1995, he fought back to respectability in 1994, with two runner-up finishes and $540,162 in earnings (29th). Last season, he played 29 times, with nine top 25s, four top 10s and a T3 at the Buick Challenge. He finished 54th on the money list with $453,928.

The Man

Hal Evan Sutton, 6'1", 185 lbs. Born Shreveport, LA, April 28, 1958. Resides Shreveport, LA. Wife, Ashley; daughter, Samantha Jean. Attended Centenary College. Enjoys horses, hunting and fishing. Turned pro in 1981; Q School in 1981.

The Stats

On the plus side: third in greens in regulation (70.9%), second in total driving, 36th in all-around, fifth in par-3 birdie leaders (17.1%), 17th in total birdies, first in ball striking, 13th in bounce back. Unfortunately, treachery lurks in the putter — he was 147th among putting leaders (1.802) and steered an average of 29.91 putts around the green each round (184th). Gag us with a Bullseye.

The Scorer's Tent

Sutton may be 40 years old but he's happy and that is the key to his game. Born into a wealthy family, he always played for the fun of it. While we think he is a better player than 54th, we worry about a return to the form of '96 when he was 109th. Such a fine player from tee to green, especially with the irons. Such a pity about the putting. Poolsters: It's your call.

Tommy Tolles

Unpretentious might be the best way to describe Tommy Tolles, the pride of Flat Rock, NC. After the pressure-packed weeks on TOUR, Tolles likes the quiet, uncomplicated life in Flat Rock where, he says, "you can count the number of stoplights on one fist." He's also straightforward about the decision-making process he used to come on TOUR. That direction was chosen "the day I flunked out of college." But this dropout is no deadbeat. In 1996, he posted six top-10 finishes, including a T2 at The Players Championship and a T3 at the PGA. As a result, he shot 100 places up the money list to 16th. In 1997, he boosted his top 10s to nine (fourth best on TOUR) and made $825,793 (27th). Notable among his best placings were a third at The Masters, a T4 at the Memorial and a T5 at the U.S. Open.

The Man

Thomas Louis Tolles, Jr., 6'1", 195 lbs. Born Fort Myers, FL, Oct. 21, 1966. Resides Flat Rock, NC. Wife, Ilse; son, Wiekus. Attended University of Georgia. Enjoys fishing and boating. Turned pro in 1988; Q School in 1994.

Off the Tee

His 275-yard average was 33rd on TOUR although hitting fairways remained a challenge (63.9%, 160th).

Hitting the Green

Tolles was 70th in GIR (66.1%) but did some damage once he got there. He was 11th among birdie leaders, averaging 3.83 per round. He was also 11th among par breakers (birdies and eagles per holes played) at 21.7% (348/1,602). While he wasn't stellar on par 3s, his overall birdie conversion rate was 32.6% (seventh).

In Trouble

While he obviously is doing a lot of things right, Tolles' bunker game is a weak spot. His sand-save average of 56.4% was 67th on TOUR and his scrambling stat of 58.3% was 109th. He was 33rd in the bounce-back category (making birdie or better after a bogey or worse).

Flatstick Facts

Tolles was 16th among putting leaders, averaging 1.756 putts when he hit a green in regulation. His average number of putts per round was a very different story — 29.24 (95th).

The Scorer's Tent

In relatively short order, we think Tolles will have as many majors as Flat Rock, NC, has stoplights. He's got all the tools, including a great attitude, and is just hitting his golfing prime. Check out his results against the strongest fields in the game. Aside from an aversion to the West Coast (which may disappear the longer he is on TOUR), he looks to be a fixture at or near the top of the money list. He plays a lot of events and makes most of the cuts (22/25 in '97).

David Toms

Why did David Toms decide at the '97 Quad Cities Classic that it was time to win after nine years and 150 TOUR events? He says the birth of his son "gave me incentive to play well. A child is expensive from what I've been told." Duh. Toms was a TOUR member from 1992 through 1994, but was demoted to the NIKE TOUR in 1995 after finishing 164th on the money list. He earned his return ticket by finishing third on the NIKE TOUR money list and he obviously doesn't want to go back. The Quad Cities' win staked him to $460,355 in 1997 (49th).

The Man

David Wayne Toms, 5'10", 160 lbs. Born Monroe, LA, Jan. 4, 1967. Resides Shreveport, LA. Wife, Sonya; son, Carter Phillip. Attended Louisiana State University. Enjoys hunting and fishing. Turn pro in 1989; Q School in 1991.

The Stats

Toms' 272.3-yard average was 50th-best on TOUR but he trailed 171 other players when it came to hitting the ball where he wanted to (62.8%). His GIR stat was 143rd (62.8%) but his birdie conversion rate of 32.1% was 13th. He can putt: he stood 20th among putting leaders (1.761) and required 28.58 putts during an average round.

The Skinny

It might be another nine years before the planets are aligned properly for Toms to win again. Or maybe he and his wife should plan to have a child every year. In any case, Toms doesn't possess the consistency at present to rise very far above his station in '98. At 31, however, time is on his side. If he has the determination to rise to the next level, he might very well become a TOUR mainstay. Wait and see.

KIRK TRIPLETT

There's no denying Kirk Triplett is consistent. Last season was the third out of the last four that he finished among the top 40 money winners on TOUR ($541,023, 39th). It was also the 11th year in which he's played at least one TOUR event that he hasn't won. That's 210 tournaments. Yuck. He did win a total of three times in the late '80s when he was playing the Canadian, Australian and Asian tours. He recalls those days with fondness and recommends that route to young, aspiring pros: "I wouldn't trade the experience for anything. I learned so much, not only about golf, but about myself." On the brighter side, Triplett made 19 of 26 cuts and posted 10 top-25 finishes.

The Man

Kirk Alan Triplett, 6'3", 200 lbs. Born Moses Lake, WA, March 29, 1962. Resides Scottsdale, AZ. Wife, Cathi; sons, Conor Logan and Samuel Jacob. Attended University of Nevada. Enjoys basketball, reading and computers. Turned pro in 1985; Q School in 1989.

Off the Tee

Big strong player who doesn't hit it all that far — his 263.7-yard average was 137th on TOUR — but his accuracy is commendable. He hit 74.5% of the fairways (24th) and was 51st in total driving.

Hitting the Green

Good performance in the GIR department: 68% (27th). Triplett was 26th among birdie leaders, notching one every 3.68 holes and 32nd among par breakers (frequency of birdies and eagles).

In Trouble

Triplett was ninth in scrambling (63.7%) but 96th in bounce back. His sand-save average of 56.9% was 56th on TOUR.

Flatstick Facts

Like all his stats, his putting is good, not great. He was 57th among putting leaders at 1.775 and needed an average of 29.2 putts per round (89th).

The Scorer's Tent

We have as much trouble figuring out why Triplett hasn't won on TOUR as we do understanding why he insists on looking like a doofus with that floppy hat and shirts buttoned to his Adam's apple. His stats are all good, but he does have a disturbing habit of firing a big number in the final round to take himself out of contention. We recommend he lose the lid, loosen the shirt collar and stop hanging around with Jeff Maggert. If he follows those instructions, we predict Triplett will win in '98.

Bob Tway

Say, didn't you used to be ... Bob Tway? You know, the guy who won four events and finished second on the money list in his second year on TOUR? The guy who gutted Greg Norman — join the crowd — by holing a bunker shot to win the '89 PGA Championship? Yep, you're the guy. Where've you been? Oh, we see ... dropped to 179th on the list in 1992 and went without a win from 1991 through 1995. Welcome back. Last season marked the third straight year you finished in the top 50 ($507,523, 43rd) and you made a run at another win with five top 10s. A T5 at the U.S. Open and a T10 at the Memorial? Good for you. Although we expect nothing less from 1995's Comeback Player of the Year and a three-time all-American. We'll be seeing you around.

The Man

Robert Raymond Tway, 6'4", 195 lbs. Born Oklahoma City, OK, May 4, 1959. Resides Edmond, OK; plays out of Oak Tree GC. Wife, Tammie; son, Kevin; daughter, Carly Paige. Attended Oklahoma State University. Enjoys snow skiing, fishing and all sports. Turned pro in 1981; Q School in 1984.

Off the Tee

Tway just doesn't have it with the driver: his distance ranking was 64th (270.3 yards) and his accuracy rating was 69.2% (84th). Who's flashing the bunt sign at this guy? He was 38th in total driving.

Hitting the Green

Now we're cooking. His 70.1% success rate in hitting greens in regulation was sixth on TOUR last season. He was 17th in the ball striking category which combines total driving with GIR.

In Trouble

He's lucky he hits all those greens. His sand-save percentage was 53.1% (110th). He was 76th in scrambling and 86th in bounce back.

Flatstick Facts

His 1.775 putts per GIR ranked him 57th and he needed 29.54 putts per round on average (146th).

The Scorer's Tent

He's back in his comfort zone, but we're wondering how far that zone extends. After his personal purgatory, Tway rocketed from 146th in 1994 to 20th in 1995, including winning the MCI Classic. In 1996, he dropped to 35th and last season he was 43rd on the money list. Comfortable or complacent? He fights hard to make the cut, with a 70.28 stroke average on Thursday and Friday, and then nods off on the weekend. So what? He made 21 of 26 cuts and is just happy to be cashing a check.

Grant Waite

Grant Waite is one of those players who puzzles a lot of observers. He can shoot the lights out — he had a 60 at the '96 Phoenix Open — but more often the lights are on, but nobody's home. How can someone spend the first nine months of the '97 TOUR in serious danger of losing his card and then earn almost $200,000 in the next three weeks to finish 68th on the money list ($362,320)? Waite won two events in '92 — once in Australia and once in Canada — and then claimed the '93 Kemper Open. He was 35th on the money list in '93 and looked to be the real deal. He plummeted to 172nd in '94 before rebounding to 76th the next year and 72nd in 1996. That's improvement, all right, but this three-time all-American can do much better.

The Man

Grant Osten Waite, 6'0", 190 lbs. Born Palmerston North, New Zealand, Aug. 11, 1964. Resides Palmerston North, NZ. Wife, Lea; sons; Osten Holland and Tanner Brian. Attended University of Oklahoma. Enjoys wind surfing, reading, skiing and fitness. Turned pro in 1987; Q School in 1989 and 1992.

The Stats

Frustratingly inappropriate for the 68th player on the money list: 16th in driving distance, 22nd in greens in regulation, third in total driving, eighth in ball striking ... but he can't putt (178th among putting leaders, 1.82/GIR).

The Skinny

Waite turns 34 this year. He's going to wake up some morning and realize he's wasted a lot of God-given talent and some great opportunities. Maybe a strategically applied cattle prod would be appropriate. His four top-10 finishes in '97 came in the 22 of 30 cuts he survived (one DQ). We wouldn't Waite for this player to blossom in '98.

Duffy Waldorf

After four runs through the hellish PGA TOUR Qualifying School, Duffy Waldorf decided that was that. He was the medalist there in 1990 and although he dipped down into the mid-80s for a couple of seasons, he seems to have found his own personal comfort zone. He finished 23rd in '92 with eight top 10s and his one and only TOUR win, the 1995 LaCantera Texas Open, boosted him to 35th. Waldorf finished 51st on the '97 list with $458,074 on the strength of four top 10s, including T2 at the Buick Invitational and the Michelob Championship at Kingsmill. One of the most recognizable golfers around because of his, shall we say, eclectic choice of apparel, Waldorf has his family and friends write inspirational notes on his "lucky cap." His wife and kids write similar messages on the balls he uses.

The Man

James Joseph Waldorf, Jr., 5'11", 225 lbs. Born Los Angeles, CA, Aug. 20, 1962. Resides Newhall, CA. Wife, Vicky; sons, Tyler Lane, Shea Duffy, Justin James; daughter, Kelli Ann. Attended UCLA. Enjoys wine collecting. Turned pro in 1985; Q School in 1986, '87, '88 and '90.

The Stats

Fifteenth on TOUR in distance (279.0 yards) and 89th in accuracy, for a 13th ranking in total driving. Not a bad combination. Waldorf was also 13th in ball striking which combines the total driving and GIR rankings. He was 27th in GIR (68%) and 24th among eagle leaders, notching one every 178 holes.

The Skinny

Great guy with some real decent stats, so why is he in the TOUR's second 50? Somebody should take Duffy aside and point out that TOUR events are at least 72 holes long. His scoring average before the cut was 70.63 (40th); 131st in the third round and an abysmal 162nd on Sunday. That inability to finish the job cost him at least two and maybe three titles in 1997. Repeat after us, Duffy, two plus two equals...? A win? Why don't you write that on your hat?

Tom Watson

Man, was this guy something in his prime. (Hey Tiger. You've got a long way to go, pal.). Thirty-three TOUR victories since 1974, and from 1977 through 1982, he won at least three a year. Five British Opens (1975, '77, '80, '82 and '83), two Masters (1977 and '81) and the 1982 U.S. Open. Note that he won both the British and U.S. opens in 1982. That put him in elite company — only Bobby Jones, Gene Sarazen, Ben Hogan and Lee Trevino have also done it. He was the TOUR money leader five times, including four years in a row (1977-80), won three Vardon Trophies for lowest stroke average and was PGA of America Player of the Year six times. So what if his last win prior to the '96 Memorial was the 1987 Nabisco Championships of Golf? In 1997, he played in 16 events, making 12 cuts and posting five top-10s and eight top-25s, including a fourth at The Masters. For the 22nd time out of 25 TOUR campaigns, Watson finished in the top 50 money winners ($479,146, 45th). It's not about the money, is it, Tom? But then it never was. In a couple of years, Watson and a few of his cronies hook up with the Senior TOUR. Now *that* will be fun to watch.

The Man

Thomas Sturges Watson, 5'9", 160 lbs. Born Kansas City, MO, Sept. 4, 1949. Resides Mission Hills, KS. Wife, Linda; daughter, Meg; son, Michael Barrett. Attended Stanford University. Enjoys hunting and fishing. Turned pro 1971; Q School 1971.

Off the Tee

Hits it not so long, but pretty straight: 266.5 yards on average (104th) and in the fairway 71.5% of the time (55th).

Hitting the Green

Legendary accuracy still there: 67.8% GIR is good for 34th spot. Watson was 12th among birdie leaders (3.81), fourth among par-3 birdie leaders (17.2%) and 23rd in scoring (70.14). Believe it.

In Trouble

A bit of a black hole here. His sand-save percentage is abysmal (50%, 134th) as is his scrambling stat (56.5%, 148th).

Flatstick Facts

Enough about his putting already. He ranked 75th in putting (1.780) but 138th in average putts per round (29.5). And, no, we have no advice for you, Tom.

The Scorer's Tent

What do you want us to say? He's about a par 5 away from the Senior TOUR, he's got admirable respect for the traditions of the game, he's always been his own man, they love him in Britain (but then again, they like haggis and blood pudding, too) and he's eighth on the career money list with more than $8 million. We hope he plays well in '98 and we'd like him to adopt us.

Tiger Woods

After demolishing every amateur in his path during his collegiate career, Tiger leaped full-blown onto the pro scene in 1996, winning the Las Vegas Invitational and the Walt Disney World/Oldsmobile Classic. Those wins and three other top-10 finishes came in only eight starts. Last season started in similar fashion when he won the inaugural event, the Mercedes Championship, in January. A runner-up finish in the AT&T Pebble Beach National Pro-Am was a prelude to a runaway, record-setting, 18-under-par victory at The Masters. He would also claim the GTE Byron Nelson Classic and the Motorola Western Open in his first full year on TOUR.

But, as they say, "horses for courses"; some telltale knotholes appeared in Woods in 1997. Tight layouts troubled him: he missed his first cut at the Bell Canadian Open at restrictive Royal Montreal, struggled at the U.S. Open at constricted Congressional and was a Ryder Cup liability (1-3-1) at vexatious Valderrama. Having said that, he may just win the next 10 Masters and, indeed, any other tournament played on more wide-open tracks. Observers who focus on his occasional lack of discipline on course may be wise to remember he is only 22 years old ... it was only 19 years ago when he shot 48 for nine holes. A week before the Ryder Cup, he posted a 13-under 59 playing with Mark O'Meara at Orlando's Isleworth. Maybe his more vocal critics should look in the mirror for a greenish tinge of envy?

The Man

Eldrick T. Woods, 6'2", 155 lb. Born Dec. 30, 1975, in Cypress, CA. Resides Orlando, FL. Attended Stanford University. Enjoys basketball, fishing and all sports. Turned professional and joined the TOUR in 1996.

Off the Tee

Although Tiger stood second in TOUR driving distance in 1997 with an average of 294.8 yards, 95 other players were more accurate than him off the tee, thus explaining his problem with tight courses. He's long, but he has to

learn to harness that power, just as Davis Love III has. (Now that's a scary thought: he was ninth in total driving on TOUR even with his relative wildness.) His longest measured drive was 361 yards, just 11th best on TOUR last year.

Hitting the Green

Tiger managed to rank fourth on TOUR in greens in regulation, and he hit some of them from some pretty deep cabbage. His iron accuracy is astounding and, as a result, he led the TOUR in holes birdied per average round (4.25 or 344 birdies in 81 rounds).

In Trouble

Despite the widely held myth that he is already a master of the short game, Tiger often struggles with delicate pitches and chips. For example, he was 180th on the list in sand saves last year, but who cares, when you hit as many greens as he does?

Flatstick Facts

Tiger averaged 29.35 putts per round in 1997 but before you applaud, let us remind you that was more than 116 of his colleagues on TOUR.

The Scorer's Tent

His 69.75 scoring average was best on TOUR. He was 83rd on the money list with $2,857,427...no, wait, that's the career money list. Woods, of course, led all 1997 money winners on TOUR ($2,066,833).

SENIOR PGA TOUR

Bud Allin

You may have wondered why golf writers commit suicide. Guys with quotes like Bud Allin are the reason. You're rushing to meet a deadline after his first tournament win and the best thing Allin comes up with is, "You have to win one before you win two." And the players say we ask dumb questions ... But we digress, yet again. Allin, a Vietnam vet with a Bronze Star and an Air Medal, came to the Senior TOUR in 1995 after an undistinguished 12 years on the PGA TOUR (five wins). He was in financial straits until he made it through Q School. In his rookie year of 1995, he posted 10 top-10 finishes in 34 events and earned $585,142 — more than he made in his entire PGA TOUR career. He finished 17th overall that year, dropping to 37th in '96 and 29th in '97, when he won his first event in more than 20 years.

The Man

Brian Thomas Allin, 5'8", 134 lbs. Born Oct. 13, 1944, in Bremerton, WA. Resides Boulder City, NV. Wife, Carol; daughters, Evamarie and Erica; son, Aaron. Three grandchildren. Attended Brigham Young University. Turned pro in 1969; joined PGA TOUR in 1970, Senior TOUR in 1994.

The Stats

The last two years, I haven't used the same swing thought two days in a row.

— Allin explaining the secret of consistency.

Scoring 71.88 (44th); Driving 254.6 (69th); Driving Accuracy 74.7% (12th); Total Driving 81 (T36); GIR 63.1% (54th); Putting 1.797 (T31); Sand saves 42.4% (66th); Eagles 855 (73rd); Birdies 3.04 (T44); All Around 393 (56th).

The Skinny

Allin caught fire at the '97 American Express Invitational, shooting 68-68-69 to edge Jim Colbert by a shot. We don't see that happening again. He'll struggle to stay in the top 31 this year.

Isao Aoki

The Isao Aoki countdown continues. Each year he has been on the Senior TOUR, he has improved his position, but now it's getting ominous: fifth in '95, fourth in '96, third in '97. Does he have the ability to vault past Hale Irwin and Gil Morgan? Aoki won once last season, edging Morgan with a birdie on the first playoff hole at the Emerald Coast Classic. That was the same event that he set a Senior TOUR record with a 60 in the second round. "I started thinking about 59," he said through his interpreter. "My putter was shaking. Very nervous. Wouldn't you be?" Although his handsy putting stroke with the toe of the club almost vertical is unorthodox, he is confident over the ball and ranked fifth on the tour last season in that department. Aoki has won a total of seven events on this tour and one ('83 Hawaiian Open) on the PGA TOUR. However, his grasp does not exceed his reach: he has also won on the European Tour, Australasian Tour, Japan PGA Tour and the Japan Senior Tour.

The Man

Isao Aoki, 6'0", 170 lbs. Born Abiko, Chiba, Japan, April 17, 1942. Resides Tokyo, Japan. Wife, Chie; daughter, Joanne. Enjoys fishing and golf course design. Turned pro in 1964; joined PGA TOUR in 1981, Senior TOUR in 1992.

The Stats

No, no. Top secret.

— Aoki's response when asked what kind of old putter he had returned to service, using it to win the Emerald Coast Classic.

Scoring 70.03 (third); Driving 268.6 (17th); Driving Accuracy 71.9% (22nd); Total Driving 39 (T3); GIR 69.4% (eighth); Putting 1.763 (fifth); Sand saves 64.7% (first); Eagles 602.0 (82nd); Birdies 4.20 (third); All Around 141 (fifth).

The Skinny

The countdown reverses itself in '98. While there's no doubt Aoki is solid, posting tons of top 10s (18/28 in '97), he doesn't cash the top check often enough.

Hugh Baiocchi

Hugh Baiocchi is full of surprises. With a name like Baiocchi (by-OCK-ee), you expect him to hail from Italy. How about South Africa? And coming from South Africa, he'd be a cricket fan, right? Nope, try baseball. And being a Monday qualifier at the start of his first Senior TOUR season, you would figure he'd manage to scrape by, right? In what was perhaps the second-biggest surprise of the '97 Senior TOUR season (after Hale Irwin's $2-million year), Baiocchi clicked for 14 top 10s in 25 events, one win and eighth place on the money list. While this is a guy whose biggest check from the PGA TOUR was a $2,275 whopper for placing T22 at the 1975 Masters, he is no pigeon. Baiocchi spent 22 years on the European Tour, winning seven times, and added 11 victories on the South African Tour.

The Man

Hugh John Baiocchi, 6'0", 184 lbs. Born Aug. 17, 1946, in Johannesburg, South Africa. Resides Johannesburg, South Africa. Wife, Joan; daughter, Lauren; son, Justin. Attended University of the Witwatersrand. Enjoys tennis, boxing, baseball and jogging. Turned pro in 1971; joined Senior TOUR in 1996.

The Stats

Scoring 70.66 (eighth); Driving 262.8 (39th); Driving Accuracy 73.3% (17th); Total Driving 56 (12th); GIR 72.2% (fourth); Putting 1.814 (T52); Sand saves 48.7% (35th); Eagles 711 (72nd); Birdies 3.52 (T14); All Around 241 (15th).

The Skinny

Baiocchi stunned a lot of people when he arrived. He and fellow Monday rabbit Bob Duval put pressure on the big boys at every opportunity. Baiocchi pushed Bruce Crampton to a three-hole playoff in May and had a two-hole overtime duel with Bruce Summerhays in August. Then — wouldn't you know it? — he had to edge Duval, of all people, in a six-hole playoff to win the Pittsburgh Senior Classic. Baiocchi's got the experience, the tools and the relative youth to make his mark out here in the next couple of years.

JOHN BLAND

Who was named South African golfer of the year in 1996? Ernie Els? No. David Frost? Uh-uh. How about John Bland, the European Tour vet who won four times on the Senior TOUR and was named rookie of the year, finishing third on the money list. Last season, he didn't win a thing, but set a record for earning the most money without winning an event — $1,169,707 — and ended up sixth on the list. Bland, who never joined the PGA TOUR, has 23 international victories to his credit. During that time, he defeated the likes of Seve Ballesteros and Bernhard Langer. He lost the Senior British Open last year in a playoff to Gary Player after posting three runner-up finishes over here.

The Man

John Louis Bland, 5'9", 176 lbs. Born Sept. 22, 1945, in Johannesburg, South Africa. Resides Knysna, South Africa. Wife, Helen; son, John-Mark; daughters, Bonney and Candice. Attended St. John's Boscoe College. Enjoys rugby and gardening. Turned pro in 1969 and joined Senior TOUR in 1996.

The Stats

Scoring 70.39 (fifth); Driving 255.5 (T66); Driving Accuracy 81% (first); Total Driving 67 (T19); GIR 72% (fifth); Putting 1.783 (T19); Sand saves 56.1% (eighth); Eagles 468 (55th); Birdies 3.42 (22nd); All Around 181 (eighth).

The Skinny

So he didn't win. That's hard on the ego, but it all came down to bounces: he didn't get them last year. He still deposited almost $1.2 in official money, led all players in sub-par rounds (for the second straight year) and had 30 top-25 finishes in 33 events (17 top 10s). He'll win at least one this year and stay well up in the top 10 money winners.

Bob Charles

Hoo. A two-pager in the *Senior PGA TOUR Media Guide*. Now that's impressive. As well it should be, since Bob Charles has been a force internationally in golf for almost half a century. That's right: An 18-year-old Charles won the 1954 New Zealand Open. He also won it in '66, '70 and '73 and hopes to compete again in 2004, the 50th anniversary of his first victory. Charles, the most successful southpaw golfer ever, has notched somewhere in the neighborhood of 75 titles worldwide, including five on the PGA TOUR and 23 on the Senior TOUR. He also won the '63 British Open. In 1997, Charles finished 21st on the money list, making it into the top 31 list for a record 12th year. While he didn't win in '97, he has won every previous year on the Senior circuit except 1986 and '94. In '88 and '89, he won five events each year.

The Man

Robert James Charles, 6'1", 175 lbs. Born March 14, 1936, in Carterton, New Zealand. Resides Oxford, New Zealand, and Palm Beach Gardens, FL. Wife, Verity; daughter, Beverley; son, David. Enjoys farming. Turned pro in 1960; joined PGA TOUR in 1962, Senior TOUR in 1986.

The Stats

Scoring 71.21 (19th); Driving 253.4 (T73); Driving Accuracy 74.4% (13th); Total Driving 86 (T44); GIR 69.1% (T9); Putting 1.826 (61st); Sand saves 51% (T24); Eagles 516 (T59); Birdies 2.94 (T53); All Around 311 (40th).

The Skinny

Charles has been a great ambassador for golf and the people of New Zealand for a long time. While he still has that kind, gracious demeanor, the much-feared golf game is gradually dwindling. Will this determined competitor be content to gear back, worrying only about the MasterCard Champions (the tournament-within-a-tournament for seniors 60 and over) and not about the overall competition? We don't think so, any more than we think he will contend in '98 and beyond.

Jim Colbert

The leading money winner in '95 and '96 was raring to kick some serious Senior butt early in '97 when prostate cancer was detected. Talk about a reality check. Colbert's surgery in June was successful and he returned to action in October, finishing 27th on the money list ($556,000) with six top 10s (two seconds) in 19 starts. It was a far cry from the two previous years when he led the money list, earned a total of $3 million and won a total of nine tournaments. Indeed, Colbert's worst year since he joined the Senior TOUR in 1991 was '93 when he was seventh overall. In addition to his eight wins on the PGA TOUR between 1966 and 1987, Colbert has won a total of 18 Senior events, banking more than $7 million.

The Man

James Joseph Colbert, 5'9", 165 lbs. Born March 9, 1941, in Elizabeth, NJ. Resides Las Vegas, NV. Wife, Marcia; daughters, Debbie, Christy and Kelly. Six grandchildren. Attended Kansas State University. Turned pro in 1965; joined PGA TOUR in 1966, Senior TOUR in 1991.

The Stats

Scoring 71.4 (T25); Driving 255.6 (65th); Driving Accuracy 73.6% (T15); Total Driving 80 (T33); GIR 64.3% (45th); Putting 1.778 (13th); Sand saves 46.1% (45th); Eagles 270 (27th); Birdies 3.37 (27th); All Around 262 (T26).

The Skinny

Colbert was cocky before the cancer scare and he will regain that "me against the world" attitude as the memory of his brush with mortality fades. He fatigued easily after the surgery but he will be competitive again this year. The time off might have benefited his chronically sore back, which he injured as a teenager. He's been in the limelight too long to let Irwin, Morgan, et al take his turf away from him. Top-10 finish in '98 with a win or maybe two.

Frank Conner

We could be wrong, but we think Frank Conner picked the right sport. You see, Conner is one of only two men to play in the U.S. Open of both golf and tennis (the late Ellsworth Vines was the other). And again, we may be mistaken, but we haven't heard a lot lately about that Senior Tennis Tour. (Bobby Riggs, where are you now?) Conner bounced around the PGA TOUR and the NIKE TOUR before hitting 50 and qualifying for the Senior circuit in 1996. He still hasn't won, but he has earned in excess of $500,000 each year he's played, finishing 20th in '96 and 30th in '97.

The Man

Frank Joseph Conner, 5'10", 195 lbs. Born Jan. 11, 1946, in Vienna, Austria. Resides San Antonio, TX. Wife, Joy; daughters, Michelle and Nicole. Attended Trinity University. Enjoys tennis. Turned pro in 1972; joined PGA TOUR in 1975, Senior TOUR in 1995.

The Stats

Scoring 71.52 (32nd); Driving 268.5 (18th); Driving Accuracy 59.1% (84th); Total Driving 102 (T65); GIR 64.6% (44th); Putting 1.764 (sixth); Sand saves 43.2% (64th); Eagles 285.4 (31st); Birdies 3.7 (fifth); All Around 284 (31st).

The Skinny

Conner almost didn't make this book. He was in 36th spot on the list late in the season, but posted four top-10 finishes in his final five events to sneak in under the wire. Only the top 31 Senior players are fully exempt for the following year. Despite Conner's admirable stats in the putting and birdie departments, we're not convinced he's not content just to exchange lobs without going for the overhead kill shot. We think it's dicey whether he'll even stay in the top 31, much less win this year.

Jim Dent

Talk about the long and the short of it. Jim Dent has always been known as a long hitter, but few people realize just how deadly he is on the putting surface. Maybe that's the key to Dent; what you see is not necessarily what you get. You see a hulking guy who looks like an offensive lineman, with a stony facial expression? How about a softhearted man who, with his wife Willye, adopted two infant children a couple of years ago? We were sure he had won on the PGA TOUR but they tell us his best finish was T2 behind Nicklaus at the '72 Walt Disney World Open Invitational. So, you kind of expect a journeyman when he hits the Senior loop in '89? How about winning twice, with 10 other top 10s in 24 starts for 12th spot on the money list and a rookie of the year trophy. Since then Dent has finished in the top 31 (those who gain automatic exemptions into next season's events) every year. In '97 he won again, beating Lee Trevino and Larry Gilbert in a playoff. His $590,646 got him to 22nd spot on the list, which was his worst-ever ranking. The money boosted him to a total of $5,492,510 (ninth) on the Senior TOUR career list.

The Man

James Lacey Dent, 6'3", 224 lbs. Born May 9, 1939, in Augusta, GA. Resides Tampa, FL. Wife, Willye; daughters, Radiah Laceyette and Victoria; sons, James Antonio and Jamie. Attended Paine College. Enjoys fishing and listening to jazz. Turned pro in 1966; joined PGA TOUR in 1970, Senior TOUR in 1989.

The Stats

The winner's circle is everything.

— Jim Dent

Scoring 71.41 (T27); Driving 273.3 (T10); Driving Accuracy 62.1% (T76); Total Driving 86 (T44); GIR 65.2% (39th); Putting 1.779 (T14); Sand saves 43.8% (61); Eagles 209.3 (T15); Birdies 3.55 (T11); All Around 253 (19th).

The Skinny

This guy's turning 60 next spring, right? Two comments: 1) we hope we hit it 273 off the tee when we're in our late 50s (you can't do that now, knucklehead); and 2) he will finish 16th or better overall in '98. If you don't think he can do it ... *you* tell him.

Bob Duval

Sure would like to tap into some of those Duval genes. Bob's headed for great things in his second full year with the Seniors, son David is one of the PGA TOUR's dominant young players, James is a PGA professional in Florida, Grandpa Henry (Hap) was a life member of the PGA of America. Whether it's the genes or just determination, the Duval family has it in spades. Bob Duval never played the PGA TOUR, but was an outstanding club pro who moved onto the elder loop through the qualifying school. His 1997 season was rewarding, as he earned more than $500,000, good for 28th spot and a full exemption for this season.

The Man

Robert Thomas Duval, 5'11", 175 lbs. Born Oct. 9, 1946, in Schenectady, NY. Resides Neptune Beach, FL. Wife, Shari; son, David; daughter, Deirdre. Attended Florida State University. Enjoys reading. Turned pro in 1968; joined Senior TOUR in 1996.

The Stats

Scoring 71.12 (16th); Driving 278.6 (fifth); Driving Accuracy 63.7% (67th); Total Driving 72 (24th); GIR 67.8% (16th); Putting 1.804 (39th); Sand saves 55.2% (10th); Eagles 148 (fourth); Birdies 3.65 (sixth); All Around 163 (seventh).

The Skinny

Did you happen to notice that Duval was among the top 10 Senior players in five separate statistical categories? Here's a guy who's worked in a pro shop, dithered around on the mini-tours and suddenly is teeing it up beside former PGA TOUR stars. Might have had some first-year jitters in '97. We think Duval is acclimated now and will finish somewhere in the mid-teens on the money list with oodles of top 10s, but no wins — not this year, anyhow.

Bob Eastwood

Just another tough, ornery redhead who came on the Senior TOUR with little fanfare in 1996 when he finished 32nd on the money list. Last season, people started to take notice when he blasted up the list to 11th ($833,908), winning the Bell Atlantic Classic and Raley's Gold Rush Classic. Eastwood is taking a rocket to stardom, especially considering that it took him 13 years to win his first PGA TOUR event. We should have known something was coming when his first 10 rounds as a senior were at par or better.

The Man

Robert Fred Eastwood, 5'10", 185 lbs. Born Feb. 9, 1946, in Providence, RI. Resides Ft. Worth, TX. Wife, Dell; sons, Scott and Steven. Attended San Jose State University. Enjoys hunting and fishing. Turned pro in 1969; joined PGA TOUR in 1969, Senior TOUR in 1996.

The Stats

Scoring 70.91 (11th); Driving 266.1 (T25); Driving Accuracy 66.1% (T51); Total Driving 76 (T26); GIR 68.9% 11th); Putting 1.807 (43rd); Sand saves 59.0% (fourth); Eagles 313.2 (T35); Birdies 3.38 (T25); All Around 205 (11th).

The Skinny

Eastwood can roar out of the starting gate (his first-round average is 70.89, seventh on TOUR) and then post some really low numbers, like 64s and 65s. Two wins in '97 surprised most observers but we think this ex-military man has some more bullets in his gun.

Dave Eichelberger

When most of the guys out here talk about a second career, they're referring to golfing on the Senior TOUR. Then there's 54-year-old Dave Eichelberger. Not only is he getting another crack at pro golf, his wife gave him a second chance at being a father last October when she presented him with twins! (We don't know for sure, but we think Eichelberger will be playing the full Senior TOUR schedule this year.) Did we mention he's due to become a grandfather this March thanks to his first incarnation as a father? This family's going to need Norman Schwartzkopf to organize their family reunions. Now back to golf ... Eichelberger has relied on a power game for his entire career. When the timing's not there, neither is Dave. In his final years on the PGA TOUR, he missed 22 consecutive cuts. Last season, he had only one top-10 finish in the first half of the season, but after finding a new driver he loved, wrapped up the year with 10. As a result, he had his best year on the Senior TOUR, finishing 13th on the list with $794,322.

The Man

Martin Davis Eichelberger, 6'1", 195 lbs. Born Sept. 3, 1943, in Waco, TX. Resides Waco, TX. Wife, D.C.; sons, Martin and Clinton; twins, Emalia and Davis. Attended Oklahoma State University. Enjoys fishing and hunting. Turned pro in 1966; joined PGA TOUR in 1967, Senior TOUR in 1993.

The Stats

Never in my wildest dreams would I have imagined this.

— Eichelberger, after being told he now led the Senior TOUR in twins.(Just kidding. He was talking about his fine year in '97.)

Scoring 71.32 (24th); Driving 268.2 (19th); Driving Accuracy 61.3% (80th); Total Driving 99 (61st); GIR 65.8% (33rd); Putting 1.782 (T17); Sand saves 45.5% (47th); Eagles 171.8 (ninth); Birdies 3.47 (19th); All Around 248 (16th).

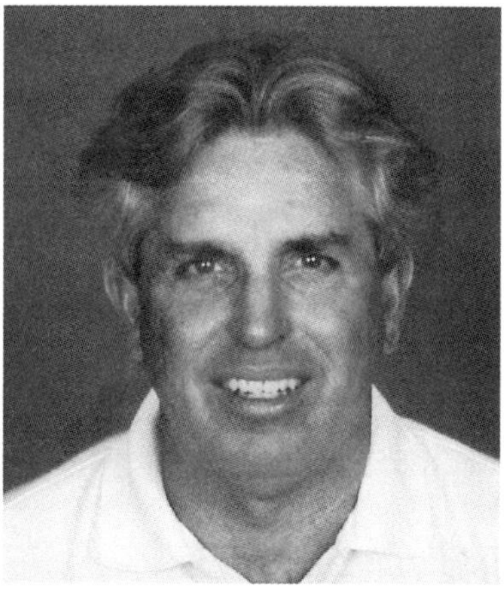

The Skinny

Eichelberger seems to show up on alternate years (his finishes since 1994 have been 20th, 16th, 40th, 13th) with the lows getting lower and the highs higher. With the blessed distractions of his young daughter and son, we think he might not make golf his priority this season. We'll bet on an off year, but wish him and his new family all the best. See you next year, Dave.

VICENTE FERNANDEZ

Put simply, the synopsis is, "Where the hell did this guy come from?" The answer to that is, "He was here for a cup of coffee until he blew out his knee at the '77 Canadian Open during his first year on TOUR." He never thought of suing the organizers because they were trying "to promote golf, my profession, the sport I love." He also never returned fulltime to the PGA TOUR. "My idols are people who do things for others without asking for anything back," says the cheery, gregarious Argentinian gentleman who was born with a partially paralyzed right leg. So it's no wonder we're pleased to see "Chino" win an event in both years he's been on the Senior loop. In '97, he edged up one spot to 17th overall with $689,915. Despite his lack of PGA TOUR experience, he has plenty of battle scars, having played the European Tour for more than 20 years, winning five times. All in all, he has almost 100 career victories. He caddied for Chi Chi Rodriguez in the '62 World Cup in Argentina and it's our humble opinion that some of the snots on both TOURs (you know who you are) should caddy for Fernandez at least once. Maybe some of that selfless, joyful attitude would rub off. On second thought, we doubt it.

The Man

Vicente Fernandez, 5'10", 170 lbs. Born Corrientes, Argentina, April 5, 1946. Resides Buenos Aires, Argentina. Wife, Esther; sons, Gustavo and Norberto. Enjoys sports and music. Turned pro in 1964; joined Senior TOUR in 1996.

The Stats

Scoring 70.98 (13th); Driving 263.2 (36th); Driving Accuracy 65.7% (T53); Total Driving 89 (T50); GIR 69.1% (T9); Putting 1.783 (T19); Sand saves 51.3% (22nd); Eagles 327.6 (39th); Birdies 3.46 (20th); All Around 211 (13th).

The Skinny

Despite being a phantom to North Americans, Fernandez has made his mark elsewhere and it didn't take him long to feel at home on the Senior circuit: he won in only his eighth start. We like his stats overall and while we may be letting our positive feelings overwhelm our usually cynical logic, we see him bumping up another couple of spots, at least, on the money list this season.

Raymond Floyd

Yeah, right. A synopsis of Ray Floyd's career? OK, boss, we'll give it a try (with heartfelt thanks to the anonymous authors of the *Senior PGA TOUR Media Guide*): Winner of 13 Senior events and 22 PGA TOUR events; second to Lee Trevino in all-time combined money; loves the big stage — on the Senior circuit, has won the '94 Tradition, '95 PGA Seniors Championship and the '96 Ford Senior Players Championship, and on the PGA TOUR, he won the '76 Masters, '86 U.S. Open, the '69 and '81 PGA Championship and the '81 Players Championship; the first player ever to win on both Tours in the same year (1992); only he and Sam Snead have won TOUR events in four different decades; only he, Trevino and Don January have won the low stroke-average award on both TOURs; shares with Bruce Summerhays and Trevino the Senior TOUR record for consecutive rounds at par or better, 27; won three times in seven starts in his Senior rookie season; oldest player ever to compete in Ryder Cup competition (51). In '97, he had no wins but 10 top 10s in 20 events, good for $584,755 (23rd).

The Man

Raymond Loran Floyd, 6'1", 200 lbs. Born Sept. 4, 1942, in Fort Bragg, NC. Resides Palm Beach, FL. Wife, Maria; sons, Raymond Jr. and Robert Loran; daughter, Christina Loran. Attended University of North Carolina. Turned pro in 1961; joined PGA TOUR in 1963, Senior TOUR in 1992. Member, World Golf Hall of Fame.

The Stats

Scoring 70.92 (12th); Driving 278.3 (seventh); Driving Accuracy 64.6% (64th); Total Driving 71 (T22); GIR 66.6% (T26); Putting 1.768 (seventh); Sand saves 54.5% (T11); Eagles 192 (14th); Birdies 3.64 (seventh); All Around 148 (sixth).

The Skinny

We think Floyd's lost interest in this TOUR and its perceived lack of drama. He can still rise to the occasion; witness his five straight Senior Skins Game victories. He plays about 20 events each year, the stats are good but the spirit seems unwilling and the body may be weak.

Larry Gilbert
(In Memoriam)

As this book was going to press, the PGA TOUR issued a release which read in part: "Larry Gilbert, a prominent member of the Senior PGA TOUR, died Jan. 21 of lung cancer. The 55-year-old Gilbert was diagnosed with cancer Sept. 2 and underwent chemotherapy in Nashville, TN. The cancer was deemed inoperable. Prior to the discovery of this medical condition, Gilbert was enjoying the finest season of his professional career. He finished ninth on the 1997 money list with earnings of $902,816. However, Gilbert's biggest thrill came when he won the Ford Senior Players Championship in July at the Tournament Players Club of Michigan in Dearborn. 'I was thinking of so many things,' Gilbert said when asked about his emotions as he played the final hole. 'All those times on the practice tee when you're dreaming of being on the 18th green playing for a championship. And I thought of my mother and father and how proud they would be of me.' "

Lawrence Allen Gilbert. Born Nov. 19, 1942. Died Jan. 21, 1998. Golf was proud to have him.

David Graham

Not a bad start to a second career: David Graham, winner of eight PGA TOUR events between 1972 and '83, made the most of his first full year on the elder loop by winning three times, finishing fifth on the money list ($1,444,994). Graham won two of his titles on the final regulation hole, once with an eagle and again with a birdie. His regular TOUR wins were anything but ordinary; two of the eight were the '79 PGA Championship and the '81 U.S. Open. He and close pal Bruce Devlin have teamed to win the World Cup and Graham was also on two winning Dunhill Cup teams. His talent extends beyond playing the game. One of his course designs, Grayhawk GC in Scottsdale, AZ, played host to the Andersen Consulting World Championships of Golf in January.

The Man

David Anthony Graham, 5'10", 170 lbs. Born may 23, 1946, in Windsor, Australia. Resides in Dallas, TX. Wife, Maureen; sons, Andrew and Michael. Enjoys course design, California wines and quail hunting. Turned pro in 1962; joined PGA TOUR in 1971, Senior TOUR in 1996.

The Stats

Scoring 70.4 (sixth); Driving 278.4 (sixth); Driving Accuracy 67.3% (45th); Total Driving 51 (10th); GIR 70.0% (sixth); Putting 1.787 (T22); Sand saves 48.6% (36th); Eagles 108.0 (first); Birdies 3.77 (fourth); All Around 126 (fourth).

The Skinny

Graham hasn't missed a beat since arriving in the promised land. Fifth on the list? $1.4 million? Look at those stats. He'll be on the money leaders' heels like one of those Australian cattle dogs and will win once, probably twice this season.

Hubert Green

"Return with me now to those thrilling days of yesteryear..." If you're old enough to remember that line, then you're old enough to remember when Hubert Green was one of the world's top players. Two decades ago, Green was in the midst of winning 19 PGA TOUR events, including the '77 U.S. Open and the '85 PGA Championship, which would be his last hurrah on the regular TOUR. Rookie of the year in 1971, he won three consecutive tournaments in '76 and was a Ryder Cupper in '77, '79 and '85. As a Senior TOUR rookie last season, he was uneven, with only nine top-10 finishes in 28 events. He did pocket enough ($556,402) to finish 26th on the money list which, by the way, was more than twice what he made during his best year on the PGA TOUR. Ain't inflation grand?

The Man

Hubert Myatt Green, 6'1", 175 lbs. Born Dec. 28, 1946, in Birmingham, AL. Resides Panama City, FL. Sons, Hubert Myatt Jr., Patrick and J.T. Attended Florida State University. Enjoys fishing and gardening. Turned pro in 1970; joined PGA TOUR in 1970, Senior TOUR in 1996.

The Stats

Scoring 71.42 (29th) Driving 246.5 (85th); Driving Accuracy 76.7% (sixth); Total Driving 91 (T53); GIR 62.3% (T60); Putting 1.775 (T9); Sand saves 49.6% (32nd); Eagles 516 (T59); Birdies 3.16 (T38); All Around 318 (42nd).

The Skinny

Talk about licking your chops. Green has been waiting a dozen years to get to this happy hunting ground. He was never the longest hitter, but featured a good short game — what a great combination for the shorter courses of this tour. He threw a scare into his new colleagues during the second round of his first Senior event: he shot 66 with 18 putts, holing out twice, chipping in once and one-putting 12 times. He'll win one and finish in the top 15 this year.

Mike Hill

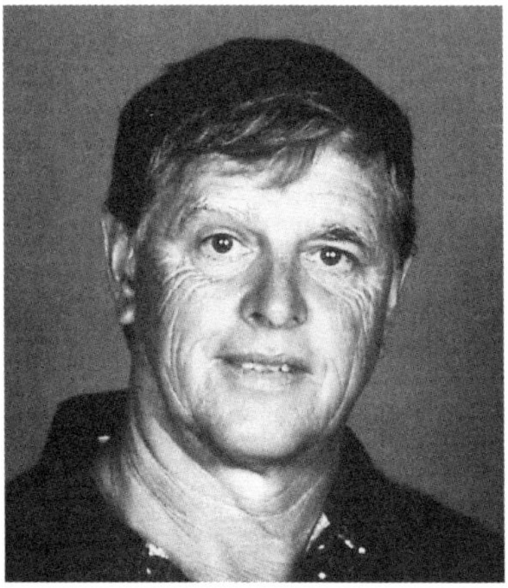

Mike Hill is nothing if not durable. While he was no roaring hell in his 22 years on the PGA TOUR, winning only three times, he keeps chugging along on the Senior loop, notching 18 titles. He even led the money list back in '91 and had back-to-back five-win seasons in '90 and '91. He has never finished lower than 22nd on the money list since moving in with the old boys in 1989, banking $6,336,905 in career earnings. Although he didn't win in '97 for the first time since 1990, he still finished 20th ($678,640). Senior tourist Dave Hill is his brother.

The Man

Michael Joseph Hill, 5'10", 170 lbs. Born Jan. 27, 1939, in Jackson, MI. Resides Brooklyn, MI. Wife, Sandra; daughters, Kimberly and Kristen; son, Michael Jr. Attended Arizona State University. Enjoys hunting and fishing. Turned pro in 1967; joined PGA TOUR in 1968, Senior TOUR in 1989.

The Stats

Scoring 71.05 (15th); Driving 257.6 (58th); Driving Accuracy 72.6% (20th); Total Driving 78 (29th); GIR 67.6% (T17); Putting 1.787 (T22); Sand saves 53.6% (14th); Eagles 382.5 (48th); Birdies 3.53 (13th); All Around 207 (12th).

The Skinny

Hill has had a great run on this TOUR, but he's in his 60th year and that usually brings the curtain down. There are the exceptions, of course, and Hill might be one of them. Chances are that he will slide down the list closer to 30th than 20th in '98. Just don't bet against him in a playoff; he's 5-1.

Hale Irwin

Get back, Tiger! Hale Irwin will live in history as the first pro golfer to win $2 million in a single season — and he did it on the Senior PGA TOUR with its less lucrative events. "When I started out [on the PGA TOUR in 1968] I didn't think $200,000 was attainable. To add another zero is mind boggling," Irwin said after setting the record on his wedding anniversary in front of his hometown fans. (Talk about the planets being in alignment!) That historic win, at the Vantage Championship last October, was the eighth of nine titles Irwin collected last year in 21 starts. Peter Thomson had the same won-lost record in 1985. By way of comparison, it took Irwin from 1968 until 1983 to with the same amount on the regular PGA TOUR — and he won 15 tournaments in that span. "I'm playing some of the best golf of my career," he says. "Granted, it's against fellow old guys, but we can play." Irwin could always play. He won 20 TOUR events from 1971 through 1994, including three U.S. Opens. When he won the '90 Open, he became the oldest winner at age 45. He has also won eight times overseas, including two World Match Play titles. From 1975 through 1978, he survived 86 straight cuts, third best in PGA TOUR history. Since joining the Senior TOUR in 1995, he has won a total of 13 tournaments. He won the '97 PGA Seniors Championship by 12 shots. For the record, he earned a grand total of $2,343,364 in '97.

The Man

Hale Irwin, 6'0", 180 lbs. Born Joplin, MO, June 3, 1945. Resides Frontenac, MO. Wife, Sally Stahlhuth; daughter, Becky; son, Steven. Attended University of Colorado. Enjoys fishing, hunting and golf course design. Turned pro in 1968; joined PGA TOUR in 1968, Senior TOUR in 1995.

The Stats

I've got the shots, I've got the experience.

- Hale Irwin.

He's right — on both counts.
Scoring 69.82 (first); Driving 266.1 (T25); Driving Accuracy 76.5% (seventh); Total Driving 32 (first); GIR 76.2% (first); Putting 1.734 (first); Sand saves 49.4% (33rd); Eagles 190.3 (13th); Birdies 4.41 (first); All Around 82 (second).

The Skinny

The distinctive glasses may be gone, but not the intensity that always lurked behind them. Although Gil Morgan did his best to unseat Irwin in '97, the former college defensive back didn't retreat. He kept hitting those crisp iron shots and a slight adjustment to his putting grip in July helped. Irwin will again go neck and neck with Morgan this season. Despite late-season biceps tendinitis (sore right shoulder), the former standout college athlete has kept in relatively good shape — he won the U.S. Open at 45 — and will maintain this level for several more years.

John Jacobs

The woods are full of long hitters, right? Let us introduce you to John Jacobs, winner of more than 100 long-drive contests worldwide, who was the 12th leading money winner on the Senior TOUR in 1997. Jacobs, whose brother Tommy plays the elder loop as well, bombed a drive 378 yards at last year's Las Vegas Senior Classic. His season average was a TOUR-leading 290.7 yards and his scoring average was 7.1.19, 18th best. The tall, powerfully built Jacobs moved up from 23rd spot in '96 and almost won his first event, until David Graham eagled the final hole at the Southwestern Bell Dominion to edge him out. He played the PGA TOUR for a number of years, recording five runner-ups, but spent most of his time overseas, becoming the first American to win the Asian Golf Circuit Order of Merit in 1984.

The Man

John Alexander Jacobs, 6'3", 225 lbs. Born March 18, 1945, in Los Angeles, CA. Resides Scottsdale, AZ. Wife, Valerie. Attended University of Southern California. Enjoys opera and classical music. Turned pro in 1967; joined PGA TOUR in 1968, Senior TOUR in 1995.

The Stats

Scoring 71.19 (18th); Driving (290.7 (first); Driving Accuracy 57.6% (88th); Total Driving 89 (T50); GIR 67.6% (T17); Putting 1.813 (51st); Sand saves 39% (79th); Eagles 267.4 (26th); Birdies 3.5 (17th); All Around 297 (T35).

The Skinny

Jacobs can take that ball deep! As a result, he converted more par-5 birdie opportunities than any other player (175/385, 45.5%). He hits his share of greens and, while his putting is shaky, we think he has the ability to break into the winner's circle as well as the top-10 money winners in '98.

Jack Kiefer

Jack Kiefer is another example of what is becoming a familiar story on the Senior TOUR: a guy who's making a pretty decent living but never played on the PGA TOUR. In eight seasons, he's won $3,079,621. That was helped along by his career-best finish in '97 — 16th on the list with $732,735 with a win at the du Maurier Champions in Canada. And, like so many of his ilk, he plays very close to the full schedule. Kiefer teed it up in 34 tournaments last year, posting nine top 10s and 20 top 25s.

The Man

Leo Charles Kiefer, 5'10", 175 lbs. Born Jan. 1, 1940, in Columbia, PA. Resides Stuart, FL. Wife, Jan; daughter, Jennifer. Attended Millersville State College. Enjoys deep-sea fishing. Turned pro in 1967; joined Senior TOUR in 1990.

The Stats

Scoring 71.43 (30th); Driving 265.7 (30th); Driving Accuracy 69.5% (34th); Total Driving 64 (T16); GIR 66.0% (T31); Putting 1.784 (21st); Sand saves 47.5% (T40); Eagles 381.6 (47th); Birdies 3.45 (21st); All Around 254 (T20).

The Skinny

Much has been made of Jack Kiefer's pro career as a knuckleball pitcher for the Detroit Tigers. Attention: He was in camp for three days. Much has also been made of him winning the '97 du Maurier Champions. Attention: He's lucky it was a 72-hole event, seeing that he was leading after 51 holes, then went bogey-bogey-bogey to drop into a tie for second. While we think Kiefer is OK, we have this uneasy feeling that there are a lot of smoke and mirrors involved here. Look for him to find his level in the second 20 in '98. And by the way, how does a guy named "Leo Charles" end up being called "Jack"?

Graham Marsh

We have it on good authority that the Queen didn't call Graham Marsh by his nickname ("Swampy") when she awarded him with the title Member of the British Empire. We also have it on good authority that Marsh (swampy marsh, get it?) deserved the honor. In addition to working with his junior golf foundation in Australia and dabbling in course design, he has found time (up to the end of '97) to win 61 times on five tours and 14 countries. Breaking that down, there were 24 on the Japan PGA Tour, 16 on the Australasian, 15 on the European, one PGA TOUR and five on the Senior TOUR. One of his Senior wins was the '97 U.S. Senior Open where he went to the wire with John Bland. The end result was a seventh-place finish on the money list ($1,128,578).

The Man

Graham Vivian Marsh, 5'11", 187 lbs. Born Jan. 14, 1944, in Kalgoorlie, Australia. Resides Dalkeith, Australia. Wife, Julie; sons, Tony and Jeremy; daughters, Jenni and Stephanie. Attended University of Western Australia and Claremont Teachers College. Enjoys skiing, tennis and watching cricket. Turned pro in 1969; joined PGA TOUR in 1977, Senior TOUR in 1994.

The Stats

Scoring 70.47 (seventh); Driving 268 (20th); Driving Accuracy 71.4% (24th); Total Driving 44 (T5); GIR 68.8% (T12); Putting 1.756 (third); Sand saves 50.9% (26th); Eagles 209.3 (T15); Birdies 3.59 (10th); All Around 117 (third).

The Skinny

Hasn't been out of the top 10 since his rookie year and we don't see that happening in '98. If anything, he might creep up a spot or two. Great stats, lots of experience and getting used to that $1-million-plus annual income that comes with at least one win a year.

JERRY McGEE

Jerry McGee doesn't get a lot of ink and he probably likes it that way. In '97, he matched his best finish on the Senior TOUR at 25th spot ($562,794), his first $500,000-plus season. McGee played the PGA TOUR from '67 to '81 before hypoglycemia put an end to his touring career. He then worked as director of golf at an Ohio club while he waited for his 50th birthday. Even though you may not have heard of him, he can play: he won four times on the PGA TOUR (including two wins in '79), was on the '77 Ryder Cup team and has won five cars at various tournaments for being closest to the hole on par 3s.

The Man

Jerry McGee, 5'10", 179 lbs. Born July 21, 1943, in New Lexington, OH. Resides East Palestine, OH. Wife, Jill; daughters, Roxane and Michelle; son, Mike. One grandchild. Attended Ohio State University. Turned pro in 1966; joined PGA TOUR in 1966, Senior TOUR in 1993.

The Stats

Scoring 71.23 (21st); Driving 263 (T37); Driving Accuracy 63.1% (T70); Total Driving 107 (70th); GIR 65.6% (T35); Putting 1.776 (12th); Sand saves 59.1% (third); Eagles 477 (57th); Birdies 3.4 (23rd); All Around 258 (23rd).

The Skinny

Although his peers call him "Magoo," McGee's eyes are the least of his worries. His progress has been hindered by recurring thumb, neck and back pain and arthritis. We're afraid that's not going to magically disappear. McGee will have trouble holding his position in the top 31 this year.

Gil Morgan

Only $170,000 separated Gil Morgan — we have a problem with this "Dr. Gil" thing — from Hale Irwin at the end of the '97 Senior PGA TOUR season. He won six events, including the last two of the season, and then tacked on the first tournament of '98, the MasterCard Championship, leaving Irwin T2 with Gibby Gilbert. Now he has won as many times on the Senior loop as he did on the PGA TOUR from 1977 through 1990. Eleven days after he turned 50, he won his first Senior title, the Ralphs Senior Classic, becoming the youngest winner ever on this tour. That shouldn't have been surprising, because he had already played 18 PGA TOUR events, recording two top 10s, including a T4 at the FedEx St. Jude Classic. His biggest win was the 1978 World Series of Golf when he beat Hubert Green (who now is on the Senior TOUR as well) in a playoff. Morgan is a two-time Ryder Cupper who has nine holes in one. He has been hampered by a series of ailments throughout his career, having missed nine months after rotator cuff surgery in 1986. The ultimate was last June when he had the gall to say, "My vision isn't very good. I don't see the slope and contours [of greens] as good as other players." "Dr. Gil" is a non-practicing optometrist, for heaven's sake. Physician, heal thyself!

The Man

Gil Morgan, 5'9", 175 lbs. Born Wewoka, OK, Sept. 25, 1946. Resides Edmond, OK. Wife, Jeanine; daughters, Molly, Maggie and Melanie. Attended East Central State College. Enjoys cars. Turned pro in 1972; joined PGA TOUR in 1973, Senior TOUR in 1996.

The Stats

Overall, my confidence level is up.

-Gil Morgan

If we had stats like this, a lot of things would be up.

Scoring 69.29 (second); Driving 281.8 (fourth); Driving Accuracy 69.1% (T35); Total Driving 39th (T3); GIR 74.1% (second); Putting 1.746 (second); Sand saves 54.5% (T11); Eagles 158.0 (sixth); Birdies 4.28 (second); All Around 64 (first).

The Skinny

Could fellow Senior TOUR player George Archer have a career as a psychic? Last season, he predicted 10 wins for Morgan in '98. If he stays healthy, the money title is a distinct possibility. If he really wants 10 wins, he may just get them. But he'd better get them this year, because there's an invasion about to start from some pretty strong players from the regular TOUR. In '98, it will be Morgan and Irwin, neck and neck, the same as in '97. They better keep checking their rear-view mirrors — there might be a few players gaining on them.

Walter Morgan

You know Walter Morgan. He's the muscular, black, ex-Army officer who smokes an average of half-a-dozen stogies every round. He's the guy who bought his first set of clubs in his mid-20s, then went out and hit balls for six months. When he finally teed it up on a course in Hawaii, he shot 79 in his first-ever round. You can't blame him for ignoring golf; he thought baseball might be his future. After all, Joe Morgan, the Hall of Famer, is his cousin. Morgan was the '97 Senior TOUR ironman, playing in 36 events, the same number as Bobby Stroble, but posting 113 rounds, two more than Stroble. Although he didn't cash a winner's check for the first time since '94 (he has a total of three wins, two of them in '96), he finished 18th on the money list.

The Man

Walter T. Morgan, 5'9", 200 lbs. Born May 31, 1941, in Haddock, GA. Resides Ponte Vedra beach, FL. Wife, Geraldine; daughter, Felicia; son, Michel; stepchildren, Ilene Pritchett, Wallace T. Parham and Keith L. Parham; six grandchildren. Attended LaSalle College. Enjoys fishing and lawn work. Turned pro in 1991; joined the Senior TOUR in 1991.

The Stats

Scoring 71.44 (31st); Driving 261.5 (43rd); Driving Accuracy 74.8% (11th); Total Driving 54 (11th); GIR 65.0% (T40); Putting 1.791 (T24); Sand saves 54.1 (13th); Eagles 508.5 (58th); Birdies 3.15 (40th); All Around 260 (25th).

The Skinny

The guy spends 20 years in the Army, two tours in Vietnam ... how tough can this golf thing be? Despite roaming up and down the money list, Morgan seems comfortable taking his place in the top 20. He should stay there for this year and maybe next, but then it's the big six-oh.

Bob Murphy

Bob Murphy's infectious smile and seemingly blasé attitude hide a tough guy who has battled severe arthritis for years. He has accomplished much at every level of golf but you have to wonder what his potential was without arthritis. He won the '65 U.S. Amateur, the '66 NCAA, played on the '75 Ryder Cup team, won five PGA TOUR events and claimed 11 Senior titles. When he was named Senior TOUR rookie of the year in 1993 (he had two wins and 15 top10s), he became the first player to win that honor on both the PGA and Senior tours. He's won at least once every year with the roundbellies, but '97 was his low point: one win, seven top 10s and $685,611 (19th). The circumstances of the win are well worth mentioning. He rolled in an 80-foot birdie putt on the ninth playoff hole to beat Jay ("Mr. Personality") Sigel at the Toshiba Senior Classic. Way to go, Murph.

The Man

Robert J. Murphy Jr., 5'10", 200 lbs. Born Feb. 14, 1943, in Brooklyn, NY. Resides Delray Beach, FL. Wife, Gail; daughter, Kimberly. One granddaughter. Attended University of Florida. Enjoys fishing and the stock market. Turned pro in 1967; joined the PGA TOUR in 1968, Senior TOUR in 1993.

The Stats

Scoring 71.81 (T38); Driving 256.2 (61st); Driving Accuracy 76.9% (T3); Total Driving 64 (T16); GIR 65.3% (T37); Putting 1.791 (T24); Sand saves 49.7% (31st); Eagles 282 (29th); Birdies 3.22 (36th); All Around 259 (24th).

The Skinny

Magnets, medication, etc., etc. Is the arthritis winning the war? You can trace Murphy's inconsistency to his physical burden. He's a warm-weather player almost exclusively now, and he can afford to pick his opportunities, having won a total of $4.6 million on the Senior TOUR. Why does he keep beating himself up by entering 30 events a year?

Jimmy Powell

We're really glad Jimmy Powell got into the top 31 Senior TOUR money winners of '97, because we only include the top 31 in this book. Do you want to know why we're really glad he made it? So we can anoint him with our "Dink of the Links Award" for 1997. Here's the scenario: After receiving a two-stroke penalty for grounding his club in a hazard at the Transamerica, he said (and we quote): "I didn't make a mistake. I'm going to get an attorney and see what the courts have to say." Now, that's really in the spirit of the grand old game. (Gosh, we'd better be careful. He might pull that attorney thing on us.) Anyhow, here's Powell's resumé for those of you who think he might redeem himself this year: Finished 31st on the '97 money list in his 13th Senior season; four Senior TOUR wins ('90, '92, '95 and '96); likes to practice. Blah, blah, blah.

The Man

Jimmy Dale Powell, 6'1", 200 lbs. Born Jan. 17, 1935, in Dallas, TX. Resides Incline Village, NV. Wife, Dolores; seven children; 12 grandchildren. Attended North Texas State University. Enjoys calling his attorney. Turned pro in 1959; joined PGA TOUR in 1959, Senior TOUR in 1985.

The Stats

Scoring 71.79 (37th); Driving 255 (68th); Driving Accuracy 70.2% (33rd); Total Driving 101 (T63); GIR 63.3% (53rd); Putting 1.793 (T26); Sand saves 56.5% (seventh); Eagles 612 (67th); Birdies 3.04 (T44); All Around 335 (45th).

The Skinny

We hope he doesn't get infected with foot-in-mouth disease in '98. Other than that, we think he is a non-factor this year and we're glad.

JAY SIGEL

We don't know what kind of life Jay Sigel had as a big-shot insurance executive and world-class amateur golfer prior to joining the Senior TOUR in 1994, but we'll wager it wasn't nearly as much fun as winning $3.5 million playing on the tour since. Sigel never played on the PGA TOUR, but combined a successful business with a stellar amateur career: he won the 1979 British Amateur, the '82 and '83 U.S. Amateurs, three U.S. Mid-Amateurs and was on nine Walker Cup teams, serving as playing captain twice. He was on seven World Amateur teams and was low amateur at three Masters, one British Open and a U.S. Open. Since joining the tour, he has won four times, counting the two titles he picked up last season on his way to fourth spot on the money list ($1,294,838).

The Man

Robert Jay Sigel, 6'1", 208 lbs. Born Nov. 13, 1943, in Narberth, PA. Resides Berwyn, PA. Wife, Elizabeth; daughters, Jennifer, Amy and Megan. Attended Wake Forest University. Joined Senior TOUR in 1994.

The Stats

Thirteen is my lucky number. I was born on the 13th, my first hole-in-one was on the 13th, I became the 13th player to win the U.S. and British amateurs.

— Sigel explaining why he was happy to play in Group 13 on the last two days on his way to winning the Bruno's Memorial Classic.

Scoring 70.37 (fourth); Driving 285.3 (third); Driving Accuracy 67.6% (T42); Total Driving 45 (seventh); GIR 73.3% (third); Putting 1.809 (T46); Sand saves 41.5% (71st); Eagles 158.7 (seventh); Birdies 3.52 (T14); All Around 190 (ninth).

The Skinny

Hits it long (he broke Jim Dent's six-year stranglehold on the distance title in '96 and has been known to poke the odd one about 340) and finds a lot of greens. Putting the only question mark, but it's not a big hurdle, obviously. Plays a lot of events (30 on average) and makes a habit of finishing in the top 10 (19/31 in '97). Calling Sigel taciturn, laconic and efficient is being kind; we wouldn't buy an insurance policy from this drugstore Indian. Nonetheless, we will buy the prediction that he will be third on this year's money list, too.

DAVE STOCKTON

Dave Stockton just keeps making history, quietly. Last season he became the first Senior TOUR player to win at least once for six straight years. He's one of only five players with more than $6 million in Senior winnings and one of 10 players with combined career earnings in excess of $7 million. He'd added 13 Senior wins to 11 PGA TOUR titles. But in mid-'97 things weren't going so well. His son Ronnie gave him a list of 15 tips to improve his long game and five more on putting. Then he dropped the bombshell, telling Dad that he had a "terrible" attitude. That put Stockton back on track and he won the Franklin Quest Championship. In addition to the win, Stockton had eight top 10s in 29 events including one second and two thirds. But his performance wasn't up to his usual standards. He finished 10th on the money list — his worst finish since his rookie year — with $854,611, breaking his skein of four consecutive $1-million-plus years.

The Man

David Knapp Stockton, 5'11", 180 lbs. Born Nov. 2, 1941, in San Bernardino, CA. Resides Mentone, CA. Wife, Catherine; sons, David and Ronald. Attended University of Southern California. Turned pro in 1964; joined PGA TOUR in 1964, Senior TOUR in 1991.

The Stats

Scoring 70.78 (10th); Driving 253.3 (75th); Driving Accuracy 71.1% (25th); Total Driving 100 (62nd); GIR 64.8% (43rd); Putting 1.762 (fourth); Sand saves 52.8% (19th); Eagles 534 (62nd); Birdies 3.51 (16th); All Around 254 (T20).

The Skinny

Stockton's got two sons who are pretty good pros in their own right and that may keep him motivated. (Just try to catch the old man.) He keeps ticking along at 56 and if Ronnie keeps giving him those tips and his bison ranch in Northern California doesn't require too much of his time, Stockton just might cash another seven-figure deposit this year.

Bruce Summerhays

Bruce Summerhays is one of those guys you really like and admire ... you just don't want to be him. Following a computerized daily agenda, he organizes his time so well he can spend two hours a day on his fitness regimen — stair-climber, weights, stretching — and still practice his game, play golf, communicate with his family via his laptop computer's e-mail, listen to music, watch a game on TV and, as a devout Mormon, do his daily devotions. Sheesh, we're exhausted just writing about it. Summerhays is a former club pro and college golf coach who never played the PGA TOUR, but he sure has made up for that since joining the Senior TOUR. From 1995 through '97, he played 109 events. Last season, he played 35, missing the 36th because of a tender back. He also won his first event after 102 tries when he made up a six-shot deficit at the Saint Luke's Classic to tie Hugh Baiocchi, beating him in a two-hole playoff. (We wonder about divine intervention there: devout Mormon ... Saint Luke ... and Summerhays' tee shot on the final hole stays in play when it bounces off some guy's elbow and a beer can ... hmmm.)

The Man

Bruce Patton Summerhays, 5'9", 175 lbs. Born Feb. 14, 1944, in St. Louis, MO. Resides Heber City, UT. Wife, Carolyn; daughters, Shelly, Rachel, Susanna, Carrie; sons, Bryan, Joseph, William, Bruce, Jr. Ten grandchildren. Attended University of Utah. Enjoys family, fishing, music, sports and church. Turned pro in 1966; joined Senior TOUR in 1994.

The Stats

Scoring 71.18 (17th); Driving 269.5 (14th); Driving Accuracy 63.1 (T70); Total Driving 84 (T41); GIR 66.2% (29th); Putting 1.782 (T17); Sand saves 44.4% (58th); Eagles 247.5 (22nd); Birdies 3.55 (T11); All Around 238 (14th).

The Skinny

Like everyone who knows him, we like Bruce Summerhays. We don't envy his schedule, but we understand it — if we had eight kids, we'd be on the road for eight weeks straight, too. Not having played the PGA TOUR, he's packing everything into this opportunity. His game is decent but, despite the dedication to fitness, we wonder if his 54-year-old body can stand the pace. That back problem last August concerns us. Despite his 14th-place finish in '97 ($776,804), we think he may drop 10 spots or so this season.

LEE TREVINO

Where do we start? Ignoring for the moment his stellar PGA TOUR career and at the risk of ticking off some of the other players, Lee Trevino raised both the profile and the bar of the Senior TOUR when he arrived in 1989. Although he limped through last season without a win (the first time in seven years that has happened), he remains the winningest Senior tourist in both numbers (27) and dollars ($7,449,561). He also retired humungous Herman Mitchell, his caddie for 20 years, and is paying him a pension. Unfortunately, it seems the Merry Mex Hex — recurring injuries — are catching up with Buck Trevino. Thumb, neck and, most insistently, back ailments have dogged him for most of his career; not to mention being struck by lightning in 1975. Hard to believe it was 30 years ago this year that he won his first PGA TOUR event, the '68 U.S. Open, and followed that up with 26 more. Remember when he won the Triple Crown in 1971 — the U.S., British and Canadian opens? How about when he aced that par 3 called Alcatraz at the '87 Skins Game? Wasn't it fun to listen to him banter with fans at every TOUR stop? Is there a golf fan anywhere who doesn't have a favorite story about him? Thanks, Mr. Trevino.

The Man

Lee Buck Trevino, 5'7", 180 lbs. Born Dec. 1, 1939, in Dallas, TX, Resides Dallas, TX. Wife, Claudia; sons, Richard, Troy, Tony Lee, Daniel Lee; daughters, Lesley Ann and Olivia Leigh. Enjoys fishing. Turned pro in 1960; joined PGA TOUR in 1967, Senior TOUR in 1989. Member, World Golf Hall of Fame.

The Stats

Scoring 70.99 (14th); Driving 256.9 (60th); Driving Accuracy 73.9% (14th); Total Driving 74 (25th); GIR 65.7% (34th); Putting 1.772 (eighth); Sand saves 44.5% (T55); Eagles 313.2 (T35); Birdies 3.30 (30th); All Around 250 (T17).

The Skinny

Thankfully, the reports of Lee Trevino's demise are greatly exaggerated. Sure, he finished 15th on the '97 money list with almost three-quarters of a million. But the feisty pride of Hardy's Driving Range in Dallas will rise again. If he can keep all his various body parts from falling off unexpectedly, the 58-year-old Trevino will be back this year. He might not play much more than the 19 times he did in '97, but we can expect a win and — who knows — a dozen top 10s? Number five on the money list next fall?

Tom Wargo

Former club professional Tom Wargo was unheralded when he joined the Senior TOUR back in '93. Although he was named PGA Club Professional of the Year the year before, he had never played fulltime on the PGA TOUR. Eight events into the season, Wargo had his first win, a playoff victory over Bruce Crampton at the PGA Seniors Championship. He finished 16th on the money list that year. He won again in '94, using that and 25 top 10s in 36 events to earn more than $1 million, good for sixth on the list. His final victory came in '95 and signaled the slide down the ladder, apparently. Wargo, with his gunslinger moustache and hat, ended up 24th in '97.

The Man

Amos Tom Wargo, 6'0", 200 lbs. Born Sept. 16, 1942, in Marlette, MI. Resides Centralia, IL. Wife, Irene; daughter, Michelle. Two grandchildren. Enjoys cooking and bowling. Turned pro in 1976; joined Senior TOUR in 1993.

The Stats

Scoring 71.29 (T22); Driving 261.3 (44th); Driving Accuracy 68.7% (38th); Total Driving 82 (T38); GIR 67.5% (19th); Putting 1.808 (T44); Sand saves 47.6% (T38); Eagles 360 (T43); Birdies 2.98 (T49); All Around 297 (T35).

The Skinny

No matter what direction he goes this year, Wargo, a former steel fitter, bartender and autoworker, has had a good ride. He's 20th on the Senior career list with $3,670,425. Although he's only 55, we think he's peaked.

LPGA

Donna Andrews

Despite rumblings of ongoing physical problems, Donna Andrews finished 13th on the '97 LPGA money list ($393,567). Most players would be satisfied with that, but not Andrews. In 1996 she was fifth, ninth in '93 and, then, in '94, she topped the list, winning three times, including a major (Nabisco Dinah Shore). Coincidentally, it was in the '97 edition of that major that she was dinged two strokes for slow play; the penalty dropped her from seventh spot to 11th, costing her a top-10 finish (she had 10 overall in '97) and $11,000. She missed only two cuts out of 26 events last year: the first of the year (HealthSouth Inaugural) and the Weetabix Women's British Open. Her victory at the Welch's/Circle K Championship in March brought her career win total to five.

The Woman

Donna Andrews, 5'8", born April 12, 1967, in Lynchburg, VA. Resides Pinehurst, NC. Husband, John Reeves. Attended University of North Carolina. Enjoys skiing, tennis, fishing, swimming and basketball. Joined LPGA in 1989.

The Stats

Low nine hole score, 30; low 18, 65; low 54, 202; low 72, 271; total birdies, 317 (eighth); total eagles, four (27); fairways hit, 944/1,193 (3); GIR, 1,097/1,530 (5); putting average, 29.94 (43); sand saves, 22/52 (53); driving average, 230.56 (137).

The Skinny

Andrews' stroke average when she led the '94 money list was 71.18; in 1997, that had dropped to 71.10 and she finished 13th. That's an indication of how tough this tour is getting. Andrews' putting remains a challenge and she is losing distance off the tee. At 31, she should be peaking unless those murmurs about her injuries were accurate. Nevertheless, we look for her to finish in the top 10 on the money list in '98.

Tina Barrett

In her rookie season of 1989, Tina Barrett must have thought that there was nothing to this professional golf thing. What's the big deal? You come out and go wire to wire to win an event and take home 40 grand at the end of the year. All pumped up the next year, you plummet to 121st on the money list. Unlike a lot of others, Barrett heard the wake-up call. In '91, she rebounded to 32nd spot, 28th in '92 and 19th in '93. A couple of dry years ensued before she turned it around again, going to 28th in '96. Her breakthrough might have occurred last year when she posted seven top 10s in 27 events, including a solo second at the Welch's/Circle K Championship and a T2 at the Chick-Fil-A Charity Championship. She was on the winning team at the Nichirei International in November.

The Woman

Tina Barrett, 5'4½", born June 5, 1966, in Baltimore, MD. Resides Scottsdale, AZ. Husband, Dan Friedman. Attended Longwood College. Enjoys watching the Baltimore Orioles and Phoenix Suns. Joined LPGA in 1988.

The Stats

Low nine hole score, 32; low 18, 66; low 54, 204; low 72, 274; total birdies, 306 (12th); total eagles, two (89th); fairways hit, 875/1,215 (47th); GIR, 1,096/1,566 (11th); putting average, 30.46 (107); sand saves, 42/95 (41st).

The Skinny

We like Barrett's resilience; we just can't watch her putt. If she can hit a few more fairways and keep her approach shots real tight to the stick, she'll be posting at least another seven top 10s and maybe another win.

Brandie Burton

Brandie Burton burst onto the LPGA scene in 1991, finishing in 22nd spot on the money list, with eight top-10 finishes, and was named rookie of the year. In 1992, she vaulted into fourth place — winning the Ping Welch's Championship and finishing second four times — and moved up another spot a year later when she claimed the Jamie Farr Toledo Classic and a major, the du Maurier Ltd. Classic. But nagging injuries to wrist, ribs and back took their toll, as she slid down the ladder to 31st and 27th in subsequent years. With her 24th-place finish in '97 ($300,311), it looks like the recuperation period is over and Burton is taking aim at top spot.

The Woman

Brandie Burton, 5'7", born Jan. 8, 1972, in San Bernadino, CA. Resides Rialto, CA. Attended Arizona State University. Enjoys fishing, softball and all sports. Joined LPGA in 1990.

The Stats

Low nine hole score, 31; low 18, 64; low 54, 207; low 72, 280; total birdies, 306 (12th); total eagles, eight (fifth); fairways hit, 745/1,163 (135th); GIR, 968/1,494 (64th); scoring average, 71.53 (19th); putting average, 29.34 (second); sand saves, 37/86 (50th), driving average, 245.52 (28th).

The Skinny

Despite her injuries, Burton never dropped too far down the ladder. She's used to winning at every level — she won the '87 and '89 World Junior Championship, the '90 North and South Amateur and won six of the seven collegiate events she played in. Now that she's totally healthy, she will have to iron out some of the inconsistencies in her game. She's got adequate length and her putting is great, but her accuracy is suspect. Nevertheless, we see her matching the eight top-10 finishes she had in '97 and probably winning — if she can string three or four good rounds together. That's something she had a big problem with last year.

Laura Davies

How much fun would it be to tee it up with Laura Davies some afternoon, play a quick 18 and then zip over in her BMW to the casino, play a few hands and have a few cocktails? That about sums up Davies' ideal day. (It would be even better if you could fit in a soccer match. Born in England, she loves the game. Last year, she played the first six minutes for the Myrtle Beach Sea Dawgs men's team in a U.S. Inter-Regional Soccer League game. They lost 4-1.) A dominant force on both sides of the Atlantic, she led the women's European Tour standings in '85, '86 and '96. Over here, she led the LPGA list in '94, was second in '95 and '96 and eighth in '97 ($483,571). She's won 15 times as an LPGA member, including four straight Standard Register PING titles from 1994-'97. Three of those titles are majors: two McDonald's LPGA Championships and one du Maurier Ltd. Classic. Prior to joining the LPGA, she won the 1987 U.S. Open, after which the LPGA wisely rewrote its rules to allow her automatic membership. She also has 35 international victories. Like countryman Nick Faldo on the PGA TOUR, Davies was named a Member of the British Empire by Queen Elizabeth II, one of the highest honors that can bestowed upon a British citizen.

The Woman

Laura Davies, 5'10", born Oct. 5, 1963, in Coventry, England. Resides West Byfleet, England. Joined LPGA in 1987.

The Stats

Low nine hole score, 31; low 18, 66; low 54, 203; low 72, 275; total birdies, 291 (19th); total eagles, six (13th); fairways hit, 481/852 (177th); GIR, 755/1.098 (17th); scoring average, 70.86 (seventh); putting average, 29.9 (40th); sand saves, 24/60 (73rd).

The Skinny

Right from the time she appeared on the pro golf scene, she has infused enthusiasm and awe into every event she plays. And while that's not all that frequently — 21 events in '97 — she misses very few cuts, only two last year, while posting seven top 10s. Her initials — L.D. — could well stand for Long Distance. While she led the LPGA in driving distance in 1996 (262.26 yards), she has backed off the driver a touch, often preferring to hit irons for increased accuracy. Judging from her stats, she might want to return to the big stick. She's got the power and the finesse. And she has fun out there. We hope she wins half-a-dozen times this year. She just might.

Cindy Figg-Currier

Hard to believe Cindy Figg-Currier is 38 years old. It seems not so long ago that she came onto the tour full of potential. Well, it only took 14 years and 314 LPGA tournaments for Figg-Currier to fulfil that potential. Her win at the State Farm Rail Classic on Labor Day, plus five other top 10s, bumped her season's earnings to $317,392. Her 20th position on the money list matched her previous best finish, in 1990. She was also selected most valuable player at the Nichirei International team event in November. While her performance between 1984 and 1994 was spotty, there's a good explanation for her 177th finish on the '95 list — she played in only four events after the birth of her daughter. Back on the circuit in '96, she popped up to 97th.

The Woman

Cindy Figg-Currier, 5'8", born Feb. 23, 1960, in Mt. Pleasant, MI. Resides Austin, TX. Husband, Patrick Currier; daughter, Kaitland Elizabeth. Enjoys weight training and cooking. Joined LPGA in 1983.

The Stats

Low nine hole score, 31; low 18, 63; low 54, 200; low 72, 280; total birdies, 305 (15th); total eagles, three (49th); fairways hit, 922/1,315 (62nd); GIR, 1,151/1,692 (22nd); scoring average, 71.9 (24th); putting average, 30.4 (100th); sand saves, 48/122 (85th); driving average, 237.23 (85th).

The Skinny

Figg-Currier is gregarious and likeable. It was great to see her finally win in '97. Inspired by her young daughter and dedicated to a fitness regimen, she could have another half-dozen years like '97 ahead of her. She plays a lot of events — 30 last year, missing only five cuts — and may use the confidence she earned through her first win to repeat as a winner this season. We're rooting for her, and not only because she specializes in two of our favorite cuisines: Tex-Mex and Cajun. A weight-lifting, gourmet-cooking, child-raising professional golfer. Cool.

Jane Geddes

Jane Geddes has been the picture of consistency during her 15-year LPGA career. After her rookie season, she has never finished lower than 36th on the money list, getting as high as third in 1987. That was the year she won five times, incuding the Mazda LPGA Championship. The previous year, she was fifth after winning the U.S. Open. In 1989, she had an incredible 12 top-10 finishes in just 25 events. In 1997, she was 17th on the money list ($330,424), which is right in her comfort zone these days.

The Woman

Jane Geddes, 5'5", born Feb. 5, 1960, in Huntington, NY. Resides Boca Raton, FL. Attended Florida State University. Enjoys playing piano, photography and all sports. Joined the LPGA in 1983.

The Stats

Low nine hole score, 31; low 18, 64; low 54, 202; low 72, 267; total birdies, 278 (28th); total eagles, seven (eighth); fairways hit, 717/1,112 (129th); GIR, 996/1422 (10th); scoring average, 71.34 (13th); putting average, 30.28 (87th); sand saves, 42/95 (41st); driving average, 261.25 (second).

The Skinny

Geddes is 38 and firmly ensconced in the top 15 to 20 money winners each season. Age doesn't appear to be catching up with her: she hit her average drive almost 10 yards farther in '97 than she did in '96. Long off the tee, good iron player, suspect putting — it all adds up to the eighth-leading money winner in LPGA history ($3,305,616).

Tammie Green

After an excruciating '96 where she endured a divorce and surgery to remove an ovarian cyst, Tammie Green blasted through the '97 season with two wins, two seconds, a T2 and a T3. When the smoke had cleared, she was fifth on the money list ($595,077), her best placing in her 11-year career. On balance, Green's career has been excellent, but there have been flashes of absolute brilliance for the 1987 LPGA rookie of the year. Take, for example, 1989, when she won a major, the du Maurier Ltd. Classic in Canada. Or how about 1993, when she won twice?

The Woman

Tammie Green, 5'8", born Dec. 17, 1959, in Somerset, OH. Resides Somerset, OH. Attended Marshall University. Enjoys fishing, gardening, horseback riding and sports. Joined LPGA in 1986.

The Stats

Low nine hole score, 31; low 18, 64; low 54, 202; low 72, 273; total birdies, 292 (18th); total eagles, five (19th); fairways hit, 806/1,144 (60th); GIR, 1,012/1,476 (19th); scoring average, 71.24 (10th); putting average, 29.63 (19th); sand saves, 34/72 (22nd); driving average, 239.41 (65th).

The Skinny

You know destiny is on your side when you're a golfer whose surname is "Green" and you have nine siblings, all of whom have first names starting with "T". But Tammie Green has a lot more going for her now than destiny; she has her enthusiasm and her health back. Her game has rounded into form as well, so we look for another top-10 ranking for her at the end of this season.

Lisa Hackney

Lisa Hackney arrived on the '97 LPGA Tour as a 29-year-old rookie who had played on the European Tour since 1991 and had two international victories under her belt. The first of her eight top-10 finishes in her 22 starts last season came in the fourth event of the season. Those results earned her the 16th spot on the money list ($351,272) and propelled her to the rookie of the year award — the eighth foreign-born player in the last 10 years to win that distinction.

The Woman

Lisa Hackney, 5'6", born Sept. 24, 1967, in Stoke-on-Trent, England. Resides Stoke-on-Trent, England. Attended University of Florida. Enjoys music and all sports. Joined LPGA in 1996.

The Stats

Low nine hole score, 32; low 18, 66; low 54, 205; low 72, 279; total birdies, 240 (46th); total eagles, four (27th); fairways hit, 652/934 (67th); GIR, 785/1,206 (61st); scoring average, 71.34 (14th); putting average, 29.88 (37th); sand saves, 24/66 (124th); driving average, 245.97 (26th).

The Skinny

Smart girl. Got her education and exposure to U.S. competition while at the University of Florida, then went back to Europe to hone her game. There's something to be said for getting some seasoning in the minor leagues before moving up to the big show. Her stats are more than adequate and we think she will join the rest of the winning English contingent on tour this year.

Pat Hurst

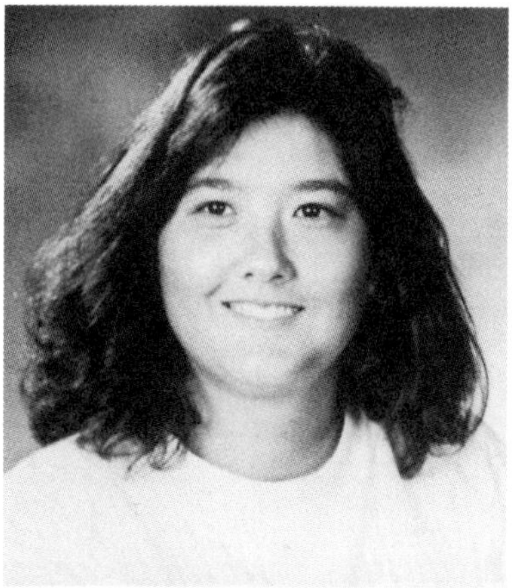

Pat Hurst is on a mission. In 1996, she vaulted from 49th spot in her rookie-of-the-year '95 season to 24th. Last season, she had an uneven start to the season before cashing her first victory check at the Oldsmobile Classic in June. Although she had only one more top 10 between then and November, she took eventual winner Annika Sorenstam to a playoff at the ITT LPGA TOUR Championship, ending up T2 with sophomore sensation Lorie Kane. She was 19th on the money list last year ($325,299). Hurst turns 29 this year and is building her LPGA game on a sound foundation. She was the 1986 USGA Junior champ, 1989 U.S. Amateur medalist, 1990 USGA Amateur champ and received top honors at the 1989 NCAA individual and team championships. After college, she worked as a teaching pro at La Quinta CC and competed on the Players West mini-tour where she won five events.

The Woman

Pat Hurst, 5'6", born May 23, 1969, in San Leandro, CA. Resides San Leandro, CA. Husband, Jeff Heitt. Attended San Jose State University. Enjoys music, friends and family. Joined LPGA in 1994.

The Stats

Low nine hole score, 31; low 18, 64; low 54, 209; low 72, 277; total birdies, 288 (21st); total eagles, eight (fifth); fairways hit, 692/1,109 (147th); GIR, 983/1,422 (16th); scoring average, 72.14 (30th); putting average, 30.58 (118th); sand saves, 26/87 (171st); driving average, 251.47 (11th).

The Skinny

Hurst is a powerful player with an exceptional attitude who should win an average of one tournament a season for the next decade. Our only concern is the occasional inconsistency in her tee game and the suspicion that her putting stroke is less than first class. She played in 26 events in '97 with five top 10s and only three missed cuts.

Juli Inkster

Few players have come to the LPGA with the credentials of Juli Inkster. She was the first person, male or female, to win three consecutive U.S. Amateurs (1980-82), played on Curtis and World Cup teams and was a four-time all-American. It was no surprise, then, that she won her first tournament in just her fifth start during her rookie year of 1984. That same year, she became the first LPGA rookie to win two majors in her first year — the Nabisco Dinah Shore and the du Maurier Ltd. Classic. In 1986, she won four times; twice in 1988 and '89. There was a bunch of others in between that first win and her victory at the '97 Samsung World Championship, which brought her career win total to 16. Significantly, the Samsung was her first win since 1992. Despite taking time off for the birth of two daughters, Inkster has remained in the top 50 money winners since 1991. In 1997, she finished sixth with $557,888 on the strength of the win, 10 top-10 finishes and no missed cuts in 24 tournaments.

The Woman

Juli Inkster, 5'7", born June 24, 1960, in Santa Cruz, CA. Resides Los Altos, CA. Husband, Brian Inkster. Attended San Jose State University. Enjoys basketball, racquetball, fishing and skiing. Joined LPGA in 1983.

The Stats

Low nine hole score, 30; low 18, 66; low 54, 203; low 72, 271; total birdies, 329 (sixth); total eagles, three (49th); fairways hit, 779/1,129 (79th); GIR, 1,017/1,458 (12th); scoring average, 70.64 (fourth); putting average, 29.34 (third); sand saves, 46/100 (28th); driving average, 251.63 (10th).

The Skinny

Inkster had a magical year. She was a marvel of consistency and her play brought back the image of the athlete who was one of the LPGA's dominant players in the late '80s. Only 38 this season, Inkster has the ability, will and experience to duplicate her '97 performance at least until the millenium.

Chris Johnson

In 1997, Chris Johnson celebrated the veracity of the truism, "You're not getting older, you're getting better," by delivering the best season of her 18-year LPGA career. Not that Johnson's previous campaigns had been truly odiferous: She had been out of the top 50 money winners only four times in almost two decades, winning seven times, most recently in 1995. However, she had apparently peaked a decade ago, when she finished eighth on tour in '86 and '87. She kicked off last season with four top-10 finishes in the first dozen events, then winning the McDonald's LPGA Championship in a two-hole playoff over Leta Lindley. It was an appropriate tournament for the solid, unspectacular, efficient Johnson to claim: a burger and fries win, if you will, definitely not filet migon avec champignons. In the next 12 events, she would finish in the top 10 six times, withdraw twice, and then win the Safeway LPGA Golf Championship in September. In all, Johnson would have 15 top 10s out of 29 events and finish fourth on the money list with $722,330.

The Woman

Chris Johnson, 5'11", born April 25, 1958, in Arcata, CA. Resides Tucson, AZ. Husband, Bill Shearman. Attended University of Arizona. Joined LPGA in1980.

The Stats

Low nine hole score, 31; low 18, 66; low 54, 206; low 72, 275; total birdies, 363 (second); total eagles, 11 (second); fairways hit, 460/688 (82nd); GIR, 558/864 (66th); scoring average, 70.84 (sixth); putting average, 30.17 (71st); sand saves, 36/91 (80th); driving average, 249.4 yards.

The Skinny

Either Johnson dumped her husband in favor of Ponce de Leon, or 1997 was a tremendous blip on an otherwise steady, workmanlike career screen. Although she bested her career best stroke average, set in 1994, by almost one full stroke to 70.84 and reduced her average putts per round by exactly one, we think Johnson — who turns 40 this spring — has had her moment in the sun.

Rosie Jones

If the LPGA had a statistical category for consistency, Rosie Jones might very likely be at the bottom. Consider this start in 1997: T6, T35, cut, T75, cut, T7, T63, T27, cut ... win (LPGA Corning Classic). How are you supposed to figure this game out? And why aren't more pro golfers jumping off high buildings? While not quite that erratic, Jones' career has bounced around a bit, too. In 1990, she was sixth on the money list, then dropped as low as 42 in '94, before rebounding to 15th last season.

The Woman

Rosie Jones, 5'7", born Nov. 13, 1959, in Santa Ana, CA. Resides Atlanta, GA. Attended Ohio State University. Enjoys fishing, dancing, woodworking, flower gardening, arts and crafts. Joined LPGA in 1982.

The Stats

Low nine hole score, 31; low 18, 65; low 54, 201; low 72, 267; total birdies, 267 (31st); total eagles, one (126th); fairways hit, 816/1060 (seventh); GIR, 903/1368 (43rd); scoring average, 71.77 (22nd); putting average, 29.86 (36th); sand saves, 34/83 (62nd); driving average, 227.22 (156th).

The Skinny

Thirty-nine of Jones' 87 tournament rounds were under par and she missed only three cuts, posting seven top 10s. So what's with the roller-coaster season last year? We haven't figured it out, but will keep an eye on this one. If she maintains her equilibrium this year, she'll be in the top five money winners. If not, she will be joining the grinders down the ladder.

Lorie Kane

Is Lorie Kane destined to become the David Duval of the LPGA? We hope not, since it took the PGA TOUR star 93 tries to win his first event. We thought Kane was going to outlast Annika Sorenstam to win the ITT LPGA Tour Championship, but she was edged out on the third playoff hole, registering her third T2 of her sophomore season. Kane hails from Prince Edward Island, a tiny speck off Canada's east coast and exudes the characteristic optimism and enthusiasm typical of that province. In 1996, she made it into only nine events and had to return to the LPGA qualifying tournament to return to the tour in '97. And return she did, big time: eight top 10s and only two missed cuts, good for 11th on the money list ($425,964). Now she's here to stay.

The Woman

Lorie Kane, 5'6", born Dec. 19, 1964, in Prince Edward Island, Canada. Resides Prince Edward Island, Canada. Attended Acadia University. Enjoys all sports, friends and family. Joined LPGA in 1995.

The Stats

Low nine hole score, 32; low 18, 65; low 54, 200; low 72, 274; total birdies, 336 (fifth); total eagles, six (13th); fairways hit, 1024/1367 (16th); GIR, 1225/1764 (14th); scoring average, 71.47 (16th); putting average, 30.22 (80th); sand saves, 44/92 (17th); driving average, 243.29 (43rd).

The Skinny

Let's get the petty stuff out of the way right now: What is with the get-up? Short black socks, black shoes, black, black, black ... Some sort of Johnny Cash/Gary Player fixation? Kane will not be the female Duval, neither will she be the distaff Jeff Maggert, with his stable of runner-up finishes. She missed only two cuts, had 56 of 105 rounds under par (fifth) and 25 of those were in the 60s (seventh). Her putting could stand some work, but she has the game and the disposition to win early and often, starting this season.

Betsy King

There are some players you don't even try to editorialize about and Hall of Famer Betsy King is one. Since joining the LPGA in 1977, King has had a superb career. Although it took her seven years to notch her first victory, she made the most of the opportunity. Consider these, her multi-win seasons: two in each of '85, '86 and '91; three in each of '84, '88 and '90; four in '87; and six in 1989. She clinched her Hall of Fame spot with her 30th win, the 1995 ShopRite LPGA Classic. From 1985 through 1995, she never dropped out of the top 10 money earners. After a one-year hiatus in '96 where she dropped to 45th (she says she fixed her swing by adopting a more upright address position), she finished 10th in '97, winning a major to boot (the Nabisco Dinah Shore).

The Woman

Betsy King, born Aug. 13, 1955, in Reading, PA. Resides Limekiln, PA. Attended Furman University. Inducted into LPGA Hall of Fame in 1995. Enjoys theater, concerts and all sports. Joined LPGA in 1977.

The Stats

Low nine hole score, 31; low 18, 65; low 54, 201; low 72, 271; total birdies, 357 (fourth); total eagles, three (49th); fairways hit, 901/1367 (121st); GIR, 1180/1764 (36th); scoring average, 71.52 (17th); putting average, 29.62 (17th); sand saves, 50/133 (108th); driving average, 246.72 (21st).

The Skinny

King hits 43 this year but shows no sign of slowing down. Not only is she an outstanding golfer, she is a humanitarian who has worked with relief agencies around the world. She is a credit to the game and we hope she plays forever. She may not crack the top 10 again, but she sure won't drop off the face of the earth, either.

Hiromi Kobayashi

Kobayashi waited four years after her 1989 debut to win on the LPGA — she won twice in 1993, in fact — so no one worried about granting her another four-year interval. But she didn't win in 1997, although she had two runner-up finishes among her seven top 10s. She did, however, make another $261,814 (30th), which appears to be her target in recent years. In 27 events, she missed only one cut.

The Woman

Hiromi Kobayashi, 5'8", born Jan. 8, 1963, in Fukushima, Japan. Resides Ibaraki, Japan. Enjoys reading and shopping. Joined LPGA in 1989.

The Stats

Low nine hole score, 32; low 18, 67; low 54, 206; low 72, 280; total birdies, 307 (11th); total eagles, two (89th); fairways hit, 934/1229 (10th); GIR, 1068/1584 (28th); scoring average, 71.59 (20th); putting average, 29.76 (28th); sand saves, 35/92 (102nd); driving average, 236.93 (31st).

The Skinny

Kobayashi didn't pick up a golf club until she was 18 years old, so she can't be burned out. Maybe that $240,000 she averages each year on the tour satisfies her shopping jones. Will she ever win again? Not this year.

Nancy Lopez

Hard to believe Hall of Famer Nancy Lopez almost walked away from golf a few months before she won her 48th tournament, the '97 Chick-Fil-A Charity Championship. But it says a lot about Lopez that she didn't, choosing instead to drop 40 pounds, hit the gym and practice like crazy. The results speak for themselves: the victory was her first since 1993, she battled Alison Nicholas down to the wire at the U.S. Open and she had nine top-10 finishes in the 16 events she played, missing two cuts. After battling knee and elbow problems, she declared: "I'm in the best shape I've ever been in." That covers a lot of ground, seeing that she was 12 when she started winning tournaments (the New Mexico Women's Amateur). In her first season on tour, she won an incredible nine times, including the LPGA Championship. The next year, she relaxed a bit, winning only eight times. She had five wins in '85, three in '80, '81, '88 and '89. The other years netted only one or two victories on average. Lopez, one of the most personable LPGA members, finished the '97 season in ninth spot with $470,386. That was her best ranking since 1992 when she was eighth.

The Woman

Nancy Lopez, 5'5", born Jan. 6, 1957, in Torrance, CA. Resides Albany, GA. Husband, Ray Knight; daughters, Ashley Marie, Erinn Shea and Torri Heather. Attended Tulsa University. Inducted LPGA Hall of Fame in 1987, PGA World Golf Hall of Fame in 1989. Received 1998 Bob Jones Award from USGA in recognition of distinguished sportsmanship. Joined LPGA in 1977.

The Stats

Low nine hole score, 30; low 18, 66; low 54, 203; low 72, 274; total birdies, 197 (80th); total eagles, three (49th); fairways hit, 534/723 (28th); GIR, 683/936 (fourth); scoring average, 70.7 (fifth); putting average, 30.23 (81st); sand saves, 22/51 (49th); driving average, 245.52 (28th).

The Skinny

While Lopez can't really be called "the skinny," she says she feels as good as she looks after dropping those extra pounds. It showed in her game last year and the competitive fire was back in her eyes, especially when she became the first woman to fire four rounds in the 60s at the U.S. Open — and still lost. She will be back with a vengeance in '98, playing a limited schedule, but always contending.

Michelle McGann

If you can't recognize Michelle McGann instantly, then are you sure you're a golf fan? Even without the trademark wide-brimmed straw hat, McGann's tawny hair and flashing, infectious smile makes her stand out. Her 5'11" stature and powerful game make her fellow competitors notice her, too. McGann joined the LPGA as an 18-year-old. She was 130th on the money list in her rookie season of 1989 and although she didn't win until 1995, she moved up the list like wildfire. Two wins in '95, three in '96 and another duo in '97 have helped position her at 22nd spot on the career money list ($2,362,097). She had seven top 10s in 26 starts, missing four cuts, on her way to 12th spot in '97 ($421,133).

The Woman

Michelle McGann, 5'11", born Dec. 30, 1969, in West Palm Beach, FL. Resides Singer Island, FL. Enjoys traveling, shopping and working out. Joined LPGA in 1988.

The Stats

Low nine hole score, 31; low 18, 64; low 54, 201; low 72, 277; total birdies, 311 (10th); total eagles, five (19th); fairways hit, 678/1174 (172nd); GIR, 1052/1512 (13th); scoring average, 71.52 (18th); putting average, 30.05 (59th); sand saves, 49/96 (eighth); driving average, 256.22.

The Skinny

McGann dropped out of the top 10 money winners for the first time since 1994 and that may motivate her. Lord knows she's got the game to absolutely dominate any event — if she wants to. Exhibit A: She is 4-0 in playoffs. She may look at some of the newcomers on tour and realize that she is in danger of being overtaken by them. Has never been given the credit she deserves.

Barb Mucha

We think Barb Mucha would win more often if she would focus on golf and forget about the Women's Professional Bowlers Tour. We're not kidding. Not to be confused with Deion Sanders, Bo Jackson and other two-sport athletes, Mucha wants to knock down some pins of another kind after she retires from the LPGA. Seriously. "I'd like to do it some day for a living," she says about bowling. Mucha would be hard-pressed to match the income she's getting from golf: $309,684 (23rd) in 1997 brought her career earnings to $1,457,932 in 11 seasons. She does have a total of four wins, the last being the '96 Chick-fil-A.

The Woman

Barb Mucha, 5'6", born Dec. 1, 1961, in Parma, OH. Resides Orlando, FL. Attended Michigan State University. Enjoys fishing, bowling and Christian fellowship. Joined LPGA in 1986.

The Stats

Low nine hole score, 31; low 18, 65; low 54, 206; low 72, 277; total birdies, 277 (29th); total eagles, five (19th); fairways hit, 854/1156 (24th); GIR, 1055/1494 (eighth); scoring average, 71.4 (15th); putting average, 30.01 (55th); sand saves, 40/85 (23rd); driving average, 234.43 (109th).

The Skinny

After finishing 15th on the tour in '96, Mucha might have been looking for even more improvement in '97. But her stats just don't illustrate a star game. They're OK, but not exceptional. In a couple of years, as she approaches the dreaded 40, she may want to think more seriously about the pro bowling tour.

Terry-Jo Myers

Terry-Jo Myers has been through what she calls "a living hell" since she contracted the bladder disease interstitial cystitis in 1983. In addition to intense pain, the disease also caused Myers to suffer from serious depression — so serious that she considered suicide. Although interstitial cystitis is incurable, a new drug has helped Myers regain control of her life and her golf. Her last win prior to 1997 was in 1988. But last January she broke through, winning the Los Angeles Women's Championship. During a tearful celebration she said, "My emotion is not about going so long without a win. It's connected more with overcoming a very serious disease and actually being able to win again." She definitely made the most of her new situation: Last May 11, Mother's Day, she won the Sara Lee Classic in a five-hole playoff. Those two wins and two other top-10 finishes in 22 starts earned Myers $313,015 (22nd). Her previous best season was when she finished 40th in 1988. Myers now is a national spokesperson for the Interstitial Cystitis Association and carries its phone number (1-800-HELP-ICA) on her bag.

The Woman

Terry-Jo Myers, 5'9", born July 23, 1962, in Ft. Myers, FL. Resides Ft. Myers, FL. Husband, Gary Mundy, Jr.; daughter Taylor-Jo. Attended Florida International University. Joined LPGA in 1985.

The Stats

Low nine hole score, 30; low 18, 66; low 54, 205; low 72, 277; total birdies, 196 (83rd); total eagles, one (126th); fairways hit, 568/909 (146th); GIR, 791/1170 (27th); scoring average, 72.43 (49th); putting average, 30.6 (120th); sand saves, 41/80 (seventh); driving average, 246.04 (24th).

The Skinny

Life and golf are fun again for Myers, who has won the biggest victory she could ever imagine. The fact that she missed seven cuts in 22 starts may concern others, but she is focused on her family and her renewed health. Although her stats weren't overwhelming in '97, she won twice. Chances are she won't win again this year, but we think she'll be in the top 30 money winners as her overall game comes around.

LISELOTTE NEUMANN

Her nickname is pronounced "Lotta." Her last name is pronounced "Noi-man." She pronounces: "I still have a lot of expectations of myself and I believe I still have what it takes to win," after winning 10 times on the LPGA and 13 times internationally. Wins No. 9 and 10 came in '97, bumping Neumann to seventh on the money list ($497,841). Along with her first LPGA win, the '88 U.S. Open, she became only the 12th player to win the Open as her first win. It goes without saying she was rookie of the year, finishing in 12th spot on the money list.

The Woman

Liselotte Neumann, 5'7", born May 20, 1966, in Finspang, Sweden. Resides Boca Raton, FL. Enjoys music, tennis, Miami Dolphins, decorating, wine collecting and traveling. Joined LPGA in 1987.

The Stats

Low nine hole score, 30; low 18, 64; low 54, 203; low 72, 273; total birdies, 320 (seventh); total eagles, eight (fifth); fairways hit, 784/1177 (111th); GIR, 996/1512 (46th); scoring average, 71.28 (11th); putting average, 29.36 (fourth); sand saves, 46/95 (16th); driving average, 243.54 (41st).

The Skinny

Neumann's a determined competitor with a taste for victory. She's strong and durable, and is only 32 this year. She won't want to be left in countrywoman Annika's slipstream, so look for some good battles between them this season.

Alison Nicholas

You can call her Bulldog, Pocket Battleship or Big Al (as her good friend Laura Davies does). If you don't know who we're talking about, look for a cheery English golfer about the same height as some of the drivers LPGA players are using these days. At five-foot-nothing, Nicholas's height belies her strength. She is very strong, fit and feisty, as Nancy Lopez found when they were battling for the '97 U.S. Open title. In the end, it was Nicholas who prevailed, becoming the first golfer — man or woman — to shoot 10 under par in a U.S. Open. Her win also marked the first time in history that Americans were shut out of their men's, senior men's and women's open championships in the same year. The 18 events she played over here last season were the most since she joined the tour in 1989. She took a hiatus in '91-'92 and concentrated on the European tour, where she has won a total of 13 times, including the 1987 Weetabix Women's British Open. Nicholas ended up 18th on the LPGA money list, missing four cuts.

The Woman

Alison Nicholas, 5'0", born March 6, 1962, in Gibraltar. Resides Birmingham, England. Enjoys skiing, scuba diving and ornithology. Joined LPGA in 1989.

The Stats

Low nine hole score, 30; low 18, 66; low 54, 203; low 72, 274; total birdies, 186 (97th); total eagles, three (49th); fairways hit, 555/773 (49th); GIR, 657/990 (49th); scoring average, 72.31 (42nd); putting average, 30.42 (103rd); sand saves, 26/66 (83rd); driving average, 241.7 (51st).

The Skinny

In her U.S. Open victory, Nicholas belted the ball an average of 243 yards off the tee and lagged her putts beautifully. She seems to come up big in the majors, although she missed the cut at the '97 du Maurier Classic shortly after her Open win. She turns 36 in June and has had her moment in the sun on this side of the Atlantic. And unlike Barb Mucha, we don't think Nicholas is planning to change sports in the near future. She tried tennis, but "it's tough when you can't see the opponent on the other side of the net." Like we said, a career change would be shortsighted (sorry).

Dottie Pepper

Intense, focused, hyper ... Dottie Pepper. What an appropriate surname for this spicy shotmaker. She won four times in '96 before a divorce and assorted physical ailments took their toll. At the end of last season, her best finish was T2 (although she did have seven top 10s in 24 events) and she dropped out of the top five money earners for the first time since 1990, ending up 26th. But the word is out that all is well once again (she married caddie Ralph Scarenzi in January). "Watch out for this one next year," said Juli Inkster after she partnered Pepper to a win at December's Diners Club Matches. "She has the eye of the tiger." There's no question she knows how to win, notching 14 LPGA wins in her 10-year career.

The Woman

Dottie Pepper, 5'6", born Aug. 17, 1965, in Saratoga Springs, NY. Resides Glassy Mountain, SC. Attended Furman University. Enjoys gardening, music, sports cars and downhill skiing. Joined LPGA in 1987.

The Stats

Low nine hole score, 31; low 18, 66; low 54, 205; low 72, 271; total birdies, 264 (32nd); total eagles, three (49th); fairways hit, 859/1187 (39th); GIR, 1093/1530 (sixth); scoring average, 71.34 (12th); putting average, 30.39 (97th); sand saves, 40/103 (92nd); driving average, 236.78 (91st).

The Skinny

Inkster's comment at the Diners Club Matches summed it up. Pepper, who decided at age eight that she would be a pro golfer, will not be denied. The happy marriage and the healthy body are new, but the win-at-all-costs attitude and the high-energy, fundamentally sound golf game have always been there. Back to the top 10 in '98.

Michele Redman

Looks like Michele Redman subscribes to the philosophy a friend of ours describes as "Win ... or pick up." Twenty-five events in '97 led to her first win, five other top-10 finishes and nine missed cuts. She must have something better to do on those nine weekends. Was the JAL Big Apple Classic in July an aberration? Maybe, just like the 64 she shot in the first round to blow the competition away. Redman, who had never been higher than 34th on the money list in her six-year career, finished '97 in 25th spot with $293,831.

The Woman

Michele Redman, 5'8", born April 15, 1965, in Zanesville, OH. Resides Port St. Lucie, FL. Attended Indiana University. Enjoys snow skiing. Joined LPGA in 1991.

The Stats

Low nine hole score, 30; low 18, 64; low 54, 202; low 72, 272; total birdies, 256 (36th); total eagles, four (27th); fairways hit, 899/1187 (11th); GIR, 997/1530 (59th); scoring average, 72.17 (33rd); putting average, 30.69 (131st); sand saves, 48/95 (10th); driving average, 231.63 (128th).

The Skinny

Redman has been a middle-of-the-pack grinder for half a dozen years. Then for a couple of rounds in mid-summer, she's possessed by the spirit of Ben Hogan and goes 64-67-71-70 to win her first tournament. Nice person, intense, works hard ... that's fine, but we don't see a return trip to the winner's circle for another six years. Nine missed cuts?

Deb Richard

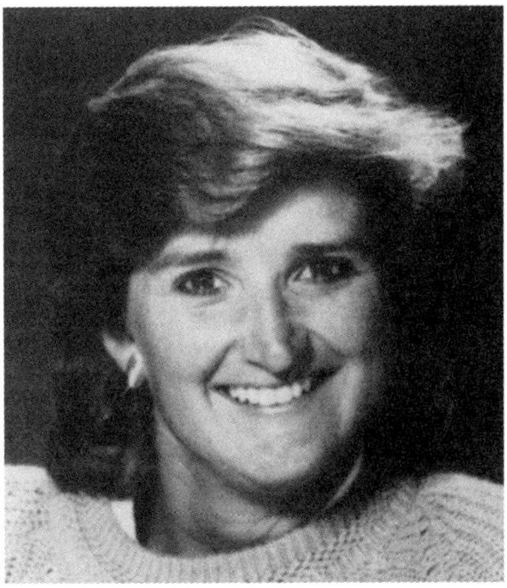

That's not "Richard" as in "Richard Simmons." (Thank goodness.) That's "Ri-shard" as in ... "Henri Richard." When you're born in Cajun country, you become very sensitive about things like that, cher. Richard came onto the LPGA scene in 1986, registering six top-10 finishes. She won in her second year and added three more wins in the intervening seasons, usually posting a ranking in the low teens. While she hasn't won since '94, she seems to have figured out the system: she posts a few top 10s and banks about 200 grand every year. Nice work if you can get it. In '97, she made $268,539 (28th), making the top 10 four times in 29 events and missing seven cuts.

The Woman

Deb Richard, 5'6", born Abbeville, LA, June 3, 1963. Resides Ponte Vedra Beach, FL. Attended University of Florida. Joined LPGA in 1985. Works with the Deb Richard Foundation, which awards college scholarships to kids with juvenile arthritis.

The Stats

Low nine hole score, 32; low 18, 66; low 54, 208; low 72, 277; total birdies, 280 (26th); total eagles, four (27th); fairways hit, 818/1226 (109th); GIR, 1033/1584 (57th); scoring average, 72.22 (37th); putting average, 29.8 (33rd); sand saves, 60/134 (35th); driving average, 237.67 (79th).

The Skinny

Destined to stay in the top 30 or so money winners for the next three or four years. May fluke a win in that span, but unlikely.

Kelly Robbins

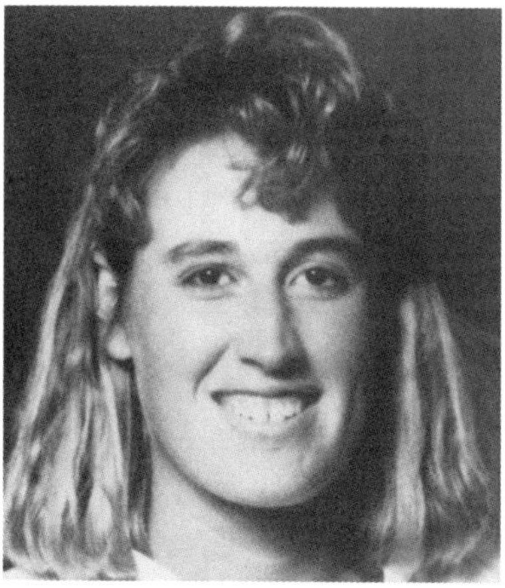

Kelly Robbins has been hobbling around — figuratively speaking — for years now with the ominous cloud of "potential superstar" hovering over her. Granted, she made a big impact when she arrived on tour, posting seven top 10s as a rookie. Three years later, she was No. 3 on the money list and had won her third tournament — the McDonald's LPGA Championship. She won in '96 and then twice in '97: the Diet Dr. Pepper in February (66-69-69-67) and then went 67-64-67-67 to claim the Jamie Farr Kroger Classic. That win set an LPGA record for lowest 72-hole score. Hate to say it, but that kinda sounds like superstar stuff to us.

The Woman

Kelly Robbins, 5'9", born Sept. 29, 1969, in Mt. Pleasant, MI, Resides Mt. Pleasant, MI. Attended University of Tulsa. Enjoys fishing, swimming, tennis and basketball. Joined LPGA in 1991.

The Stats

Low nine hole score, 31; low 18, 64; low 54, 198; low 72, 265; total birdies, 383 (first); total eagles, 17 (first); fairways hit, 863/1245 (73rd); GIR, 1260/1602 (first); scoring average, 70.35 (third); putting average, 29.9 (39th); sand saves, 35/78 (34th); driving average, 255.97 (sixth).

The Skinny

Turning 29 this year, Robbins is definitely ready to break out. She led the tour in total birdies, eagles, rounds in the 60s (46/96) and was second in rounds under par (61/96) and top 10s (18/28). She won't be denied. Three wins this year plus a major? Could be.

Annika Sorenstam

LPGA Commissioner Jim Ritts calls Annika Sorenstam "the baby-faced assassin." Apt description. She's a cute, quiet killer who has yet to reach her potential despite winning six times in '97 to boost her total wins in four years to 12. Her "major" disappointment last season was failing to defend her two consecutive U.S. Open crowns. Coming from the Swedish system where players are taught that shooting 54 is not impossible, it's not surprising that Sorenstam says, "I personally feel I can improve even more. I know what to work on. I really look forward to climbing the ladder even higher." Her Swedish bestseller is titled *Dare To Be Great*. How apropos. She wound up '97 by smashing the mythical $1-million mark ($1.2367 million to be exact) and, of course, was No. 1 on the list.

The Woman

Annika Sorenstam, 5'6", born Sept. 10, 1970, in Stockholm, Sweden. Husband, David Esch. Attended University of Arizona. Enjoys sports, music and cooking. Joined LPGA in 1993.

The Stats

Low nine hole score, 30; low 18, 65; low 54, 204; low 72, 272; total birdies, 317 (eighth); total eagles, three (49th); fairways hit, 737/977 (12th); GIR, 923/1260 (third); scoring average, 70.04 (second); putting average, 29.67 (22nd); sand saves, 26/55 (21st); driving average, 249.0 (14th).

The Skinny

When she stunned herself — and everybody else — by missing the cut at the U.S. Open (her first MC in 62 starts), Sorenstam revealed that she is human after all. But just barely. She had 16 top 10s in 22 starts and missed only two cuts. She's one of those "once in a generation" players who just might lap the field.

Sherri Steinhauer

Steinhauer, a former all-American at the University of Texas, appeared mired in the journeyman (journeyperson?) category until she slowly started to creep up the money list in the early '90s. By 1994, her best year thus far, she was seventh. But the rarified air of the top 10 must have gotten to her, because she plummeted to 62nd in '96. Last season was more to her liking, with a 29th-place finish and a tidy $267,739.

The Woman

Sherri Steinhauer, 5'7", born Dec. 27, 1962, in Madison, WI. Resides Madison, WI. Attended University of Texas. Enjoys sports and music. Joined LPGA in 1985.

The Stats

Low nine hole score, 31; low 18, 65; low 54, 202; low 72, 277; total birdies, 295 (17th); total eagles, four (27th); fairways hit, 926/1382 (103rd); GIR, 1263/1782 (seventh); scoring average, 72.3 (41st); putting average, 31.09 (167th); sand saves, 41/99 (57th); driving average, 236.92 (90th).

The Skinny

Tough competitor who won a major (1992 du Maurier Ltd. Classic) for her first victory and has flirted with serious success. Putting woes appear terminal, which is a real shame when you look at how many greens she hits. Hope we're wrong, but doubt it.

Kris Tschetter

After a 12th-place finish on the '95 money list and a 13th in '96, it looked like Kris Tschetter ("Chedder") was starting to like the view from the top. But she must have pushed the down button in '97 as she plunged to 27th spot, missing nine cuts in 28 events and posting five top 10s. That's not a good sign for the woman who was in the top 10 13 times in '96.

The Woman

Kris Tschetter, 5'7", born Dec. 30, 1964, in Detroit, MI. Resides McLean, VA. Husband, Kirk Lucas. Attended Texas Christian University. Enjoys ballet, cooking and reading. Joined LPGA in 1987.

The Stats

Low nine hole score, 30; low 18, 64; low 54, 200; low 72, 278; total birdies, 306 (12th); total eagles, seven (eighth); fairways hit, 685/1118 (154th); GIR, 981/1440 (20th); scoring average, 72.10 (29th); putting average, 30.57 (117th); sand saves, 48/96 (10th); driving average, 256.98 (fourth).

The Skinny

Tschetter should be hitting her prime. She drives the ball a ton, hits a lot of greens, gets up and down out of bunkers — and struggles with her putter, to say the least. There are rumblings about vision problems, but we would be surprised if that's the whole story. How can someone who is this close have won only once, six years ago? Might be ready to have a career year.

Colleen Walker

Strange game, this golf. Colleen Walker has had a pretty good career on the LPGA; she was in the top 10 money winners four times in the 16 years she's been on tour. Up to 1993, she had won seven times, but then the drought set in. That drought ended with a bang last August when she won her first major, the du Maurier Ltd. Classic, and then claimed the very next event on the schedule, the Star Bank LPGA Classic. "Life begins at 40," she smiled as she, her husband and their toddler climbed into the family truck to head for the next tour stop. Walker played in 28 events, had five top-10 finishes including her wins, and missed eight cuts. She finished 14th on the money list with $384,882.

The Woman

Colleen Walker, 5'5", born Aug. 16, 1956, in Jacksonville, FL. Resides Brandon, FL. Husband, Ron Bakich; son, Tyler. Attended Florida State University. Enjoys football. Joined LPGA in 1982.

The Stats

Low nine hole score, 32; low 18, 65; low 54, 203; low 72, 278; total birdies, 263 (33rd); total eagles, one (126th); fairways hit, 885/1203 (26th); GIR, 980/1584 (95th); scoring average, 72.31 (43rd); putting average, 29.58 (15th); sand saves, 47/115 (65th); driving average, 230.04 (142nd).

The Skinny

Walker was full value for those two wins, but we know from personal experience that that "life begins at 40" crap is just that. She was a great story in '97, but will start the inexorable slide down the earnings escalator.

Karrie Webb

"I don't feel I have anything to prove anymore." Pretty cocky for someone in her rookie LPGA season, wouldn't you say? What if we mentioned that Karrie Webb said that last year after winning her second British Open in three years? And that she was well on the way to almost equaling the previous season when she was not only the LPGA rookie of the year, but also the leading money winner. And not just the leading money winner, but the first to win $1 million in a single season, based on four wins and 12 top-five finishes in 25 events. In 1997, she won three times in 25 starts with 21 top 10s. While Annika Sorenstam reclaimed the earnings title, Webb finished second with $987,606 and set a new season scoring record of 70.00.

The Woman

Karrie Webb, 5'6", born Dec. 21, 1974, in Ayr, Queensland, Australia. Resides Ayr, Queensland, Australia. Enjoys reading, basketball and fishing. Joined LPGA in 1995.

The Stats

Low nine hole score, 29; low 18, 63; low 54, 198; low 72, 269; total birdies, 363 (second); total eagles, 11 (second); fairways hit, 873/1210 (44th); GIR, 1176/1566 (second); scoring average, 70.00;putting average, 30.2 (72nd); sand saves, 27/71 (103rd); driving average, 254.59 (seventh).

The Skinny

She is sooo good. Only 23 years old, she will continue to set the LPGA on its ear. Battles among Webb, Sorenstam, McGann and some of the other newcomers should go a long way to revitalize the tour. Who will prevail in '98? A coin flip between Webb and Sorenstam.

1997
STATISTICS

PGA Tour

MONEY WINNERS

1997 Schedule
Through Tour Championship (Nov. 2)

Rank	Player	Trn	Money
1	Tiger Woods	21	$2,066,833
2	David Duval	29	$1,885,308
3	Davis Love III	25	$1,635,953
4	Jim Furyk	27	$1,619,480
5	Justin Leonard	29	$1,587,531
6	Scott Hoch	22	$1,393,788
7	Greg Norman	15	$1,345,856
8	Steve Elkington	17	$1,320,411
9	Ernie Els	19	$1,243,008
10	Brad Faxon	23	$1,233,505
11	Phil Mickelson	21	$1,225,390
12	Jesper Parnevik	19	$1,217,587
13	Mark O'Meara	22	$1,124,428
14	Mark Calcavecchia	27	$1,117,365
15	Loren Roberts	24	$1,089,140
16	Vijay Singh	21	$1,059,236
17	Nick Price	16	$1,053,845
18	Stuart Appleby	23	$1,003,356
19	Tom Lehman	21	$960,584
20	Steve Jones	24	$959,108
21	Paul Stankowski	29	$929,405
22	Bill Glasson	19	$926,552
23	Frank Nobilo	19	$891,315
24	Lee Janzen	27	$877,832
25	Scott McCarron	26	$852,459
26	Jeff Maggert	27	$835,884
27	Tommy Tolles	25	$825,793
28	John Cook	28	$815,903
29	Stewart Cink	31	$809,580
30	Andrew Magee	29	$752,007
31	Billy Andrade	28	$665,602
32	Phil Blackmar	27	$642,400
33	Tim Herron	31	$640,997
34	Jeff Sluman	29	$634,203
35	Tom Kite	22	$631,252
36	David Ogrin	27	$593,683
37	Colin Montgomerie	9	$578,991
38	Fred Funk	33	$544,419
39	Kirk Triplett	26	$541,023
40	Payne Stewart	23	$538,289
41	Craig Stadler	21	$525,304
42	Tom Byrum	27	$525,161
43	Bob Tway	26	$507,523
44	Steve Lowery	30	$480,467
45	Tom Watson	16	$479,146
46	Russ Cochran	29	$470,929
47	Michael Bradley	28	$465,887
48	Chris Perry	32	$460,984
49	David Toms	27	$460,355
50	David Frost	24	$458,700
51	Duffy Waldorf	26	$458,074
52	Kevin Sutherland	27	$455,860
53	Robert Damron	32	$455,604
54	Hal Sutton	29	$453,928
55	Fred Couples	15	$448,385
56	Dan Forsman	27	$443,034
57	Jay Haas	24	$437,895
58	Nick Faldo	15	$431,326
59	Lee Rinker	31	$415,442
60	Dudley Hart	28	$410,188
61	Paul Goydos	30	$396,241
62	Brent Geiberger	29	$395,472
63	Craig Parry	20	$387,603
64	Doug Martin	30	$383,593
65	Jay Don Blake	28	$378,484
66	Brad Fabel	30	$375,122
67	Mike Brisky	30	$367,112
68	Grant Waite	31	$362,320

69	Bob Estes	19	$340,057
70	Brandel Chamblee	26	$334,664
71	Brian Henninger	25	$329,864
72	Rick Fehr	22	$327,204
73	Mike Reid	25	$325,551
74	Skip Kendall	31	$320,800
75	Mike Standly	28	$318,939
76	Mike Hulbert	30	$317,247
77	Len Mattiace	35	$315,656
78	Don Pooley	19	$312,660
79	Billy Mayfair	30	$304,083
80	Ted Tryba	34	$303,399
81	Brad Bryant	24	$295,365
82	Peter Jacobsen	25	$294,931
83	David Edwards	23	$292,096
84	David Sutherland	28	$288,663
85	Mark Wiebe	25	$285,139
86	Robert Gamez	28	$283,434
87	Darren Clarke	4	$282,816
88	Jim Carter	29	$279,834
89	Gabriel Hjertstedt	23	$279,624
90	Kenny Perry	26	$270,081
91	Billy Ray Brown	24	$268,709
92	Kelly Gibson	36	$267,230
93	Paul Azinger	20	$262,045
94	Olin Browne	33	$261,810
95	Steve Pate	28	$261,436
96	Phil Tataurangi	26	$256,930
97	Clarence Rose	32	$256,481
98	Glen Day	29	$248,323
99	Larry Mize	21	$246,773
100	Joe Durant	31	$240,936
101	Rocco Mediate	24	$240,521
102	Fulton Allem	21	$237,051
103	Jerry Kelly	33	$234,257
104	Ronnie Black	28	$230,224
105	P.H. Horgan III	30	$226,249
106	Donnie Hammond	21	$224,799
107	Frank Lickliter	30	$221,049
108	Mark Brooks	30	$213,516
109	Scott Gump	33	$209,672
110	Pete Jordan	33	$209,020
111	Nolan Henke	24	$205,859
112	Michael Christie	33	$204,883
113	Omar Uresti	32	$203,516
114	Joey Sindelar	31	$200,069
115	Joe Ozaki	19	$199,207
116	Doug Barron	31	$198,051
117	Larry Nelson	18	$196,981
118	Wayne Levi	20	$195,820
119	Mike Springer	22	$191,422
120	Guy Boros	27	$191,139
121	Willie Wood	27	$190,283
122	Lennie Clements	28	$189,958
123	John Adams	28	$188,986
124	Larry Rinker	33	$188,281
125	Neal Lancaster	34	$179,273
126	Jose Maria Olazabal	6	$173,589
127	Tom Pernice, Jr.	30	$173,012
128	Brett Quigley	34	$172,023
129	Curtis Strange	20	$171,092
130	Steve Stricker	20	$167,652
131	Tommy Armour III	30	$163,664
132	Jimmy Johnston	30	$163,202
133	Tom Purtzer	23	$161,393
134	John Morse	30	$161,363
135	J.P. Hayes	29	$160,722
136	Bernhard Langer	7	$158,508
137	Lanny Wadkins	20	$155,962
138	Lee Westwood	5	$155,645
139	Greg Kraft	35	$152,109
140	Bruce Fleisher	17	$151,902
141	John Huston	28	$151,840
142	Bradley Hughes	27	$142,793
143	Blaine McCallister	30	$140,966
144	Jim McGovern	32	$140,756

145	Jim Gallagher, Jr.	28	$137,654
146	Dave Stockton, Jr.	32	$136,159
147	Robin Freeman	20	$135,702
148	Fuzzy Zoeller	16	$134,776
149	Scott Simpson	25	$128,448
150	Brian Claar	18	$121,273

SCORING LEADERS

The number (e.g., 68.96) is not a pure scoring average, but is adjusted to the average score of the field each week. If the field is under par, each player's score is adjusted upward a corresponding amount; if the field is over par, the score is adjusted downward. This keeps a player from receiving any advantage for playing a schedule of easier-than-average courses.

Rank	Player	Rounds	Avg.
1	Nick Price	58	68.98
2	Tiger Woods	81	69.10
3	Greg Norman	51	69.16
4	Davis Love III	90	69.47
5	Tom Lehman	72	69.62
6	Jesper Parnevik	70	69.63
7	Jim Furyk	98	69.64
8	Scott Hoch	87	69.70
9	Justin Leonard	101	69.76
10	Phil Mickelson	76	69.83
11	Loren Roberts	82	69.88
12	Ernie Els	62	69.90
13	David Duval	98	69.91
14	Lee Janzen	99	69.96
15	Brad Faxon	75	69.97
16	Mark Calcavecchia	97	70.00
17	David Ogrin	96	70.06
18	Payne Stewart	87	70.07
T19	Steve Elkington	62	70.09
T19	Bob Estes	69	70.09
21	Bob Tway	93	70.10
22	Fred Couples	57	70.13
23	Tom Watson	52	70.14
24	Don Pooley	72	70.15
25	Craig Parry	71	70.17
26	Vijay Singh	83	70.18
27	Mark O'Meara	78	70.23
28	Craig Stadler	69	70.29
29	Bill Glasson	68	70.33
T30	John Cook	99	70.35
T30	Jay Haas	80	70.35
32	Tommy Tolles	89	70.36
33	Stuart Appleby	78	70.37
34	Frank Nobilo	64	70.41
35	Billy Andrade	101	70.43
36	Paul Azinger	62	70.44
37	Tom Byrum	98	70.46
38	Brent Geiberger	93	70.48
39	Stewart Cink	99	70.49
40	Andrew Magee	102	70.50
41	Peter Jacobsen	87	70.51
42	Scott McCarron	81	70.52
43	Chris Perry	106	70.53
44	Steve Lowery	99	70.54
T45	Doug Martin	102	70.56
T45	Kirk Triplett	88	70.56
T47	Jay Don Blake	91	70.57
T47	Bruce Fleisher	61	70.57
49	Jeff Maggert	93	70.58
T50	Steve Jones	78	70.60
T50	Kevin Sutherland	85	70.60
52	Russ Cochran	103	70.62
53	Jeff Sluman	98	70.63
54	Phil Blackmar	92	70.66
T55	Tom Kite	74	70.69

T55	Larry Mize	69	70.69
57	Hal Sutton	96	70.70
T58	Fred Funk	115	70.72
T58	Paul Stankowski	101	70.72
60	Paul Goydos	100	70.73
61	Nick Faldo	49	70.74
T62	Michael Bradley	88	70.77
T62	Mike Reid	81	70.77
T64	Jim Carter	98	70.80
T64	Rick Fehr	69	70.80
T66	Tim Herron	101	70.85
T66	Kenny Perry	81	70.85
T68	Ronnie Black	85	70.93
T68	Kelly Gibson	121	70.93
70	David Toms	88	70.96
71	Brian Henninger	77	70.97
72	Rocco Mediate	80	70.98
73	Robert Damron	98	70.99
74	Brad Fabel	94	71.01
T75	Wayne Levi	67	71.02
T75	Lanny Wadkins	71	71.02
77	Grant Waite	102	71.03
T78	Billy Mayfair	90	71.04
T78	Duffy Waldorf	89	71.04
T80	Keith Fergus	58	71.10
T80	Dan Forsman	84	71.10
T80	Skip Kendall	102	71.10
T80	Len Mattiace	107	71.10
T80	Fuzzy Zoeller	52	71.10
T85	David Edwards	70	71.11
T85	Nolan Henke	82	71.11
T85	David Sutherland	82	71.11
T88	Brandel Chamblee	79	71.13
T88	Steve Pate	83	71.13
T90	Mike Brisky	100	71.15
T90	Frank Lickliter	85	71.15
92	Phil Tataurangi	76	71.18
T93	Donnie Hammond	68	71.19
T93	Joey Sindelar	102	71.19
T93	Mike Standly	86	71.19
96	Mike Hulbert	98	71.20
97	Brad Bryant	78	71.22
98	Brian Claar	59	71.23
99	Steve Stricker	59	71.28
T100	Brett Quigley	111	71.30
T100	Lee Rinker	95	71.30
T102	Joe Durant	98	71.31
T102	Scott Gump	108	71.31
T104	Lennie Clements	88	71.32
T104	P.H. Horgan III	89	71.32
106	Curtis Strange	63	71.33
T107	Fulton Allem	62	71.34
T107	John Morse	92	71.34
109	Doug Barron	103	71.35
T110	Robin Freeman	65	71.36
T110	David Frost	69	71.36
T110	Pete Jordan	101	71.36
113	Tommy Armour III	94	71.37
114	David Berganio, Jr.	83	71.42
T115	Dudley Hart	79	71.43
T115	Neal Lancaster	101	71.43
117	Robert Gamez	82	71.46
T118	Scott Dunlap	92	71.47
T118	J.P. Hayes	95	71.47
T118	D.A. Weibring	62	71.47
121	Willie Wood	86	71.48
122	Mark Brooks	89	71.49
123	Larry Rinker	98	71.50
124	Scott Verplank	62	71.51
T125	Patrick Burke	65	71.52
T125	Gene Sauers	53	71.52
T125	Scott Simpson	80	71.52
128	Tom Pernice, Jr.	85	71.53
129	Michael Christie	95	71.54
130	Omar Uresti	101	71.55
T131	Bradley Hughes	78	71.56

T131	Mark Wiebe	77	71.56
T133	Clarence Rose	92	71.57
T133	Ted Tryba	103	71.57
T135	Olin Browne	101	71.58
T135	Naomichi "Joe" Ozaki	66	71.58
T135	Corey Pavin	63	71.58
T135	Mike Springer	66	71.58
T139	Greg Kraft	104	71.60
T139	Jim McGovern	89	71.60
T141	John Adams	81	71.61
T141	Glen Day	82	71.61
143	Dave Stockton, Jr.	99	71.65
144	Blaine McCallister	85	71.66
145	Spike McRoy	68	71.68
146	Billy Ray Brown	70	71.71
147	Jay Delsing	84	71.73
148	Jerry Kelly	92	71.74
149	Rafael Alarcon	79	71.75
T150	Marco Dawson	85	71.78
T150	Tom Purtzer	66	71.78
152	Allen Doyle	85	71.79
153	Jeff Hart	79	71.80
154	John Huston	75	71.81
155	John Wilson	91	71.82
156	Jack O'Keefe	75	71.88
T157	Joel Edwards	92	71.89
T157	Jim Gallagher, Jr.	87	71.89
159	Sonny Skinner	71	71.92
160	Ken Green	53	71.93
161	Eric Johnson	83	71.96
T162	Paul Claxton	66	71.97
T162	Jimmy Johnston	85	71.97
164	Jimmy Green	82	72.00
165	Craig Bowden	55	72.01
T166	Guy Boros	79	72.02
T166	John Maginnes	101	72.02
168	Larry Nelson	54	72.10
T169	Emlyn Aubrey	72	72.11
T169	John Daly	50	72.11
T169	Todd Demsey	74	72.11
T172	Gabriel Hjertstedt	72	72.12
T172	Bob Wolcott	71	72.12
174	Taylor Smith	81	72.13
175	Kevin Burton	74	72.20
176	Ed Fiori	50	72.25
177	Tim Simpson	63	72.26
178	Shane Bertsch	83	72.28
179	Tray Tyner	74	72.31
180	Chip Sullivan	77	72.32
T181	Steve Hart	69	72.38
T181	Howard Twitty	48	72.38
183	Woody Austin	87	72.42
184	Hideki Kase	85	72.45
185	Sandy Lyle	63	72.46
186	Dicky Pride	76	72.55
187	Hugh Royer III	83	72.59
188	Ed Dougherty	65	72.61
189	Craig Kanada	54	72.63
190	Larry Silveira	59	72.70
191	Lee Porter	81	72.75
192	Anthony Rodriguez	61	72.83
193	John Dowdall	61	72.95
194	Shaun Micheel	53	72.97
195	Chip Beck	71	73.79

DRIVING ACCURACY

This statistic calculates the percentage of a player's drives that remain on the faiway. Note that par three holes are not included.

Rank	Player	Rounds	%
1	Allen Doyle	85	80.8
2	Fred Funk	115	79.8
3	Larry Mize	69	79.5

4	Nick Price	58	79.3
5	Jim Furyk	98	79.2
6	Nick Faldo	49	78.7
7	David Edwards	70	78.2
8	Loren Roberts	82	77.7
9	John Morse	92	77.6
10	Olin Browne	101	77.2

4	Jesper Parnevik	70	3.99
5	Phil Mickelson	76	3.95
6	Mark Calcavecchia	97	3.91
7	Don Pooley	72	3.90
T8	Lee Janzen	99	3.88
T8	Greg Norman	51	3.88
10	Fred Couples	57	3.86

DRIVING DISTANCE

This statistic averages the exact distances of two tee shots on the widest par four or par five holes from the front nine and back nine.

(Avg. yards per drive)

Rank	Player	Rounds	Stat
1	John Daly	50	302.0
2	Tiger Woods	81	294.8
3	Bill Glasson	68	287.5
4	Davis Love III	90	285.8
T5	Phil Mickelson	76	284.1
T5	Chip Sullivan	77	284.1
7	Scott McCarron	81	283.8
8	Fred Couples	57	283.5
T9	John Adams	81	280.9
T9	Vijay Singh	83	280.9

BIRDIE

This statistic compiles the average number of birdies made per round.

Rank	Player	Rounds	Stat
1	Tiger Woods	81	4.25
2	Bill Glasson	68	4.18
3	David Duval	98	4.09

EAGLE LEADERS

This statistic tabulates the frequency (number of holes played between each) that a player makes an eagle.

Rank	Player	Rounds	Stat
1	Tiger Woods	81	104.1
2	Steve Lowery	99	104.8
3	Tim Herron	101	113.6
4	Fred Couples	57	114.0
5	David Berganio, Jr.	83	114.9
6	Mark Calcavecchia	97	116.4
7	John Daly	50	128.6
8	Vijay Singh	83	135.8
9	Ken Green	53	136.3
10	Billy Ray Brown	70	140.0

GREENS IN REGULATION

1997 Schedule

Through Tour Championship (Nov. 2)

Rank	Player	Rounds	Stat
1	Tom Lehman	72	72.7
2	John Cook	99	71.1
3	Hal Sutton	96	70.9
T4	Bill Glasson	68	70.3
T4	Tiger Woods	81	70.3

T6	Mark Calcavecchia	97	70.1
T6	Bob Tway	93	70.1
T6	Fuzzy Zoeller	52	70.1
9	Davis Love III	90	70.0
T10	Rocco Mediate	80	69.9
T10	Greg Norman	51	69.9

PUTTING LEADERS

1997 Schedule
Through Tour Championship (Nov. 2)

Rank	Player	Rounds	Stat
1	Don Pooley	72	1.718
2	Lee Janzen	99	1.726
3	Loren Roberts	82	1.734
4	Brad Faxon	75	1.736
5	Mark O'Meara	78	1.742
6	Jim Furyk	98	1.743
7	Mike Brisky	100	1.745
8	Phil Blackmar	92	1.747
9	Brian Claar	59	1.749
T10	Michael Christie	95	1.751
T10	Bob Estes	69	1.751

SAND SAVES

A percentage of "up-and-down" efforts from greenside sand traps only. Fairway bunkers and waste areas are not included in this category.

Rank	Player	Rounds	Stat
1	Bob Estes	69	70.3
2	Ronnie Black	85	66.3
3	Frank Nobilo	64	64.6
4	Jay Haas	80	64.5
5	Stuart Appleby	78	64.2
T6	John Morse	92	63.8
T6	Kevin Sutherland	85	63.8
8	Willie Wood	86	62.6
9	Lanny Wadkins	71	62.5
10	Jesper Parnevik	70	62.4

ALL-AROUND LEADERS

This category is created by adding each player's standing listings for all other categories.

Rank	Player	Events	Stat
1	Bill Glasson	19	282
2	Tom Byrum	27	305
3	Greg Norman	15	317
4	Tom Lehman	21	321
5	Mark Calcavecchia	27	329
6	Scott Hoch	22	337
7	Tiger Woods	21	346
8	Jay Haas	24	351
9	Andrew Magee	29	357
10	Jesper Parnevik	19	362

WORLD MONEY LIST

The World PGA Tours weekly list will use the Dow Jones currency exchange rates published each Monday to convert international currency to U.S. dollars. Earnings from official events on each of the five tour — the PGA Tour, the European PGA Tour, the Australasian PGA Tour, the PGA Tour of Japan and the FNB Tour (South Africa) — will count on the world list.

Rank	Player	Events	Money
1	Tiger Woods	22	$2,082,381
2	David Duval	29	$1,885,308
3	Ernie Els	25	$1,814,029
4	Greg Norman	20	$1,720,573
5	Davis Lovelll	25	$1,635,953
6	Jim Furyk	27	$1,619,460
7	Colin Montgomerie	27	$1,609,300
8	Justin Leonard	29	$1,587,531
9	Scott Hoch	23	$1,418,272
10	JumboOzaki	20	$1,362,433
11	Mark O'Meara	24	$1,359,480
12	Nick Price	20	$1,326,569
13	Steve Elkington	17	$1,320,411
14	Jesper Parnevik	23	$1,253,697
15	Phil Mickelson	22	$1,241,120
16	Brad Faxon	23	$1,233,505
17	Tom Lehman	25	$1,230,194
18	Vijay Singh	24	$1,201,816
19	Lee Westwood	26	$1,186,780
20	Bernhard Langer	24	$1,120,988
21	Mark Calcavecchia	27	$1,117,365
22	ShigekiMaruyama	27	$1,090,027
23	Loren Roberts	24	$1,089,140
24	Steve Jones	27	$1,025,243
25	Stuart Appleby	27	$1,009,849
26	Frank Nobilo	22	$977,809
27	Paul Stankowski	29	$929,405
28	Bill Glasson	19	$926,552
29	Joe Ozaki	31	$905,056
30	Darren Clarke	27	$878,154
31	Lee Janzen	27	$877,832
32	Scott McCarron	26	$852,459
33	Jeff Maggert	27	$835,884
34	José MariaOlazábal	23	$828,000
35	Tommy Tolles	26	$825,793
36	John Cook	28	$815,903
37	Stewart Cink	31	$809,580
38	Brian Watts	21	$809,241
39	Ian Woosnam	22	$782,275
40	Tom Watson	17	$763,942
41	Andrew Magee	29	$752,007
42	Nick Faldo	20	$737,533
43	Craig Parry	26	$706,488
44	Jeff Sluman	31	$675,387
45	Billy Andrade	28	$665,602
46	Retief Goosen	29	$661,486
47	Costantino Rocca	31	$654,768
48	Phil Blackmar	27	$642,400
49	Tim Herron	32	$640,997
50	Tom Kite	22	$631,252
51	Ignacio Garrido	26	$623,213
52	Per-Ulrik Johansson	19	$604,329
53	Padraig Harrington	30	$599,030
54	David Frost	28	$595,058
55	David Ogrin	27	$593,683
56	Fred Couples	17	$589,900
57	Payne Stewart	24	$578,897
58	Robert Karlsson	21	$560,915
59	Fred Funk	34	$553,703
60	Kirk Triplett	26	$541,023
61	BrandtJobe	18	$536,785
62	Craig Stadler	22	$531,957
63	Tom Byrum	27	$525,161
64	JetOsaki	24	$523,182
65	CarlosFranco	20	$518,480
66	Bob Tway	26	$507,523
67	ShoichiKuwabara	30	$497,056
68	Russ Cochran	30	$482,890
69	Steve Lowery	30	$480,467
70	Michael Bradley	28	$465,887
71	RobertDamron	34	$461,608
72	Chris Perry	32	$460,984
73	David Toms	27	$460,355
74	Eduardo Romero	21	$458,089
75	Duffy Waldorf	26	$458,074

76	Kevin Sutherland	27	$455,860
77	Hal Sutton	29	$453,928
78	Dan Forsman	27	$443,034
79	Jay Haas	24	$437,895
80	FrankieMinoza	20	$437,177
81	Thomas Bjørn	23	$421,293
82	Mark James	24	$420,712
83	Lee Rinker	31	$415,442
84	Peter O'Malley	26	$412,796
85	Raymond Russell	28	$410,500

ALL TIME PGA TOUR MONEY LEADERS

Rank	Player	Money
1	Greg Norman	$11,910,518
2	Tom Kite	$10,286,177
3	Fred Couples	$ 8,885,487
4	Nick Price	$ 8,794,431
5	Mark O'Meara	$ 8,506,774
6	Davis Love III	$ 8,470,982
7	Payne Stewart	$ 8,465,062
8	Tom Watson	$ 8,307,277
9	Corey Pavin	$ 8,130,356
10	Scott Hoch	$ 7,899,250
11	Mark Calcavecchia	$ 7,612,931
12	Paul Azinger	$ 7,451,410
13	Curtis Strange	$ 7,147,752
14	Ben Crenshaw	$ 7,064,604
15	Craig Stadler	$ 6,870,877
16	Jay Haas	$ 6,390,645
17	Steve Elkington	$ 6,328,138
18	David Frost	$ 6,299,819
19	Lanny Wadkins	$ 6,249,812
20	John Cook	$ 6,109,117
21	Chip Beck	$ 5,994,624
22	Hale Irwin	$ 5,902,306
23	Bruce Lietzke	$ 5,880,083
24	Brad Faxon	$ 5,842,619
25	Tom Lehman	$ 5,642,999
26	Loren Roberts	$ 5,624,104
27	Jack Nicklaus	$ 5,563,516
28	Fuzzy Zoeller	$ 5,401,176
29	Lee Janzen	$ 5,337,931
30	Mark McCumber	$ 5,290,798
31	Ray Floyd	$ 5,269,595
32	Gil Morgan	$ 5,259,164
33	Scott Simpson	$ 5,210,150
34	Larry Mize	$ 5,149,716
35	Jeff Sluman	$ 5,145,364
36	Hal Sutton	$ 5,134,238
37	Phil Mickelson	$ 5,127,731
38	Jim Gallagher, Jr.	$ 5,073,383
39	Peter Jacobsen	$ 4,969,692
40	Mark Brooks	$ 4,950,012
41	Bob Tway	$ 4,875,948
42	Wayne Levi	$ 4,629,618
43	Jeff Maggert	$ 4,411,032
44	Nick Faldo	$ 4,372,259
45	Bill Glasson	$ 4,206,807
46	D.A. Weibring	$ 4,167,691
47	David Edwards	$ 4,140,344
48	Billy Mayfair	$ 4,067,796
49	John Huston	$ 4,067,085
50	Joey Sindelar	$ 4,045,696
51	Kenny Perry	$ 4,039,232
52	Vijay Singh	$ 3,987,559
53	Steve Pate	$ 3,933,431
54	Andrew Magee	$ 3,919,085
55	Steve Jones	$ 3,899,180
56	John Mahaffey	$ 3,860,873
57	Larry Nelson	$ 3,816,001
58	David Duval	$ 3,815,010
59	Tom Purtzer	$ 3,808,670
60	Ernie Els	$ 3,736,234

61	Dan Forsman	$ 3,653,383	99	Bob Lohr	$ 2,410,252
62	Mike Reid	$ 3,618,656	100	Steve Stricker	$ 2,380,426
63	Ken Green	$ 3,569,068	101	Robert Gamez	$ 2,318,291
64	Fred Funk	$ 3,562,286	102	Dave Barr	$ 2,307,533
65	Lee Trevino	$ 3,478,328	103	Calvin Peete	$ 2,302,363
66	Russ Cochran	$ 3,471,403	104	Keith Clearwater	$ 2,247,022
67	Brad Bryant	$ 3,432,069	105	Mike Sullivan	$ 2,246,591
68	Mike Hulbert	$ 3,430,405	106	Tom Weiskopf	$ 2,241,687
69	Justin Leonard	$ 3,419,878	107	Ed Fiori	$ 2,230,823
70	Billy Andrade	$ 3,414,050	108	J.C. Snead	$ 2,219,171
71	Tim Simpson	$ 3,398,594	109	Roger Maltbie	$ 2,212,879
72	Andy Bean	$ 3,359,549	110	Gary Hallberg	$ 2,182,587
73	Gene Sauers	$ 3,242,925	111	Lennie Clements	$ 2,180,928
74	Rick Fehr	$ 3,220,587	112	Craig Parry	$ 2,163,557
75	Don Pooley	$ 3,218,134	113	John Daly	$ 2,154,618
76	Duffy Waldorf	$ 3,175,903	114	Ronnie Black	$ 2,147,112
77	Jim Furyk	$ 3,130,413	115	Tom Byrum	$ 2,064,258
78	Rocco Mediate	$ 3,083,014	116	Sandy Lyle	$ 2,024,354
79	Dan Pohl	$ 3,021,680	117	Jesper Parnevik	$ 1,978,127
80	Jay Don Blake	$ 3,002,801	118	Billy Ray Brown	$ 1,965,194
81	Blaine McCallister	$ 2,998,837	119	John Adams	$ 1,963,115
82	Donnie Hammond	$ 2,890,982	120	Wayne Grady	$ 1,959,689
83	Tiger Woods	$ 2,857,427	121	Mike Donald	$ 1,951,278
84	Jodie Mudd	$ 2,806,955	122	Jim Thorpe	$ 1,931,586
85	Bob Estes	$ 2,801,525	123	Clarence Rose	$ 1,923,074
86	Mark Wiebe	$ 2,801,101	124	Arnold Palmer	$ 1,904,668
87	Bob Gilder	$ 2,764,907	125	David Graham	$ 1,888,731
88	Johnny Miller	$ 2,747,484	126	Tommy Tolles	$ 1,863,813
89	Nolan Henke	$ 2,732,845	127	Chris Perry	$ 1,859,286
90	Howard Twitty	$ 2,704,677	128	Dave Rummells	$ 1,843,415
91	Phil Blackmar	$ 2,666,434	129	David Peoples	$ 1,841,907
92	Bobby Wadkins	$ 2,620,005	130	Gary Player	$ 1,823,282
93	Kirk Triplett	$ 2,615,567	131	Leonard Thompson	$ 1,819,028
94	Hubert Green	$ 2,591,959	132	Bill Britton	$ 1,814,615
95	Steve Lowery	$ 2,456,776	133	Michael Bradley	$ 1,804,142
96	Doug Tewell	$ 2,439,850	134	Mark Lye	$ 1,800,654
97	Fulton Allem	$ 2,430,822	135	George Burns	$ 1,781,090
98	David Ogrin	$ 2,428,882	136	Brian Claar	$ 1,779,557

137	Dudley Hart	$ 1,772,903
138	Jim McGovern	$ 1,734,085
139	Jay Delsing	$ 1,725,140
140	Mike Springer	$ 1,719,583
141	Morris Hatalsky	$ 1,703,280
142	Billy Casper	$ 1,691,583
143	Bob Murphy	$ 1,642,330
144	Willie Wood	$ 1,638,333
145	Paul Stankowski	$ 1,634,931
146	Jerry Pate	$ 1,618,874
147	Ted Schulz	$ 1,614,281
148	Gary Koch	$ 1,613,407
149	Kenny Knox	$ 1,607,180
150	Lon Hinkle	$ 1,605,646

ALL-TIME PGA TOUR MONEY RECORDS

Most money won in a single season:

$2,066,833 by Tiger Woods in 1997
$1,885,308 by David Duval in 1997
$1,780,159 by Tom Lehman in 1996
$1,697,799 by Phil Mickelson in 1996
$1,654,959 by Greg Norman in 1995
$1,635,480 by Davis Love III in 1997
$1,619,480 by Jim Furyk in 1997
$1,587,531 by Justin Leonard in 1997
$1,543,192 by Billy Mayfair in 1995
$1,499,927 by Nick Price in 1994
$1,478,557 by Nick Price in 1993
$1,458,456 by Paul Azinger in 1993
$1,429,396 by Mark Brooks in 1996
$1,395,278 by Tom Kite in 1989
$1,393,788 by Scott Hoch in 1997
$1,383,739 by Steve Stricker in 1996
$1,345,856 by Greg Norman in 1997
$1,330,307 by Greg Norman in 1994
$1,320,411 by Steve Elkington in 1997
$1,278,966 by Lee Janzen in 1995

Most money won by a rookie:

$881,436 by David Duval in 1995
$809,580 by Stewart Cink in 1997
$790,594 by Tiger Woods in 1996
$684,440 by Ernie Els in 1994
$657,831 by Vijay Singh in 1993
$574,783 by John Daly in 1991
$475,670 by Tim Herron in 1996
$461,407 by Robert Gamez in 1990

Most money won by a second-year player:

$2,066,833 by Tiger Woods in 1997
$977,079 by David Duval in 1996
$943,140 by Justin Leonard in 1996
$871,589 by Tommy Tolles in 1996
$693,658 by Billy Mayfair in 1990
$652,780 by Bob Tway in 1986
$640,997 by Tim Herron
$628,735 by Phil Mickelson in 1993

Most money won in first two seasons:

$2,857,427 by Tiger Woods (1996-1997)
$1,858,515 by David Duval (1995-1996)
$1,691,933 by Justin Leonard (1995-1996)
$1,275,894 by Woody Austin (1995-1996)
$1,038,020 by Tommy Tolles (1995-1996)
$1,116,667 by Tim Herron (1996-1997)
$983,790 by Vijay Singh (1993-1994)
$962,238 by John Daly (1991-1992)
$816,803 by Bob Tway (1985-1986)
$805,650 by Billy Mayfair (1989-1990)

Most consecutive years $100,000 or more:

23- Tom Watson (1974-present)
21- Tom Kite (1976-present)

20- Bruce Lietzke (1977-present)

Most consecutive years $200,000 or more:

15 Tom Kite (1981-present)
12 Mark O'Meara(1984-present)
12 Curtis Strange (1980-1991)
12 Tom Watson (1977-1988)
10 Payne Stewart (1984-1993)

Most consecutive years $500,000 or more:

7 Fred Couples (1989-present)
7 Paul Azinger (1987-1993)
7 Chip Beck (1987-1993)
5 Payne Stewart (1 986-1990)
5 Greg Norman (1986-1990)

Most consecutive years $1 million or more:

3 Nick Price (1992-1994)

Most consecutive years Top 10 Money List:

17 Jack Nicklaus (1962-1978)
15 Arnold Paimer (1957-1971)

Most years Top l0 Money List:

18 Jack Nicklaus
15 Arnold Palmer, Sam Snead

Most years leading Money List:

8 Jack Nicklaus

Most consecutive years leading Money List:

4 Tom Watson (1977-1980)

Most money won in a single season without a victory:

$1,619,480 by Jim Furyk in 1997
$1,217,587 by Jesper Parnevik in 1997
$1,055,050 by Brad Faxon in 1996
$1,016,804 by Fuzzy Zoeller in 1994

PLAYOFF RECORDS

Longest sudden death playoffs (holes):

(11) Cary Middlecoff and Lloyd Mangrum were declared co-winners by mutual agreement in the 1949 Motor City Open.

(8) Dick Hart defeated Phil Rodgers in the 1965 Azaiea Open.

(8) Lee Elder defeated Lee Trevino in the 1978 Greater Milwaukee Open.

(8) Dave Barr defeated Woody Blackburn, Dan Haildorson, Frank Conner, Victor Regalado in the1981 Quad Cities Open.

(8) Bob Gilder defeated Rex Caldwell, Johnny Miller, Mark O'Meara in the 1983 Phoenix Open.

Most players in a sudden-death playoff:

(6) 1994 GTE Byron Nelson Classic-Neal Lancaster defeated Curt Byrum, Mark Carnevale, David Edwards, Yoshinori Mizumaki and David Ogrin.

(5) Eight times, most recently 1996 Buick Challenge- Michael Bradley defeated John Maginnes, Fred Funk, Davis Love III and Len Mattiace.

(5) Teams at the 1985 Chrysler Team Championship.

Most playoffs, season:

(16) 1988, 1991
(15) 1972

ALL-TIME PGA TOUR PUTTING RECORDS

PUTTING RECORDS

Fewest putts, one round:

18 - Sam Trahan, at Whitemarsh Valley Country Club, in final round of 1979 IVB Philadelphia Golf Classic.

18 - Mike McGee, at Colonial CC, in first round of 1987 Federal Express St. Jude Classic.

18 - Kenny Knox, at Harbour Town GL, in first round of 1989 MCI Heritage Classic.

18 - Andy North, at Kingsmill GC, in second round of 1990 Anheuser Busch Golf Classic.

18 - Jim McGovern, at TPC at Southwind, in second round of 1992 Federal Express St. Jude Classic.

Fewest putts, four rounds:

93 - Kenny Knox in 1989 MCI Heritage Classic at Harbour Town Golf Links.

94 - Bob Tway in 1986 MCI Heritage Classic at Harbour Town Golf Links.

95 - George Archer in 1980 Sea Pines Heritage Classic at Harbour Town Golf Links.

95 - Lennie Clements in 1986 PGA Championships at the Inverness Club.

95 - Andy Bean in 1990 MCI Heritage Classic at Harbour Town Golf Links.

95 - Mark O'Meara in 1989 GTE Byron Nelson Classic at the TPC at Las Colinas.

Fewest putts, nine holes:

8 - Jim Colbert, at the Deerwood Club, on front nine of last round in 1967 Greater Jacksonville Open.

8 - Sam Trahan, at Whitemarsh Valley Country Club, on the back nine of the last round in the 1979 IVB Philadelphia Golf Classic.

8 -Bill Caltee, at Forest Oaks CC, on the back nine of the third round of the 1980 Greater Greensboro Open.

8 - Kenny Knox, at Harbour Town GL, on the back nine of the first round of the 1989 MCI Heritage Classic.

8 - John Inman, at Harbour Town GL, on the front nine of the fourth round of the 1994 MCI Heritage Classic.

ALL-TIME PGA TOUR VICTORY RECORDS

Most victories during career (PGA TOUR cosponsored and/or approved tournaments only):

81- Sam Snead

70- Jack Nicklaus

63- Ben Hogan

60- Arnold Palmer

52- Byron Nelson

51- Billy Casper

Most consecutive years winning at least one tournament:

17- Jack Nicklaus (1962-78)

17- Arnold Palmer (1955-71)

16- BillyCasper(1956-71)

Most consecutive victories:

11 Byron Nelson, from Miami Four Ball March 8-11, 1945, through Canadian Open, August 2-4, 1945. Tournament, site, dates, score, purse-Miami Four Ball, Miami Springs Course, Miami, FL, March 8-11, won 8-6, $1,500; Charlotte Open, Myers Park Golf

Club, Charlotte, NC, March 16-19, 272, $2000; Greensboro Open, Starmount Country Club, Greensboro, NC, March 23-25, 271, $1 000; Durham Open, Hope Valley Country Club, Durham, NC, March 30-April 1, 276, $1 000; Atlanta Open, Capital City Course, Atlanta, GA, April 5-8, 263, $2000; Montreal Open, Islemere Golf and Country Club, Montreal, Que., June 7-10, 268, $2000; Philadel- phia Inquirer Invitational, Llanerch Country Club, Phila., PA, June 14-17, 269, $3000; Chicago Victory National Open, Calumet Country Club, Chicago, IL, June 29-July 1, 275, $2000; PGA Championship, Moraine Country Club, Dayton, OH, July 9-15,4-3, $3750; Tam O'Shanter Open, Tam O'Shanter Country Club, Chicago, IL, July 26-29 269, $10,000; Canadian Open, Thornhill Country Club, Toronto, Ont., August 2-4, 280, $2000; Winnings for streak $30,250. NOTE: Nelson won a 12th event in Spring Lake, NJ which is not accounted as official as its $2,500 purse was below the PGA $3000 minimum.

4 Jackie Burke, Jr., in 1952: From February 14 to March 9-Texas Open, Houston Open, Baton Rouge Open, St. Petersburg Open.

3 Byron Nelson in 1944, 1945-46.

3 Sam Snead in 1945.

3 Ben Hogan in 1946.

3 Bobby Locke in 1947.

3 Jim Ferrier in 1951.

3 Billy Casper in 1960.

3 Anold Palmer in 1960, 1962.

3 Johnny Miller in 1974.

3 Hubert Green in 1976.

3 Gary Player in 1978.

3 Tom Watson in 1980.

3 Nick Price in 1993.

3 David Duval in 1997.

Most victories in a single event:

8 Sam Snead, Greater Greensboro Open: 1938, 1946, 1949, 1950, 1955, 1956, 1960, and 1965.

6 Sam Snead, Miami Open: 1937, 1939, 1946, 1950, 1951, and 1955.

6 Jack Nicklaus, Masters: 1963, 1965, 1966, 1972, 1975 and 1986.

5 Walter Hagen, PGA Championship: 1 921, 1924 1925, 1926, and 1927.

5 Ben Hogan Colonial NIT: 1946 1947, 1952, 1953, and 1959.

5 Arnold Palmer, Bob Hope Desert Classic: 1960, 1962, 1968, 1971, and 1973.

5 Jack Nicklaus Tournament of Champions: 1963, 1964, 1971, 1973, and 1977.

5 Jack Nicklaus, PGA Championship: 1963, 1971, 1973, 1975, and 1980.

5 Walter Hagen, Western Open: 1916, 1921, 1926, 1927, 1932.

Most consecutive victories in a single event:

4 Walter Hagen, PGA Championship, 1924-1927.

3 Willie Anderson, U.S. Open, 1903-1905.

3 Henry Picard, Tournament of the Gardens, 1935-1937.

3 Ralph Guidahl, Western Open, 1936-1938.

3 Gene Littler. Tournament of Champions, 1955-1957.

3 Billy Casper, Portland Open, 1959-1961.

3 Arnold Palmer, Texas Open, 1960-1962, Phoenix Open, 1961-1963.

3 Jack Nicklaus, Disney World Golf Classic, 1971-1973.

3	Johnny Miller, Tucson Open, 1974-1976.
3	Tom Watson, Byron Nelson Classic, 1978-1980.

Most victories in a calendar year:

18	Byron Nelson (1945)
13	Ben Hogan (1946)
11	Sam Snead (1950)
10	Ben Hogan (1948)
8	Byron Nelson (1944)
8	Lloyd Mangrum (1948)
8	Arnold Palmer (1960)
8	Johnny Miller (1974)
8	Sam Snead (1938)
7	11 times

Most first-time winners during one calendar year:

14	1991
13	1996
12	1979,1980,1986
11	1977,1985,1988
10	1968,1969,1971,1974,1983,1987,1990,1994

Most years between victories:

14 years, 8 months-Ed Fiori (1982-1996)

12 years, 7 months-Leonard Thompson (1977-1989)

12 years, 5 months, 21 days- Howard Twitty (1980-1993)

11 years, 2 months, 27 days- Bob Murphy (1975-1986)

Most years from first victory to last:

29 years-Sam Snead (1936-1965)

28 years, 11 months, 22 days-Ray Floyd (1963-1992)

23 years, 9 months, 26 days-Jack Nicklaus (1962-1986)

23 years, 3 months, 8 days-Gene Littler (1954-1977)

21 years, 11 months, 20 days-Art Wall (1953-1975)

21 years, 11 months, 18 days-Tom Watson (1974-1996)

Youngest winners:

Johnny McDermott, 19 years and 10 months, 1911 U.S- Open.

Gene Sarazen, 20 years and 5 days, 1922 Southern Open

Charles Evans, Jr. (amateur), 20 years 1 month, 1910 Western Open

Francis Ouimet (amateur), 20 years, 4 months, 12 days, 1913 U.S. Open

Gene Sarazen, 20 years, 4 months, 18 days, 1922 U.S. Open.

Horton Smith, 20 years, 5 months, 13 days, 1928 Oklahoma City Open.

Gene Sarazen, 20 years, 5 months, 22 days, 1922 PGA Championship

Ray Floyd, 20 years and 6 months, 1963 St. Petersburg Open.

Phil Mickelson, 20 years and 6 months, 1991 Northern Telecom Open.

Horton Smith, 20 years, 7 months, 1 day, 1928 Catalina Island Open

Tom Creavy, 20 years, 7 months, 16 days, 1931 PGA Championship

Tiger Woods, 20 years and 9 months, 1996 Las Vegas Inviational

Seve Balleateros, 20 years and 11 months, 1978 Greater Greensboro Open.

Oldest winners;

Sam Snead, 52 years, 10 months and eight

days, 1965 Greater Greensboro Open.

Art Wall, 51 years, seven months and 10 days, 1975 Greater Milwaukee Open.

Jim Barnes, 51 years three months and seven days, 1937 Long Island Open.

John Barnum, 51 years, one month and five days, 1962 Cajun Classic.

Ray Floyd, 49 years and 6 months, 1992 Doral-Ryder Open.

Widest winning margin: strokes

16 Bobby Locke, 1948 Chicago Victory National Championship.

14 Ben Hogan, 1945 Portland Invitational.
Johnny Miller, 1975 Phoenix Open-

13 Byron Nelson, 1945 Seattle Open.
Gene Littler, 1955 Tournament of Champions.

12 Arnold Palmer, 1962 Phoenix Open.
Jose Maria Olazabal, 1990 NEC World Series of Golf.

CONSECUTIVE CUTS MADE

Rank	Player	Cuts
1	Vijay Singh	47
2	Scott Hoch	24
3	Tom Byrum	14
T4	Mark Calcavecchia	12
T4	Phil Mickelson	2
6	Skip Kendall	10
T7	Isao Aoki	8
T7	John Cook	8
T7	Ernie Els	8
T7	Lee Janzen	8
T7	Rocco Mediate	8
T7	Chris Smith	8
T7	Payne Stewart	8
T14	Fred Couples	7
T14	Greg Norman	7
T14	Grant Waite	7
T17	Tommy Armour III	6
T17	Jim Carter	6
T17	Gabriel Hjertstedt	6
T17	Steve Jones	6
T17	Davis Love III	6
T17	Steve Lowery	6
T23	Bruce Fleisher	5
T23	Paul Goydos	5
T23	Jesper Parnevik	5
T23	Chris Perry	5
T23	Charlie Rymer	5
T23	David Toms	5
T29	Joe Durant	4
T29	David Duval	4
T29	Robin Freeman	4
T29	Gary Hallberg	4
T29	Craig Parry	4
T29	Nick Price	4
T29	Joey Sindelar	4
T29	Duffy Waldorf	4
T37	Andy Bean	3
T37	Olin Browne	3
T37	Keith Fergus	3
T37	Jim Furyk	3
T37	Kelly Gibson	3
T37	Bill Glasson	3
T37	Neal Lancaster	3
T37	Bruce Lietzke	3
T37	Jeff Maggert	3
T37	Blaine McCallister	3
T37	Larry Nelson	3
T37	Brett Quigley	3
T37	Bob Shearer	3
T37	Kirk Triplett	3

T37	Ted Tryba	3
T37	Bob Tway	3
T37	Tiger Woods	3
T54	Doug Barron	2
T54	Phil Blackmar	2
T54	Keith Clearwater	2
T54	Bob Estes	2
T54	Brad Fabel	2
T54	Tim Herron	2
T54	Mike Hulbert	2
T54	Hale Irwin	2
T54	Eric Johnson	2
T54	Tom Lehman	2
T54	Wayne Levi	2
T54	Billy Mayfair	2
T54	Mac McLendon	2
T54	Jack Newton	2
T54	Frank Nobilo	2
T54	Don Pooley	2
T54	Loren Roberts	2
T54	John Schroeder	2
T54	Charles Sifford	2
T54	Bob E. Smith	2
T54	Curtis Strange	2
T54	Kevin Sutherland	2
T54	Hal Sutton	2
T54	Howard Twitty	2
T54	Tray Tyner	2
T54	Bobby Wadkins	2
T80	Bud Allin	1
T80	Billy Andrade	1
T80	Stuart Appleby	1
T80	David Berganio, Jr.	1
T80	Shane Bertsch	1
T80	Jay Don Blake	1
T80	Craig Bowden	1
T80	Mark Brooks	1
T80	Patrick Burke	1
T80	George Cadle	1
T80	Mark Carnevale	1
T80	T.C. Chen	1
T80	Stewart Cink	1
T80	Bobby Clampett	1
T80	Frank Conner	1
T80	Bruce Crampton	1
T80	Marco Dawson	1
T80	Glen Day	1
T80	Jim Dent	1
T80	Scott Dunlap	1
T80	Danny Edwards	1
T80	David Edwards	1
T80	Joel Edwards	1
T80	Steve Elkington	1
T80	Nick Faldo	1
T80	Brad Faxon	1
T80	John Fought	1
T80	David Frost	1
T80	Jim Gallagher, Jr.	1
T80	Brent Geiberger	1
T80	Bob Gilder	1
T80	Hubert Green	1
T80	J.P. Hayes	1
T80	Nolan Henke	1
T80	Bradley Hughes	1
T80	John Huston	1
T80	John Inman	1
T80	Barry Jaeckel	1
T80	Justin Leonard	1
T80	Andrew Magee	1
T80	Doug Martin	1
T80	Scott McCarron	1
T80	Adam Mednick	1
T80	Larry Mize	1
T80	Gil Morgan	1
T80	Mac O'Grady	1
T80	Jack O'Keefe	1

T80	Mark O'Meara	1
T80	Naomichi "Joe" Ozaki	1
T80	Steve Pate	1
T80	Lee Porter	1
T80	Sam Randolph	1
T80	Mike Reid	1
T80	Larry Rinker	1
T80	Clarence Rose	1
T80	Bill Sander	1
T80	Tom Sieckmann	1
T80	Scott Simpson	1
T80	Mike Smith	1
T80	Ed Sneed	1
T80	Paul Stankowski	1
T80	Steve Stricker	1
T80	Jim Thorpe	1
T80	Tommy Tolles	1
T80	Greg Twiggs	1
T80	Scott Verplank	1
T80	Willie Wood	1
T80	Kermit Zarley	1

VARDON TROPHY

The Vardon Trophy is awarded each year by the PGA of America to the PGA TOUR player who posts the season's best scoring average. The system was amended in 1988 to allow all TOUR members to compete for the prestigious award provided they have played in 60 rounds. The new system also uses an "adjusted" score for purposes of computing the scoring average. The adjusted score is computed based upon the average score of the field at each tournament. As a result, a player's adjusted score may be higher or lower than his actual score. For example, a player shoots 70 each day at a tournament while the field average was 73. His 280 total would then be adjusted to 268 since he actually played 12 shots better than the field did during the tournament. The Vardon Trophy is a bronze-colored plaque measuring 39" by 27".

Year	Winner	Average
1937	Harry Cooper	1500
1938	Sam Snead	520
1939	Byron Nelson	473
1940	Ben Hogan	423
1941	Ben Hogan	494
1942-1946	No Award - World War II	
1947	Jimmy Demaret	69.90
1948	Ben Hogan	69.30
1949	Sam Snead	69.37
1950	Sam Snead	69.23
1951	Lloyd Mangrum	70.05
1952	Jack Burke	70.54
1953	Lloyd Mangrum	70.22
1954	E. J. Harrison	70.41
1955	Sam Snead	69.86
1956	Cary Middlecoff	70.35
1957	Dow Finsterwald	70.30
1958	Bob Rosburg	70.11
1959	Art Wall	70.35
1960	Billy Casper	69.95
1961	Arnold Palmer	69.85
1962	Arnold Palmer	70.27
1963	Billy Casper	70.58
1964	Arnold Palmer	70.01
1965	Billy Casper	70.85
1966	Billy Casper	70.27
1967	Arnold Palmer	70.18
1968	Billy Casper	69.82
1969	Dave Hill	70.34
1970	Lee Trevino	70.64
1971	Lee Trevino	70.27
1972	Lee Trevino	70.89

1973	Bruce Crampton	70.57
1974	Lee Trevino	70.53
1975	Bruce Crampton	70.51
1976	Don January	70.56
1977	Tom Watson	70.32
1978	Tom Watson	70.16
1979	Tom Watson	70.27
1980	Lee Trevino	69.73
1981	Tom Kite	69.80
1982	Tom Kite	70.21
1983	Raymond Floyd	70.61
1984	Calvin Peete	70.56
1985	Don Pooley	70.36
1986	Scott Hoch	70.08
1987	Dan Pohl	70.25
1988	Chip Beck	69.46
1989	Greg Norman	69.49
1990	Greg Norman	69.10
1991	Fred Couples	69.59
1992	Fred Couples	69.38
1993	Nick Price	69.11
1994	Greg Norman	68.81
1995	Steve Elkington	69.62
1996	Tom Lehman	69.32

ALL-TIME PGA TOUR SCORING RECORDS

SCORING RECORDS

72 holes

257 (60-68-64-65) Mike Souchak at Brackenridge Park Golf Course, San Antonio, TX, in 1955 Texas Open (27-under-par)

258 (62-64-65-67) Steve Jones at TPC of Scottsdale, Scottsdale, AZ, in 1997 Phoenix Open (6-under-par)

258 (64-62-63-69) John Cook at TPC at Southwind in Memphis, TN, in 1996 FedEx St. Jude Classic (26-under-par)

258 (65-64-65-64) Donnie Hammond at Oak Hills CC, San, Antonio, TX, in 1989 Texas Open (22-under-par)

259 (68-63-64-64) David Frost at Oakwood CC, Coal Valley, IL, in 1993 Hardee's Golf Classic (21-under-par)

259 (64-63-66-66) Corey Pavin at Oak Hills CC. San Antonio, TX, in 1988 Texas Open (21-under-par)

259 (63-64-66-66) Tim Norris at Wethersfield CC, Hartford, CT, in 1982 Sammy Davis (25-under-par)

259 (70-63-63-63) Chandler Harper at Brackenridge Park Golf, Course, San Antonio, TX, in 1954 Texas Open (25-under-par)

259 (62-68-63-66) Byron Nelson at Broadmoor Golf Club., Seattle, WA, in 1945 Seattle Open (1-under-par)

90 holes

325 (67-67-64-65-62) Tom Kite at four cours es, Palm Springs, CA, in 1993 Bob Hope Chrysler Classic (35-under-par).

327 (66-69-67-62-63) John Cook at four courses, Palm Springs, CA, in 1997 Bob Hope Chrysler Classic (33-under-par)

328 (64-67-66-64-67) Mark Calcavecchia at four courses, Palm Springs, CA, in 1997 Bob Hope Chrysler Classic (32-under-par)

329 (69-65-67-62-66) Andrew Magee at three courses, Las Vegas, NV, in 1991 Las Vegas Invitational (31-under-par)

329 (70-64-65-64-66) D.A. Weibring at three

courses, Las Vegas, NV, in 1991 Las Vegas Invitational, (31-under-par)

Most shots under par, 72 holes, Score

27 Mark Calcavecchia, first four rounds of 1997 Bob Hope Classic, 261

27 Mike Souchak, in winning the 1955 Texas Open, 257

27 Ben Hogan, in winning the 1945 Portland Invitational, 261

26 Steve Jones, in winning the 1997 Phoenix Open, 258

26 John Cook, in winning the 1996 FedEx St. Jude Classic, 258

26 John Huston, in winning the 1992 Walt Disney World/Oldsmobile Classic, 262

26 Chip Beck, in winning the 1988 USF&G Classic, 262

26 Robert Wrenn, in winning the 1987 Buick Open, 262

26 Gay Brewer, in winning the 1967 Pensacola Open, 262

90 holes

35 Tom Kite, in winning the 1993 Bob Hope Chrysler Classic, 325

33 John Cook, in winning the 1997 Bob Hope Chrysler Classic, 327

32 Mark Calcavecchia, in finishing second in the 1997 Bob Hope Chrysler Classic, 327

31 Andrew Magee, in winning the 1991 Las Vegas Invitational, 329

31 D.A. Weibring, in finishing second in the 1991 Las Vegas Invitational, 329

54 holes (Opening rounds)

189 (64-62-63) John Cook TPC at Southwind in Memphis, TN, in 1996 FedEx St. Jude Classic (24-under-par)

189 (63-63-63) Chandler Harper at Brackenridge Park Golf Course. San Antonio, TX, in 1954 Texas Open (24-under-par)

191 (62-64-65) Steve Jones TPC of Scottsdale, Scottsdale, AZ, in 1997 Phoenix Open (22-under-par)

191 (66-64-61) Gay Brewer at Pensacola CC, Pensacola,, FL, in 1967 Pensacola Open (25-under-par)

192 (64-63-65) Bob Gilder at Westchester CC, Harrison, NY, in1982 Manufacturers Hanover Westchester Classic (18-under-par)

192 (60-68-64) Mike Souchak at Brackenridge Park Golf Course, San Antonio, TX, in 1955 Texas Open (21-under-par)

36 holes (Opening rounds)

126 (64-62) John Cook at TPC at Southwind in Memphis, TN, in 1996 FedEx St. Jude Classic (16-under-par)

126 (64-62) Paul Azinger at Oak Hills CC, San Antonio, TX, in 1989 Texas Open (14-under-par)

126 (64-62) Tommy Bolt at Cavalier Yacht & Country Club, Virginia Beach, VA, in 1954 Virginia Beach Open (12-under-par)

36 holes (Consecutive rounds)

125 (62-63) John Cook, fourth and fifth rounds, at Indian Wells CC in Indian Wells, CA, in 1997 Bob Hope Chrysler Classic (19-under-par)

125 (62-63) John Cook, second and third rounds, at TPC at Southwind in Memphis, TN, in 1996 FedEx St. Jude Classic (19-under-par)

125 (62-63) Blaine McCallister, the middle two rounds, at Oakwood CC, Coal Valley, IL, in 1988 Hardee's Golf, Classic (15-under-par)

125 (63-62) Ron Streck, last two rounds at Oak Hills Country Club, San Antonio, TX, in 1978 Texas Open (15-under-par)

125 (64-61) Gay Brewer, the middle rounds at Pensacola CC, Pensacola, FL, in 1967 Pensacola Open (19-under-par)

18 holes

59 Chip Beck, at Sunrise Golf Club, Las Vegas, NV, third round of 1991 Las Vegas Invitational (13-under-par)

59 Al Geiberger, at Colonial Country Club, Memphis, TN, second round of 1977 Memphis Classic (13-under-par)

60 Grant Waite, at TPC in Scottsdale, Scottsdale, AZ, the final round of the 1996, Phoenix Open (12-under-par)

60 Davis Love III, at Waialae Country Club, Honolulu, HI, second round of 1994 United Airlines Hawaiian Open (12-under-par)

60 David Frost, at Randolph Park Golf Course, Tucson, AZ, second round of 1990 Northern Telecom Tucson Open (12-under-par)

60 Sam Snead, at Glen Lakes Country Club, Dallas, TX, second round of 1957 Dallas Open (11-under-par)

60 Mike Souchak, at Brackenridge Park Golf Course, San Antonio, TX, first round of 1955 Texas Open (11-under-par)

60 Tommy Bolt, at Wethersfield Country Club, Hartford, CT, second round of 1954 Insurance City Open (11-under-par)

60 Wally Ulrich, at Cavalier Yacht and Country Club, Virginia Beacn, VA, second round of 1954 Virginia Beach Open (9-under-par)

60 Ted Kroll, at Brackenridge ParK Golf Course, San Antonio, TX, third round of 1954 Texas Open (11-under-par)

60 Bill Nary, El Paso Country Club, El Paso, TX, third round of 1952 El Paso Open (11-under-par)

60 Al Brosch, Brackenridge Park Golf Course, San Antonio, TX, third round of 1951 Texas Open (11-under-par)

9 holes

27 Andy North, at En-Joie Golf Club, Endicott, NY, second nine of first round in 1975 B.C. Open (7-under-par)

27 Mike Souchak, at Brackenrdge Park Golf Course, San Antonio, TX, second nine of first round in 1955 Texas Open (8-under-par)

Best Vardon Trophy scoring average

Non-adjusted:

69.23 Sam Snead in 1950 (6646 strokes, 96 rounds)

69.30 Ben Hogan in 1948 (5267 strokes, 76 rounds)

69.37 Sam Snead in 1949 (5064 strokes, 73 rounds)

Adjusted (since 1988):

68.81 Greg Norman in 1994

68.98 Nick Price in 1997

69.10 Greg Norman in 1990

69.11 Nick Price in 1993

Most consecutive rounds under 70

19 Byron Nelson in 1945

Most birdies in a row

8 Dewey Arnette, Warwick Hills GC, Grand Blanc, MI, first round of the 1987 Buick Open

8 Fuzzy Zoeller, Oakwood Country Club, Coal Valley, IL, first round of 1976 Quad Cities Open

8 Bob Goalby, Pasadena Golf Club, St. Petersburg FL, fourth round of 1961 St. Petersburg Open

Best birdie-eagle streak

7 Webb Heintzelman, 5 birdies, eagle and 1 birdie, 1989 Las Vegas Invitational

7 Al Geiberger, 6 birdies and 1 eagle, 1977 Danny Thomas Memphis Classic

Most birdies in a row to win

5 Jack Nicklaus, 1978 Jackie Gleason Inver rary Classic, Final 5 holes

5 Tiger Woods, 1997 Mercedes Championship, Final 4 holes and first hole of playoff

PGA TOUR 1998 SCHEDULE

Date, Tournament, Location, Current or Defending (D) Champion

JANUARY

3-4 , **Andersen Consulting World Championship of Golf**, Grayhawk Golf Club, Scottsdale, AZ, Colin Montgomerie

8-11, **Mercedes Championships**, La Costa Resort Carlsbad, CA, Phil Mickelson

14-18, **Bob Hope Chrysler Classic**, Indian Wells/Bermuda, Dunes/LaQuinta, Indians Wells, CA, Fred Couples

22-25, **Phoenix Open**, TPC of Scottsdale Scottsdale, AZ, Jesper Parnevik

29-1, **AT&T Pebble Beach Natl Pro-Am**, Pebble Beach Golf Links/Spyglass Hill/Poppy Hills Pebble Beach, CA, To be completed March 2

FEBRUARY

5-8, **Buick Invitational**, Torrey Pines Golf Course, South Course/North Course, LaJolla, CA, Mark O'Meara (D)

12-15, **United Airlines Hawaiian Open**, Waialae Country Club Honolulu, HI, Paul Stankowski (D)

19-22, **Tucson Chrysler Classic**, Tucson National Golf Resort Tucson, AZ, Jeff Sluman (D)

26-1, **Nissan Open**, Valencia Country Club Valencia, CA, Nick Faldo (D)

MARCH

5-8, **Doral-Ryder Open**, Doral Resort & Country Club Miami, FL, Steve Elkington (D)

12-15, **Honda Classic**, TPC at Heron Bay Coral Springs, FL, Stuart Appleby (D)

19-22, **Bay Hill Invitational**, Bay Hill Club & Lodge Orlando, FL, Phil Mickelson (D)

26-29, **The Players Championship**, TPC at Sawgrass, Ponte Vedra Beach, FL, Steve Elkington (D)

APRIL

2-5, **Freeport-McDermott Classic**, English Turn Golf & Country Club, New Orleans, LA, Brad Faxon (D)

9-12, **Masters Tournament**, Augusta National Golf Club, Augusta, GA, Tiger Woods (D)

16-19, **MCI Classic**, Harbour Town Golf Links, Hilton Head Island, SC, Nick Price (D)

23-26, **Greater Greensboro Chrysler Classic**, Forest Oaks Country Club, Greensboro, NC, Frank Nobilo (D),

30-3, **Shell Houston Open**, TPC at The Woodlands, The Woodlands, TX, Phil Blackmar (D)

MAY

7-10, **BellSouth Classic**, TPC at Sugarloaf, Duluth, GA, Scott McCarron (D)

14-17, **GTE Byron Nelson Classic**, TPC at Las Colinas/Cottonwood Valley Irving, TX, Tiger Woods (D)

21-24, **MasterCard Colonial**, Colonial Country Club, Ft. Worth, TX, David Frost (D)

28-31, **Memorial Tournament**, Muirfield Village Golf Club, Dublin, OH, Vijay Singh (D)

JUNE

4-7, **Kemper Open**, TPC at Avenel, Potomac, MD, Justin Leonard (D)

11-14, **Buick Classic**, Westchester Country Club, Rye, NY, Ernie Els (D)

18-21, **U.S. Open Championship**, Olympic Country Club, San Francisco, CA, Ernie Els (D)

25-28, **Motorola Western Open**, Cog Hill Golf & Country Club, Lemont, IL, Tiger Woods (D)

JULY

2-5, **Canon Greater Hartford Open**, TPC at River Highlands, Cromwell, CT, Stewart Cink (D)

9-12, **Quad City Classic**, Oakwood Country Club, Coal Valley, IL, David Toms (D)

16-19, **Open Championship**, Royal Birkdale, Southport, England, Justin Leonard (D)

16-19, **Deposit Guaranty Golf Classic**, Annandale Golf Club, Madison, MS, Billy Ray Brown (D)

23-26, **CVS Charity Classic**, Pleasant Valley Country Club, Sutton, MA, Loren Roberts (D)

30-2, **FedEx St. Jude Classic**, TPC at Southwind Memphis, TN, Greg Norman (D)

AUGUST

6-9, **Buick Open**, Warwick Hills Golf & Country Club Grand Blanc, MI, Vijay Singh (D)

13-16, **PGA Championship**, Sahalee Country Club, Seattle, WA, Davis Love III (D)

20-23, **Sprint International**, Castle Pines Golf Club, Castle Rock, CO, Phil Mickelson (D)

27-30, **NEC World Series of Golf**, Firestone Country Club (South Course), Akron, OH, Greg Norman (D)

27-30, **Greater Vancouver Open**, Northview Golf & Country Club, Surrey, BC, Canada, Mark Calcavecchia (D)

SEPTEMBER

3-6, **Greater Milwaukee Open**, Brown Deer Park Golf Course, Milwaukee, WI, Scott Hoch (D)

10-13, **Bell Canadian Open**, Glen Abbey, G.C., Oakville, Ontario, Steve Jones (D)

17-20, **B.C. Open**, En-Joie Golf Club, Endicott, NY, Gabriel Hjertstedt (D)

24-27, **LaCantera Texas Open**, LaCantera Golf Club, San Antonio, TX, Tim Herron (D)

OCTOBER

1-4, **Buick Challenge**, Callaway Gardens Resort Pine Mountain, GA, Davis Love III (D)

8-11, **Michelob Championship**, Kingsmill Golf Club, Williamsburg, VA, David Duval (D)

14-18, **Las Vegas Invitational**, TPC at Summerlin/Desert Inn Golf Club, Las Vegas, NV, Bill Glasson (D)

22-25, **Walt Disney World/Oldsmobile Golf**

Classic, Magnolia, Palm & Lake Buena, Vista Golf Courses, Lake Buena Vista, FL, David Duval (D)

29-1, **The Tour Championship**, East Lake G.C., Atlanta, GA, David Duval (D)

NOVEMBER

5-8, **Subaru Sarazen World Open**, The Legends at Château Élan, Braselton, GA, Mark Calcavecchia (D)

12-15, **Franklin Templeton Shark Shootout**, Sherwood Country Club, Thousand Oaks, CA, Lietzke/McCarron (D)

19-22, **World Cup of Golf**, Gulf Harbour, Auckland, NZ, Ireland (D)

28-29, **Skins Game**, Tom Lehman (D), Tom Lehman (D),

DECEMBER

3-6, **JCPenney Classic**, Innisbrook Hilton Resort, Palm Harbour, FL, Fruhwirth/Rose (D)

11-13, **The Presidents Cup**, Royal Melbourne, Australia, U.S.A. (D)

19-20, **Wendy's Three-Tour Challenge**, Lake Las Vegas Resort, Henderson, NV, PGA (D)

TBA, Diners Club Matches, Jack Nicklaus Private Course, PGA West LaQuinta, CA, Elkingon/Maggert (D)

OFFICIAL WORLD GOLF RANKING

(Through December 21, 1997)

Position	1996 Position	Player	Country	Points Average	Total Points	1995-96 # of events	1995-96 Total	1997 Minus	1997 Plus
1	1	Greg Norman	Aus	11.49	517	45	485	-350	382
2	33	Tiger Woods	USA	10.76	452	42	155	-79	376
3	13	Nick Price	Zim	9.93	437	44	263	-186	360
4	4	Ernie Els	SAf	9.89	554	56	490	-330	394
5	9	Davis Love III	USA	9.09	482	53	384	-248	346
6	7	Phil Mickelson	USA	8.73	419	48	404	-237	252
7	3	Colin Montgomerie	Sco	8.58	489	57	528	-359	320
8	8	"Jumbo" Ozaki	Jpn	8.05	346	43	341	-227	232
9	2	Tom Lehman	USA	8.02	425	53	487	-302	240
10	10	Mark O'Meara	USA	7.98	383	48	363	-228	248
11	29	Justin Leonard	USA	7.00	413	59	253	-162	322
12	19	David Duval	USA	6.87	364	53	268	-180	276
13	15	Scott Hoch	USA	6.85	377	55	332	-217	262
14	23	Brad Faxon	USA	6.66	313	47	250	-161	224
15	20	Vijay Singh	Fij	6.54	366	56	317	-223	272
16	14	Steve Elkington	Aus	6.49	266	41	263	-211	214
17	6	Nick Faldo	Eng	6.44	277	43	359	-236	154

18	39	Jesper Parnevik	Swe	5.70	285	50	178	-121	228
19	17	Tom Watson	USA	5.47	219	40	211	-128	136
20	5	Fred Couples	USA	5.47	235	43	351	-228	112
21	16	Bernhard Langer	Ger	5.39	264	49	260	-214	218
22	49	Jim Furyk	USA	5.34	326	61	206	-136	256
23	64	Lee Westwood	Eng	5.26	342	65	159	-85	268
24	28	Steve Jones	USA	5.21	297	57	234	-129	192
25	26	Ian Woosnam	Wal	5.06	268	53	238	-134	164
26	31	Frank Nobilo	NZl	4.92	256	52	229	-147	174
27	22	Loren Roberts	USA	4.88	244	50	241	-169	172
28	38	Mark Calcavecchia	USA	4.42	265	60	221	-158	202
29	27	Jeff Maggert	USA	4.38	232	53	224	-142	150
30	21	Mark McNulty	Zim	4.22	169	40	204	-121	86
31	59	Paul Stankowski	USA	4.09	229	56	156	-83	156
32	48	Tommy Tolles	USA	3.96	214	54	163	-87	138
33	56	Shigeki Maruyama	Jpn	3.89	237	61	159	-106	184
34	32	Lee Janzen	USA	3.79	212	56	236	-184	160
35	60	John Cook	USA	3.70	207	56	141	-78	144
36	62	Darren Clarke	NIr	3.65	219	60	150	-95	164
37	50	Brian Watts	USA	3.64	182	50	156	-100	126
38	84	Tom Kite	USA	3.59	158	44	88	-52	122
39	42	Craig Stadler	USA	3.51	151	43	143	-98	106
40	52	Craig Parry	Aus	3.49	227	65	212	-147	162
41	122	Bill Glasson	USA	3.47	139	40	61	-54	132
42	220	José Maria Olazábal	Spn	3.40	146	43	33	-33	146
43	12	Steve Stricker	USA	3.30	145	44	297	-172	20
44	103	Scott McCarron	USA	3.29	184	56	90	-50	144
44	282	Stuart Appleby	Aus	3.29	207	63	33	-24	198
46	66	"Joe" Ozaki	Jpn	3.22	206	64	151	-97	152
47	34	Payne Stewart	USA	3.15	167	53	210	-147	104
48	69	Per-Ulrik Johansson	Swe	3.13	141	45	109	-74	106
49	35	Bob Tway	USA	2.98	152	51	195	-137	94
50	37	Robert Allenby	Aus	2.96	166	56	210	-130	86
51	44	Michael Bradley	USA	2.96	151	51	163	-90	78
52	57	David Frost	SAf	2.93	170	58	156	-112	126
53	24	Costantino Rocca	Ity	2.92	190	65	285	-201	106
54	107	Eduardo Romero	Arg	2.84	122	43	77	-49	94
55	220	Stewart Cink	USA	2.79	145	52	33	-20	132

56	53	Jeff Sluman	USA	2.78	178	64	193	-129	114
57	36	Jay Haas	USA	2.72	136	50	189	-141	88
58	41	Duffy Waldorf	USA	2.65	130	49	164	-110	76
59	86	CarlosFranco	Par	2.58	111	43	75	-48	84
60	110	Retief Goosen	SAf	2.56	174	68	103	-65	136
61	98	David Ogrin	USA	2.56	156	61	107	-59	108
62	18	Mark Brooks	USA	2.54	170	67	337	-191	24
63	103	Billy Andrade	USA	2.48	144	58	100	-62	106
64	25	Kenny Perry	USA	2.41	123	51	237	-156	42
65	161	PeterLonard	Aus	2.38	114	48	46	-26	94
66	73	Brandt Jobe	USA	2.36	104	44	100	-76	80
67	70	Kirk Triplett	USA	2.36	118	50	113	-87	92
68	51	Fred Funk	USA	2.30	159	69	200	-133	92
69	74	Frankie Minoza	Phi	2.23	107	48	104	-67	70
70	99	Tim Herron	USA	2.23	147	66	90	-45	102
71	268	"Jet" Ozaki	Jpn	2.22	109	49	26	-15	98
72	124	Andrew Magee	USA	2.22	129	58	81	-52	100
73	112	Thomas Bjørn	Den	2.18	120	55	76	-38	82
74	218	Phil Blackmar	USA	2.15	118	55	43	-27	102
75	87	Paul Goydos	USA	2.15	133	62	118	-65	80
76	11	Corey Pavin	USA	2.13	100	47	347	-261	14
77	94	Greg Turner	NZl	2.04	100	49	86	-58	72
78	95	Padraig Harrington	Ire	2.03	122	60	84	-42	80
79	133	Dudley Hart	USA	2.02	99	49	68	-37	68
80	245	Robert Karlsson	Swe	2.00	86	43	35	-29	80
81	155	Ignacio Garrido	Spn	1.94	99	51	61	-42	80
82	80	Stephen AmesT&	T	1.94	97	50	97	-54	54
83	131	Miguel Angel Martin	Spn	1.87	86	46	71	-37	52
84	92	Peter O'Malley	Aus	1.87	112	60	106	-82	88
85	71	Andrew Coltart	Sco	1.84	118	64	130	-78	66
86	150	Rick Fehr	USA	1.84	81	44	58	-35	58
87	178	Dan Forsman	USA	1.82	89	49	46	-31	74
88	61	Rocco Mediate	USA	1.80	81	45	103	-56	34
89	277	Tom Byrum	USA	1.78	96	54	29	-21	88
90	138	Mark James	Eng	1.77	85	48	64	-57	78
91	146	Eduardo Herrera	Col	1.72	79	46	60	-39	58
92	67	Yoshinori Kaneko	Jpn	1.70	104	61	136	-74	42
93	116	Larry Nelson	USA	1.70	73	43	68	-37	42

94	118	Steve Lowery	USA	1.67	105	63	92	-69	82
95	47	PeterSenior	Aus	1.66	93	56	188	-131	36
96	128	Hal Sutton	USA	1.64	95	58	83	-68	80
97	111	Jay Don Blake	USA	1.64	90	55	84	-58	64
98	88	Larry Mize	USA	1.63	78	48	90	-60	48
99	146	Raymond Russell	Sco	1.62	94	58	60	-30	64
100	139	Russ Cochran	USA	1.61	100	62	75	-45	70
101	303	David Toms	USA	1.58	90	57	28	-14	76
102	81	Paul McGinley	Ire	1.57	96	61	112	-66	50
103	332	Chris Perry	USA	1.55	82	53	26	-16	72
104	30	Mark McCumber	USA	1.52	61	40	164	-109	6
105	103	Paul Broadhurst	Eng	1.52	96	63	105	-67	58
106	106	Jose Coceres	Arg	1.52	76	50	82	-52	46
107	125	Paul Azinger	USA	1.51	65	43	67	-46	44
108	65	Wayne Westner	SAf	1.51	83	55	121	-70	32
109	229	Fulton Allem	SAf	1.48	65	44	34	-19	50
110	179	MichaelLong	NZl	1.48	62	42	41	-21	42
111	83	Tom Purtzer	USA	1.47	72	49	82	-46	36
112	188	Joakim Haeggman	Swe	1.47	69	47	49	-34	54
113	167	Mark Wiebe	USA	1.46	73	50	53	-34	54
114	405	Kevin Sutherland	USA	1.45	84	58	16	-8	76
115	117	HajimeMeshiai	Jpn	1.45	81	56	78	-47	50
116	90	Brad Bryant	USA	1.44	75	52	102	-79	52
117	261	Don Pooley	USA	1.44	59	41	29	-24	54
118	40	Sam Torrance	Sco	1.43	80	56	200	-168	48
119	206	Doug Martin	USA	1.42	85	60	52	-35	68
120	43	Billy Mayfair	USA	1.41	83	59	186	-151	48
121	130	Hisayuki Sasaki	Jpn	1.40	87	62	89	-60	58
122	181	Shoichi Kuwabara	Jpn	1.40	77	55	44	-23	56
122	84	Clarence Rose	USA	1.40	84	60	88	-44	40
124	738	Robert Damron	USA	1.39	78	56	0	0	78
125	162	Richard Green	Aus	1.39	71	51	47	-26	50
126	72	Miguel Angel Jiménez	Spn	1.39	75	54	125	-88	38
127	149	Brandel Chamblee	USA	1.38	72	52	66	-42	48
128	46	PeterJacobsen	USA	1.38	65	47	142	-129	52
129	428	Hiroyuki Fujita	Jpn	1.38	55	40	11	-8	52
130	127	Bob Estes	USA	1.36	64	47	71	-57	50
131	156	Mike Brisky	USA	1.35	77	57	68	-43	52

132	77	ToddHamilton	USA	1.32	70	53	112	-74	32
133	296	Patrik Sjöland	Swe	1.31	67	51	26	-13	54
134	273	Brad Fabel	USA	1.29	75	58	30	-15	60
135	187	Jamie Spence	Eng	1.29	62	48	51	-35	46
136	738	Brent Geiberger	USA	1.28	64	50	0	0	64
137	246	StephenLeaney	Aus	1.27	51	40	29	-20	42
138	159	Jarmo Sandelin	Swe	1.27	71	56	70	-51	52
139	97	Peter Mitchell	Eng	1.26	73	58	102	-61	32
140	68	John Huston	USA	1.25	69	55	123	-76	22
141	332	Edward Fryatt	Eng	1.25	50	40	20	-10	40
142	121	David Ishii	USA	1.25	71	57	77	-44	38
143	55	D.A. Weibring	USA	1.23	49	40	121	-84	12
144	302	Mike Reid	USA	1.21	58	48	27	-17	48
145	175	Mike Hulbert	USA	1.21	76	63	68	-48	56
146	144	David Gilford	Eng	1.20	59	49	67	-54	46
147	354	Ke'ro Fukabori	Jpn	1.20	66	55	20	-10	56
148	148	Glen Day	USA	1.19	70	59	80	-48	38
149	351	Steven Alker	NZl	1.17	47	40	18	-9	38
150	203	Hirofumi Miyase	Jpn	1.17	69	59	41	-26	54
151	108	Nolan Henke	USA	1.16	58	50	82	-54	30
152	499	Toshiaki Odate	Jpn	1.16	51	44	7	-4	48
153	89	Fuzzy Zoeller	USA	1.15	46	40	71	-45	20
154	145	Grant Waite	NZl	1.14	72	63	78	-54	48
155	102	Paul Lawrie	Sco	1.14	58	51	79	-43	22
155	82	Lennie Clements	USA	1.14	58	51	92	-62	28
157	210	Roger Chapman	Eng	1.13	61	54	47	-30	44
158	264	Olin Browne	USA	1.13	70	62	32	-16	54
159	95	Kaz'ko Hosokawa	Jpn	1.13	79	70	96	-61	44
160	172	David Edwards	USA	1.13	54	48	51	-37	40
161	309	Angel Cabrera	Arg	1.12	47	42	22	-11	36
162	341	Brian Henninger	USA	1.11	60	54	27	-21	54
163	113	JeanVan-de-Velde	Frn	1.09	59	54	85	-48	22
164	201	TsukasaWatanabe	Jpn	1.08	68	63	59	-39	48
165	272	Lee Rinker	USA	1.08	69	64	39	-26	56
166	177	Toru Suzuki	Jpn	1.08	70	65	64	-46	52
167	403	Eiji Mizoguchi	Jpn	1.07	60	56	20	-14	54
167	170	Sven Strüver	Ger	1.07	60	56	58	-40	42
169	153	Peter Teravainen	USA	1.07	61	57	67	-42	36

170	332	Mit'aka Kusakabe	Jpn	1.07	46	43	20	-16	42
171	241	Greg Chalmers	Aus	1.06	54	51	38	-22	38
171	238	Phil Tataurangi	NZl	1.06	54	51	30	-16	40
173	143	Jerry Kelly	USA	1.06	73	69	71	-36	38
174	75	Wayne Riley	Aus	1.05	62	59	132	-94	24
175	224	Wayne Levi	USA	1.05	43	41	34	-19	28
176	256	Len Mattiace	USA	1.05	67	64	34	-17	50
177	54	Scott Simpson	USA	1.02	50	49	138	-104	16
178	185	Russell Claydon	Eng	1.02	52	51	54	-36	34
179	264	David Carter	Eng	1.02	58	57	40	-22	40
180	123	Robert Gamez	USA	1.00	57	57	85	-58	30
180	364	Donnie Hammond	USA	1.00	42	42	19	-15	38
182	189	Jean Louis Guepy	Frn	0.98	42	43	44	-34	32
183	166	Toshimitsu Izawa	Jpn	0.96	44	46	52	-40	32
184	141	Curtis Strange	USA	0.95	42	44	64	-50	28
185	738	Kenichi Kuboya	Jpn	0.95	38	40	0	0	38
186	171	Peter Baker	Eng	0.95	56	59	63	-45	38
187	79	John Morse	USA	0.95	55	58	107	-74	22
188	238	Shinichi Yokota	Jpn	0.95	53	56	36	-25	42
189	263	Ronnie Black	USA	0.94	51	54	37	-22	36
190	76	Hidem'i Tanaka	Jpn	0.94	61	65	104	-71	28
191	232	Pete Jordan	USA	0.93	55	59	36	-23	42
191	137	Joey Sindelar	USA	0.93	55	59	70	-45	30
193	516	Clinton Whitelaw	SAf	0.93	39	42	6	-3	36
194	183	Kats'i Kuwabara	Jpn	0.92	59	64	59	-40	40
195	257	Jim Carter	USA	0.92	55	60	42	-27	40
196	194	Ross McFarlane	Eng	0.92	54	59	53	-33	34
197	259	Yosh'ri Mizumaki	Jpn	0.91	50	55	44	-30	36
198	289	KevinWentworth	USA	0.90	36	40	24	-16	28
198	151	AnthonyPainter	Aus	0.90	36	40	50	-28	14
200	114	Bradley Hughes	Aus	0.89	47	53	65	-34	16

FINAL U.S. RYDER CUP TEAM STANDINGS

Rank	Player	1996 Points	1997 Points	Total Points
1	Tiger Woods	250.000	935.000	1185.000
2	Justin Leonard	283.500	785.000	1068.500

3	Tom Lehman	592.000	430.953	1022.953
4	Davis Love III	480.000	477.167	957.167
5	Jim Furyk	172.500	775.000	947.500
6	Phil Mickelson	487.500	321.786	809.286
7	Jeff Maggert	296.625	510.000	806.625
8	Mark O'Meara	350.000	451.250	801.250
9	Scott Hoch	400.000	391.952	791.952
10	Brad Faxon	247.500	480.000	727.500

Top-10 automatically qualify for the U.S. Ryder Cup team

11	Tommy Tolles	265.000	424.286	689.286
12	Steve Jones	290.000	289.286	579.286
13	Mark Brooks	519.750	30.000	549.750
14	Paul Stankowski	115.000	388.333	503.333
15	Lee Janzen	103.500	375.000	478.500
16	David Duval	235.000	235.000	470.000
17	Fred Couples	282.500	175.536	458.036
18	Tom Watson	165.000	268.667	433.667
19	Tom Kite	45.000	375.000	420.000
20	Michael Bradley	232.500	170.000	402.500
21	John Cook	171.000	205.000	376.000
22	Kenny Perry	311.250	61.250	372.500
23	Steve Stricker	342.500	30.000	372.500
24	Jeff Sluman	108.000	260.000	368.000
25	Mark Calcavecchia	155.000	212.000	367.000
26	Scott McCarron	82.500	268.334	350.834
27	Loren Roberts	153.000	165.000	318.000
28	David Ogrin	147.500	166.667	314.167
29	Payne Stewart	154.667	158.750	313.417
30	Bob Tway	143.333	165.000	308.333
31	Craig Stadler	75.000	217.786	292.786
32	Dudley Hart	86.000	205.000	291.000
33	Phil Blackmar	50.000	230.000	280.000
34	Fred Funk	214.583	65.000	279.583
35	Paul Goydos	98.000	168.750	266.750
36	Robert Damron	0.000	265.000	265.000
37	Duffy Waldorf	185.000	55.000	240.000
38	Jay Haas	98.500	141.000	239.500

39	Billy Andrade	73.000	162.500	235.500
40	Tom Byrum	36.250	195.000	231.250
41	Corey Pavin	209.167	20.000	229.167
42	David Toms	28.750	195.000	223.750
43	Russ Cochran	65.000	147.500	212.500
44	Brandel Chamblee	45.625	160.000	205.625
45	Brad Bryant	67.500	135.000	202.500
46	Stewart Cink	7.500	194.286	201.786
47	Kirk Triplett	50.625	147.500	198.125
48	Tim Herron	102.500	90.000	192.500
49	Mark McCumber	185.833	0.000	185.833
50	Hal Sutton	0.625	180.000	180.625
51	Mike Standley	25.000	155.000	180.000
52	Mike Brisky	51.250	125.833	177.083
53	Steve Lowery	27.500	145.000	172.500
54	Robert Gamez	65.000	103.333	168.333
55	Jay Don Blake	45.000	114.286	159.286
56	Clarence Rose	78.000	80.000	158.000
57	Brad Fabel	21.000	135.000	156.000
57	Kevin Sutherland	5.000	151.000	156.000
59	Guy Boros	75.000	80.000	155.000
59	Tom Purtzer	90.000	65.000	155.000
61	Billy Ray Brown	0.000	150.000	150.000
62	John Huston	128.500	20.000	148.500
63	Lennie Clements	85.000	60.000	145.000
63	Mark Wiebe	55.000	90.000	145.000
65	Jerry Kelly	86.000	58.333	144.333
66	Rick Fehr	82.500	60.000	142.500
67	Andrew Magee	78.750	62.666	141.416
68	Lee Rinker	50.000	90.000	140.000
69	John Morse	115.000	20.000	135.000
70	Omar Uresti	17.500	110.000	127.500
71	Mike Hulbert	47.500	79.286	126.786
72	Donnie Hammond	5.000	120.000	125.000
73	Mike Springer	12.000	110.000	122.000
74	D.A Weibring	95.000	25.000	120.000
75	Rocco Mediate	91.000	27.500	118.500
76	Nolan Henke	97.500	20.000	117.500

77	Mike Reid	25.000	88.333	113.333
78	Scott Simpson	112.500	0.000	112.500
79	Olin Browne	30.833	80.000	110.833
80	Bill Glasson	25.000	85.000	110.000
81	Dan Forsman	0.000	109.286	109.286
82	Ronnie Black	34.750	73.333	108.083
83	Don Pooley	0.000	104.333	104.333
84	Larry Nelson	14.750	85.000	99.750
85	Greg Kraft	98.625	0.000	98.625
86	Jim Carter	38.500	60.000	98.500
87	Woody Austin	93.000	3.333	96.333
88	Kelly Gibson	55.000	40.000	95.000
89	Brian Henninger	5.000	83.333	88.333
90	Larry Mize	55.000	30.000	85.000
90	Skip Kendall	0.000	85.000	85.000
92	Taylor Smith	75.000	7.500	82.500
93	Willie Wood	75.000	6.000	81.000
94	Jimmy Johnston	0.000	80.000	80.000
95	Fuzzy Zoeller	77.500	0.000	77.500
96	Brian Claar	30.000	45.000	75.000
96	Ed Fiori	75.000	0.000	75.000
96	Emlyn Aubrey	75.000	0.000	75.000
96	Marco Dawson	75.000	0.000	75.000
100	Bob Estes	32.500	40.000	72.500
101	Wayne Levi	23.333	48.750	72.083
102	Frank Lickliter	15.000	55.000	70.000
102	Len Mattiace	70.000	0.000	70.000
104	Blaine McCallister	23.750	45.000	68.750
104	Chris Perry	38.750	30.000	68.750
104	Curtis Strange	3.750	65.000	68.750

SENIOR PGA TOUR

MONEY WINNERS

1997 Schedule
Through the Tour Championship

Rank	Player	Events	Money
1	Hale Irwin	23	$2,343,364
2	Gil Morgan	25	$2,160,562
3	Isao Aoki	28	$1,410,499
4	Jay Sigel	31	$1,294,838
5	David Graham	30	$1,173,579
6	John Bland	33	$1,169,707
7	Graham Marsh	29	$1,128,578
8	Hugh Baiocchi	25	$906,565
9	Larry Gilbert	23	$902,816
10	Dave Stockton	29	$854,611
11	Bob Eastwood	28	$833,908
12	John Jacobs	34	$802,942
13	Dave Eichelberger	34	$794,322
14	Bruce Summerhays	35	$776,804
15	Lee Trevino	27	$733,912
16	Jack Kiefer	34	$732,735
17	Vicente Fernandez	29	$689,915
18	Walter Morgan	36	$687,676
19	Bob Murphy	30	$685,611
20	Mike Hill	27	$678,640
21	Bob Charles	27	$623,467
22	Jim Dent	31	$590,646
23	Ray Floyd	20	$584,755
24	Tom Wargo	33	$567,419
25	Jerry McGee	34	$562,794
26	Hubert Green	28	$556,402
27	Jim Colbert	19	$556,000
28	Bob Duval	24	$555,601
29	Bud Allin	31	$535,064
30	Frank Conner	35	$528,346
31	Jimmy Powell	33	$518,576
32	Bob Dickson	33	$480,521
33	J.C. Snead	33	$476,149
34	Gibby Gilbert	29	$440,533
35	Kermit Zarley	29	$429,442
36	Dana Quigley	20	$427,774
37	George Archer	26	$407,605
38	DeWitt Weaver	33	$395,232
39	Bruce Crampton	35	$390,287
40	Leonard Thompson	30	$384,806
41	Mike McCullough	35	$373,282
42	Chi Chi Rodriguez	28	$372,359
43	Dale Douglass	31	$366,803
44	Brian Barnes	28	$354,886
45	John D. Morgan	30	$349,302
46	John Schroeder	32	$345,233
47	Simon Hobday	30	$327,085
48	Terry Dill	31	$325,522
49	Larry Nelson	6	$312,457
50	Bobby Stroble	36	$311,970
51	Bob E. Smith	29	$281,130
52	Rocky Thompson	29	$273,037
53	Jim Albus	26	$268,487
54	Buddy Whitten	30	$262,133
55	Al Geiberger	23	$260,427
56	Tom Shaw	30	$253,956
57	Larry Laoretti	29	$244,166
58	Jack Nicklaus	6	$239,932
59	Rick Acton	33	$233,541
60	Dick Hendrickson	33	$220,675
61	Charles Coody	30	$218,564
62	Gary Player	22	$208,615
63	Jose-Maria Canizares	7	$202,908
64	Butch Baird	31	$191,496
65	Bob Wynn	18	$177,874
66	Miller Barber	33	$173,113
67	Tony Jacklin	26	$171,497
68	Dan Wood	24	$165,457

69	David Oakley	34	$164,844
70	Larry Ziegler	27	$163,691
71	Walter H. Hall	8	$161,796
72	Calvin Peete	23	$160,025
73	Walter Zembriski	33	$146,573
74	Will Sowles	32	$144,159
75	Harold Henning	32	$140,153
76	David Ojala	19	$137,666
77	Don January	24	$132,947
78	Bunky Henry	19	$107,178
79	Steven Veriato	12	$103,301
80	Dennis Coscina	31	$98,462
81	Tommy Aaron	25	$93,075
82	Don Bies	18	$91,426
83	Bob Betley	10	$74,597
84	Orville Moody	24	$63,506
85	Larry Mowry	20	$62,800
86	Bobby Nichols	29	$58,999
87	Gay Brewer	27	$58,624
88	John Paul Cain	20	$57,351
89	Homero Blancas	20	$49,574
90	Ted Hayes	12	$49,250
91	Ray Arinno	5	$44,339
92	Lee Elder	28	$43,767
93	Jim Ferree	21	$42,276
94	Bruce Devlin	16	$39,063
95	Rik Massengale	6	$38,958
96	Jimmy Adams	3	$37,075
97	Tom Weiskopf	5	$36,943
98	Gene Littler	17	$36,077
99	Austin Straub	9	$33,211
100	Ben Smith	23	$32,846
101	Arnold Palmer	13	$29,052
102	Fritz Gambetta	7	$27,786
103	Deane Beman	9	$23,552
104	Roy Vucinich	2	$23,257
105	Lou Graham	25	$20,314
106	Tom Knapp	5	$19,628
107	Tommy Horton	2	$19,625
108	Robert Thomas	5	$19,480
109	Dick Rhyan	3	$18,119
110	Rives McBee	10	$17,154
111	Robert Zimmerman	3	$16,960
112	David Lundstrom	4	$16,355
113	Billy Casper	10	$15,069
114	Seiichi Kanai	1	$15,000
115	John Rech	3	$14,172
116	Kurt Cox	2	$13,366
117	Bob Panasik	4	$13,188
118	Dave Hill	4	$12,940
119	Bill Hall	5	$12,797
120	Johnny Miller	2	$11,716
121	Harry Toscano	3	$10,195
122	Bob Irving	4	$9,780
123	Ed Sneed	9	$9,543
124	Greg Powers	2	$9,315
125	Tony Perla	4	$9,290
126	Babe Hiskey	5	$9,188
127	Dick Lotz	3	$9,055
128	Masaru Amano	2	$7,920
129	Hank Cooper	1	$7,656
130	Jerry Heard	6	$7,555
131	John Irwin	1	$7,260
132	Bob Leaver	4	$7,248
133	Bill King	2	$7,246
134	Jim Jewell	2	$7,000
135	Tom Bartolec	4	$6,740
136	Pat O'Brien	3	$5,959
137	Jim Wilkinson	2	$5,720
138	Ray Carrasco	2	$5,700
139	Robert Landers	1	$5,520
140	Bill Tindall	2	$5,246
141	Marion Heck	2	$5,236
142	Art Proctor	3	$4,790
143	Don Massengale	3	$4,368
144	Steve Robbins	4	$4,153

145	Bob Lunn	5	$4,091
146	Jerry Bruner	2	$3,998
147	Bobby Mitchell	2	$3,913
148	Chuck Thorpe	1	$3,719
149	Reid Goodliffe	1	$3,700
150	Bruce Lehnhard	2	$3,600

SCORING LEADERS

1997 Schedule
Through the Tour Championship

Rank	Player	Rounds	Avg.
1	Hale Irwin	74	68.92
2	Gil Morgan	79	69.29
3	Isao Aoki	89	70.03
4	Jay Sigel	97	70.37
5	John Bland	104	70.39
6	David Graham	96	70.40
7	Graham Marsh	93	70.47
8	Hugh Baiocchi	79	70.66
9	Larry Gilbert	73	70.71
10	Dave Stockton	89	70.78
11	Bob Eastwood	87	70.91
12	Ray Floyd	64	70.92
13	Vicente Fernandez	91	70.98
14	Lee Trevino	87	70.99
15	Mike Hill	85	71.05
16	Bob Duval	74	71.12
17	Bruce Summerhays	110	71.18
18	John Jacobs	104	71.19
19	Bob Charles	86	71.21
20	Leonard Thompson	93	71.22
21	Jerry McGee	106	71.23
T22	Dana Quigley	62	71.29
T22	Tom Wargo	100	71.29
24	Dave Eichelberger	105	71.32
T25	Jim Colbert	60	71.40
T25	Kermit Zarley	90	71.40
T27	George Archer	79	71.41
T27	Jim Dent	93	71.41
29	Hubert Green	86	71.42
30	Jack Kiefer	106	71.43
31	Walter Morgan	113	71.44
32	Frank Conner	111	71.52
33	J.C. Snead	104	71.53
34	Chi Chi Rodriguez	87	71.64
35	Terry Dill	92	71.71
36	Gibby Gilbert	88	71.77
37	Jimmy Powell	102	71.79
T38	Brian Barnes	86	71.81
T38	Bob Murphy	94	71.81
T40	Al Geiberger	71	71.83
T40	Gary Player	71	71.83
T42	Mike McCullough	109	71.87
T42	John Schroeder	99	71.87
44	Bud Allin	95	71.88
45	DeWitt Weaver	103	71.89
46	John D. Morgan	94	71.96
47	Dale Douglass	95	71.99
48	Jim Albus	80	72.04
49	Simon Hobday	91	72.15
T50	Bob E. Smith	90	72.20
T50	Buddy Whitten	91	72.20
T52	Bob Dickson	102	72.22
T52	Rocky Thompson	90	72.22
54	Bobby Stroble	110	72.24
55	Charles Coody	94	72.30
56	Bob Wynn	56	72.34
57	Tom Shaw	95	72.40
58	Bruce Crampton	107	72.49
59	Dan Wood	73	72.53
60	Larry Laoretti	89	72.54
61	Tony Jacklin	79	72.67
62	Larry Ziegler	82	72.70
63	Butch Baird	95	72.74

64	Calvin Peete	69	72.78
65	David Ojala	58	72.83
66	Miller Barber	101	72.84
67	Don January	71	72.90
68	Bunky Henry	59	73.03
69	Dick Hendrickson	98	73.04
70	David Oakley	105	73.16
71	Rick Acton	100	73.21
72	Will Sowles	97	73.26
73	Harold Henning	96	73.43
74	Tommy Aaron	75	73.51
75	Walter Zembriski	98	73.57
76	Dennis Coscina	94	73.61
77	Don Bies	57	73.81
78	John Paul Cain	59	73.83
79	Homero Blancas	61	73.90
80	Orville Moody	71	73.97
81	Gay Brewer	81	74.27
82	Bobby Nichols	86	74.28
83	Jim Ferree	62	74.31
84	Bruce Devlin	49	74.35
85	Larry Mowry	58	74.66
86	Ben Smith	69	75.39
87	Gene Littler	49	75.57
88	Lee Elder	82	76.01
89	Lou Graham	74	77.82

DRIVING ACCURACY

1997 Schedule

Through the Tour Championship

Rank	Player	Stat
1	John Bland	81.0
2	Calvin Peete	78.9
3	Bob Murphy	77.0
T4	David Oakley	76.9
T4	Bob E. Smith	76.9
6	Hale Irwin	76.0
7	Hubert Green	75.9
8	Chi Chi Rodriguez	75.6
9	Walter Zembriski	75.0
10	David Ojala	74.9

DRIVING DISTANCE

1997 Schedule

Through the Tour Championship

Rank	Player	Stat
1	John Jacobs	290.7
2	Terry Dill	286.6
3	Jay Sigel	285.3
4	Gil Morgan	281.8
5	Bob Duval	278.6
6	David Graham	278.4
7	Ray Floyd	278.3
8	Dan Wood	276.3
9	DeWitt Weaver	275.4
T10	Jim Dent	273.3
T10	John Schroeder	273.3

BIRDIE LEADERS

1997 Schedule

Through the Tour Championship

Rank	Player	Stat
1	Hale Irwin	4.41
2	Gil Morgan	4.28
3	Isao Aoki	4.20
4	David Graham	3.77
5	Frank Conner	3.70
6	Bob Duval	3.65
7	Ray Floyd	3.64
8	Larry Gilbert	3.62

9	Kermit Zarley	3.61
10	Graham Marsh	3.59

EAGLE LEADERS

1997 Schedule

Through the Tour Championship

Rank	Player	Stat
1	David Graham	108.0
2	Terry Dill	110.4
3	DeWitt Weaver	142.6
4	Bob Duval	148.0
5	Leonard Thompson	152.2
6	Gil Morgan	158.0
7	Jay Sigel	158.7
8	Bob Wynn	168.0
9	Dave Eichelberger	171.8
10	Bruce Devlin	176.4

GREENS IN REGULATION

1997 Schedule

Through the Tour Championship

Rank	Player	Stat
1	Hale Irwin	76.2
2	Gil Morgan	74.1
3	Jay Sigel	73.3
4	Hugh Baiocchi	72.2
5	John Bland	72.0
6	David Graham	70.0
7	Brian Barnes	69.5
8	Isao Aoki	69.4
T9	Bob Charles	69.1
T9	Vicente Fernandez	69.1

PUTTING LEADERS

1997 Schedule

Through the Tour Championship

Rank	Player	Stat
1	Hale Irwin	1.734
2	Gil Morgan	1.746
3	Graham Marsh	1.756
4	Dave Stockton	1.762
5	Isao Aoki	1.763
6	Frank Conner	1.764
7	Ray Floyd	1.768
8	Lee Trevino	1.772
9	3 Tied with	1.775

SAND SAVES

1997 Schedule

Through the Tour Championship

Rank	Player	Stat
1	Isao Aoki	64.7
2	John Schroeder	61.7
3	Jerry McGee	59.1
4	Bob Eastwood	59.0
5	Homero Blancas	58.8
6	Don January	56.8
7	Jimmy Powell	56.5
8	John Bland	56.1
9	Simon Hobday	55.5
10	Bob Duval	55.2

1997 ALL AROUND LEADERS

Through the Tour Championship

Rank	Player	Stat

1	Gil Morgan	64
2	Hale Irwin	82
3	Graham Marsh	117
4	David Graham	126
5	Isao Aoki	141
6	Ray Floyd	148
7	Bob Duval	163
8	John Bland	181
9	Jay Sigel	190
10	Larry Gilbert	196

1997 TOTAL DRIVING LEADERS

Through the Tour Championship

Rank	Player	Stat
1	Hale Irwin	32
2	Jim Albus	38
T3	Isao Aoki	39
T3	Gil Morgan	39
T5	Larry Gilbert	44
T5	Graham Marsh	44
7	Jay Sigel	45
8	Brian Barnes	48
9	DeWitt Weaver	49
10	David Graham	51

ALL-TIME MONEY LEADERS

Through the Tour Championship

Rank	Player	Money
1	Lee Trevino	$7,449,561
2	Bob Charles	$7,244,675
3	Jim Colbert	$7,126,797
4	Dave Stockton	$6,636,029
5	Mike Hill	$6,336,905
6	Chi Chi Rodriguez	$6,068,903
7	George Archer	$5,671,991
8	Ray Floyd	$5,580,271
9	Jim Dent	$5,492,510
10	Dale Douglass	$5,140,633
11	Isao Aoki	$5,130,137
12	Hale Irwin	$4,758,308
13	Bob Murphy	$4,618,929
14	Gary Player	$4,478,607
15	Bruce Crampton	$4,391,178
16	Al Geiberger	$4,103,795
17	J.C. Snead	$4,023,511
18	Jim Albus	$3,843,798
19	Miller Barber	$3,800,297
20	Tom Wargo	$3,670,425
21	Rocky Thompson	$3,620,980
22	Jay Sigel	$3,591,156
23	Graham Marsh	$3,494,620
24	Harold Henning	$3,477,381
25	Charles Coody	$3,401,799
26	Jimmy Powell	$3,310,570
27	Gibby Gilbert	$3,258,187
28	Orville Moody	$3,255,400
29	Larry Gilbert	$3,238,187
30	Simon Hobday	$3,232,366
31	Don January	$3,149,496
32	Jack Kiefer	$3,079,621
33	Kermit Zarley	$2,966,836
34	Walter Zembriski	$2,845,480
35	John Bland	$2,712,560
36	Don Bies	$2,607,716
37	DeWitt Weaver	$2,552,059
38	Jim Ferree	$2,385,763
39	Jack Nicklaus	$2,383,180
40	Gil Morgan	$2,317,901
41	Dave Hill	$2,307,253
42	Tommy Aaron	$2,303,853

43	Dave Eichelberger	$2,286,788
44	Larry Laoretti	$2,256,766
45	Walter Morgan	$2,237,346
46	Butch Baird	$2,235,852
47	Gene Littler	$2,184,143
48	Terry Dill	$2,154,434
49	Tom Shaw	$2,136,890
50	Bruce Summerhays	$1,976,195
51	Dick Hendrickson	$1,971,316
52	Ben Smith	$1,957,877
53	Larry Mowry	$1,936,891
54	Gay Brewer	$1,912,917
55	John Paul Cain	$1,798,456
56	Bobby Nichols	$1,797,911
57	Jerry McGee	$1,795,663
58	Rives McBee	$1,711,850
59	Billy Casper	$1,705,828
60	Tom Weiskopf	$1,683,215
61	Arnold Palmer	$1,664,018
62	Dick Rhyan	$1,569,398
63	Larry Ziegler	$1,541,540
64	Lee Elder	$1,531,265
65	Bud Allin	$1,487,040
66	David Graham	$1,444,994
67	Joe Jimenez	$1,336,752
68	John Jacobs	$1,325,807
69	Vicente Fernandez	$1,295,165
70	Bob Dickson	$1,289,929
71	Bob Eastwood	$1,246,908
72	Bob Brue	$1,238,862
73	Don Massengale	$1,238,533
74	Homero Blancas	$1,225,632
75	Tony Jacklin	$1,090,343
76	Frank Conner	$1,089,812
77	Bruce Devlin	$1,082,675
78	Peter Thomson	$1,061,118
79	Bob Betley	$1,038,994
80	Bob E. Smith	$1,036,740
81	Brian Barnes	$949,604
82	Charles Sifford	$928,820
83	Ken Still	$912,016
84	Hugh Baiocchi	$906,565
85	Al Kelley	$870,136
86	John Schroeder	$831,022
87	Calvin Peete	$811,305
88	Bob Wynn	$811,126
89	Bobby Stroble	$785,598
90	Frank Beard	$779,684
91	Lou Graham	$741,633
92	John Brodie	$732,198
93	Harry Toscano	$725,458
94	Charles Owens	$708,583
95	Bob Goalby	$696,871
96	Mike Fetchick	$688,680
97	Rick Acton	$678,627
98	Mike McCullough	$668,934
99	Doug Dalziel	$625,493
100	Babe Hiskey	$613,745
101	Mike Joyce	$609,461
102	Bob Erickson	$609,416
103	Bob Duval	$569,041
104	Hubert Green	$556,402
105	Doug Sanders	$534,117
106	Howie Johnson	$533,600
107	Jim O'Hern	$516,456
108	J.C. Goosie	$498,300
109	Jack Fleck	$456,869
110	Billy Maxwell	$455,252
111	Dick Goetz	$446,335
112	Ed Sneed	$439,626
113	Dana Quigley	$427,774
114	Phil Rodgers	$426,329
115	Dick Lotz	$417,775
116	Roberto De Vicenzo	$406,858
117	Art Wall	$401,555
118	Bill Collins	$396,542

119	Leonard Thompson	$384,806
120	John D. Morgan	$376,711
121	Robert Gaona	$360,789
122	Jim King	$347,116
123	Doug Ford	$342,145
124	Fred Hawkins	$332,688
125	Bill Johnston	$330,065
126	Bunky Henry	$320,804
127	Bob Reith	$318,839
128	Larry Nelson	$312,457
129	Marion Heck	$305,575
130	Quinton Gray	$296,219
131	Chick Evans	$292,843
132	Bob Rawlins	$291,887
133	Robert Zimmerman	$289,975
134	Gardner Dickinson	$284,066
135	Bob Toski	$275,520
136	Paul Harney	$269,152
137	Buddy Whitten	$262,133
138	Dan Morgan	$261,200
139	Deane Beman	$244,281
140	Al Balding	$243,948
141	Jim Cochran	$242,178
142	George Bayer	$240,338
143	Masaru Amano	$240,319
144	Al Chandler	$235,513
145	Art Silvestrone	$222,400
146	Dow Finsterwald	$218,762
147	Bob Boldt	$218,673
148	Paul Moran	$214,303
149	Bruce Lehnhard	$208,096
150	Jose-Maria Canizares	$202,908

SENIOR PGA TOUR 1998 SCHEDULE

Date, Tournament, Location, Current or Defending (D) Champion

January 16-18, **MasterCard Championship**, Hualalai Golf Club, Kailua-Kona, HI, Gil Morgan

January 24-25, **Senior Skins Game**, Mauna Lani Resort, Kohala Coast, HI, Raymond Floyd

January 30 - Feb 1, **Royal Caribbean Classic**, Crandon Park Golf Club, Key Biscayne, FL, David Graham

February 6-8, **LG Championship**, Bay Colony Golf Club, Naples, FL, Hale Irwin (D)

February 13-15, **GTE Classic**, TPC of Tampa Bay, Lutz, FL, David Graham (D)

February 19-22, **American Express Invitational**, TPC at Prestancia Sarasota, FL, Bud Allin (D)

March 9-10, **Senior Slam**, Cabo del Sol Golf Club, Los Cabos, Mexico, Hale Irwin (D)

March 13-15, **Toshiba Senior Classic**, Newport Beach Country Club, Newport Beach, CA, Bob Murphy (D)

March 20-22, **Liberty Mutual Legends of Golf**, Golf Club of Amelia Island at Summer Beach Amelia Island, FL, John Bland/Graham Marsh (D)

March 27-29, **Southwestern Bell Dominion**, The Dominion Country Club, San Antonio, TX, David Graham (D)

April 2-5, **The Tradition Presented by, Countrywide**, Desert Mountain (Cochise Course), Scottsdale, AZ, Gil Morgan (D)

April 16-19, **PGA Seniors Championship**, PGA National Golf Club, Palm Beach Gardens, FL, Hale Irwin (D)

April 20-26, **Las Vegas Senior Classic by TruGreen-ChemLawn**, TPC at The Canyons Las Vegas, NV, Hale Irwin (D)

May 1-3, **Bruno's Memorial Classic**, Greystone Golf Club, Birmingham, AL, Jay Sigel (D)

May 8-10, **Home Depot Invitational**, TPC at Piper Glen, Charlotte, NC, Jim Dent (D)

May 15-17, **St. Luke's Classic**, Loch Lloyd Country Club, Belton, MO, Bruce Summerhays (D)

May 22-24, **Bell Atlantic Classic**, Hartefeld National Avondale, PA, Bob Eastwood (D)

May 29-31, **Pittsburgh Senior Classic**, Quicksilver Golf Club, Midway, PA, Hugh Baiocchi (D)

June 5-7, **Nationwide Championship**, The Golf Club of Georgia, Alpharetta, GA, Graham Marsh (D)

June 12-14, **BellSouth Senior Classic at Opryland**, Springhouse Golf Club, Nashville, TN, Gil Morgan (D)

June 18-21, **AT&T Canada Senior Open**, Glencoe Golf & Country Club, Calgary, Alberta, Canada, Jack Kiefer (D)

June 26-28, **Cadillac NFL Golf Classic**, Upper Montclair Country Club, Clifton, NJ, Bruce Crampton (D)

July 5-7, **State Farm Senior Classic**, Hobbit's Glen Golf Club, Columbia, Md., New event

July 9-12, **Ford Senior Players Championship**, TPC of Michigan, Dearborn, MI, Larry Gilbert (D)

July 17-19, **Ameritech Senior Open**, Kemper Lakes Golf Club, Long Grove, IL, Gil Morgan (D)

July 23-26, **U.S. Senior Open**, Riviera Country Club, Pacific Palisades, CA, Graham Marsh (D)

July 31-Aug. 2, **Franklin Quest Championship**, Park Meadows Country Club, Park City, UT, Dave Stockton (D)

August 7-9, **Burnet Senior Classic**, Bunker Hills Golf Club, Coon Rapids, MN, Hale Irwin (D)

August 14-16, **First of America Classic**, Egypt Valley Country Club, Grand Rapids, MI, Gil Morgan (D)

August 21-23, **Northville Long Island Classic**, Meadow Brook Club, Jericho, NY, Dana Quigley (D)

August 28-30, **Bank Boston Classic**, Nashawtuc Country Club, Concord, MA, Hale Irwin (D)

September 4-6, **Emerald Coast Classic**, The Moors Golf Club, Milton, FL, Isao Aoki (D)

September 11-13, **Comfort Classic**, Brickyard Crossing Indianapolis, IN, David Graham (D)

September 18-20, **Kroger Senior Classic**, The Golf Center at Kings Island Mason, OH, Jay Sigel (D)

September 26-27, **Boone Valley Classic**, Boone Valley Golf Club, Augusta, MO, Hale Irwin (D)

October 2-4, **Vantage Championship**, Tanglewood Park, Clemmons, NC, Hale Irwin (D)

October 9-11, **The Transamerica**, Silverado Resort Napa, CA, Dave Eichelberger (D)

October 16-18, **Raley's Gold Rush Classic**, Serrano Country Club, El Dorado Hills, CA, Bob Eastwood (D)

October 23-25, **Hyatt Regency Maui Kaanapali**, Classic Kaanapali Golf Course (North) Lahaina, HI, Hale Irwin (D)

October 30- Nov. 1, **Ralphs Senior Classic**, The Wilshire Country Club, Los Angeles, CA, Gil Morgan (D)

November 5-8, **Energizer Senior Tour Championship**, The Dunes Golf & Beach Club, Myrtle Beach, SC, Gil Morgan (D)

November 18-20, **Lexus Challenge**, La Quinta Resort and Club (Citrus Course), LaQuinta, CA

December 19-20, **Wendy's Three-Tour Challenge**, Lake Las Vegas Resort, Henderson, NV

LPGA

MONEY WINNERS

Through the LPGA Tour Championship
(Nov. 23)

Rank	Player	Events	Money
1.	Annika Sorenstam	22	$1,236,789
2.	Karrie Webb	25	$987,606
3.	Kelly Robbins	28	$910,907
4.	Chris Johnson	29	$722,330
5.	Tammie Green	25	$595,077
6.	Juli Inkster	24	$557,988
7.	Liselotte Neumann	27	$497,841
8.	Laura Davies	21	$483,571
9.	Nancy Lopez	16	$470,386
10.	Betsy King	30	$469,632
11.	Lorie Kane	30	$425,964
12.	Michelle McGann	26	$421,133
13.	Donna Andrews	26	$393,567
14.	Colleen Walker	28	$384,882
15.	Rosie Jones	25	$381,236
16.	Lisa Hackney	22	$351,272
17.	Jane Geddes	26	$330,424
18.	Alison Nicholas	20	$328,554
19.	Pat Hurst	26	$325,299
20.	Cindy Figg-Currier	30	$317,392
21.	Tina Barrett	27	$315,697
22.	Terry-Jo Myers	24	$313,015
23.	Barb Mucha	25	$309,684
24.	Brandie Burton	25	$300,311
25.	Michele Redman	28	$293,831
26.	Dottie Pepper	24	$292,652
27.	Kris Tschetter	28	$283,661
28.	Deb Richard	29	$268,539
29.	Sherri Steinhauer	33	$267,739
30.	Hiromi Kobayashi	27	$261,814
31.	Meg Mallon	24	$239,337
32.	Gail Graham	26	$223,040
33.	Catriona Matthew	30	$221,276
34.	Cindy Schreyer	31	$212,371
35.	Kim Saiki	29	$210,858
36.	Emilee Klein	28	$208,865
37.	Amy Fruhwirth	26	$200,419
38.	Kathryn Marshall	27	$199,187
39.	Nanci Bowen	23	$199,163
40.	Penny Hammel	29	$195,135
41.	Wendy Doolan	26	$194,506
42.	Alicia Dibos	27	$190,991
43.	Karen Weiss	29	$189,812
44.	Helen Alfredsson	20	$189,441
45.	Leta Lindley	29	$188,828
46.	Nancy Harvey	27	$187,339
47.	Dawn Coe-Jones	22	$183,903
48.	Patty Sheehan	17	$179,453
49.	Dana Dormann	27	$176,655
50.	Wendy Ward	24	$175,264
51	Danielle Ammaccapane	26	$148,352
52	Susie Redman	32	$143,688
53	RachelHetherington	28	$138,019
54	Mayumi Hirase	30	$130,547
55	Helen Dobson	26	$129,482
56	Kim Williams	26	$129,063
57	Pat Bradley	23	$127,376
58	Dale Eggeling	28	$126,888
59	Jenny Lidback	27	$125,505
60	CharlottaSorenstam	25	$118,195
61	Jan Stephenson	27	$116,793
62	VickieOdegard	29	$111,553
63	Joan Pitcock	23	$110,294
64	KristalParker	23	$110,230
65	Cathy Johnston-Forbes	27	$104,951
66	Trish Johnson	15	$104,574
67	Laurel Kean	26	$101,533
68	Marianne Morris	26	$98,272

69	Jane Crafter	22	$96,885
70	CarolineMcMillan	25	$92,480
71	Stefania Croce	24	$92,286
72	Becky Iverson	29	$90,862
73	Kris Monaghan	24	$89,282
74	BarbWhitehead	24	$85,292
75	Laurie Brower	25	$84,406
76	Missie McGeorge	25	$82,714
77	Michelle Estill	28	$81,496
78	Luciana Bemvenuti	26	$81,303
79	Hollis Stacy	22	$79,915
80	Val Skinner	27	$79,709
81	Mardi Lunn	27	$77,944
82	Tracy Hanson	21	$77,539
83	Shani Waugh	18	$74,870
84	Mitzi Edge	26	$74,126
85	Catrin Nilsmark	17	$71,479
86	Beth Daniel	9	$71,402
87	CarinKoch	27	$70,802
88	Allison Finney	26	$69,697
89	JackieGallagher-Smith	25	$68,44989
90	ErikaWicoff	26	$68,42390
91	NancyRamsbottom	24	$67,90491
92	Dale Reid	19	$67,45892
93	Amy Read	20	$66,64193
94	DeniseKilleen	28	$64,35394
95	Vicki Goetze-Ackerman	27	$63,44095
96	JoanneMorley	18	$63,21996
97	Dina Ammaccapane	21	$63,07197
98	Stephanie Maynor	27	$61,03998
99	MaggieHalpin	25	$60,45499
100	Suzanne Strudwick	27	$60,173
101	Sally Little	23	$59,028
102	Kate Golden	18	$58,044
103	KristiAlbers	24	$57,444
104	Mary BethZimmerman	23	$54,938
105	Elaine Crosby	28	$54,722
106	Jill Briles-Hinton	29	$54,592
107	Martha Nause	25	$52,570
108	Anna Acker-Macosko	24	$52,219
109	PamelaKometani	22	$52,049
110	Amy Benz	24	$52,047
111	Vicki Fergon	28	$50,984
112	CristieKerr	27	$49,058
113	Moira Dunn	29	$48,862
114	Ellie Gibson	25	$47,924
115	Lisa Kiggens	28	$47,481
116	Michelle Dobek	26	$44,060
117	Judy Dickinson	15	$43,112
118	Cindy Rarick	26	$41,686
119	Janice Gibson	21	$40,660
120	Angie Ridgeway	25	$40,117
121	Cathy Mockett	23	$39,508
122	Sherri Turner	30	$38,465
123	Julie Piers	29	$38,020
124	Missie Berteotti	24	$37,980
125	Jody Anschutz	20	$37,432
126	Patti Liscio	24	$37,377
127	Eva Dahllof	21	$35,738
128	Jennifer Wyatt	23	$34,797
129	Sherrin Smyers	17	$31,211
130	ErikaHayashida	13	$30,110
131	Jill McGill	28	$30,075
132	Muffin Spencer-Devlin	22	$29,988
133	PamWright	22	$29,172
134	Leigh AnnMills	20	$29,157
135	Renee Heiken	29	$28,994
136	Page Dunlap	10	$27,265
137	Nancy Scranton	23	$27,139
138	Lisa Walters	23	$26,976
139	Lori West	28	$26,431
140	Tina Tombs	18	$25,377
141	Corinne Dibnah	13	$25,056
142	Noelle Daghe	21	$24,597
143	Susan Veasey	27	$24,051
144	Anne MariePalli	25	$24,024

145	Robin Walton	25	$22,985
146	Tracy Kerdyk	20	$22,448
147	KatiePeterson	26	$22,199
148	Michelle Mackall	13	$18,991
149	Laurie Rinker-Graham	14	$18,933
150	Amy Alcott	16	$18,779
151	Pearl Sinn	22	$18,340
152	Leslie Spalding	18	$18,130
153	Alice Miller	27	$18,020
154	Kim Bauer	26	$17,968
155	Kathy Postlewait	24	$17,782
156	DebbiKoyama	9	$16,390
157	SmritiMehra	19	$15,352
158	Melissa McNamara	27	$15,111
159	Kathy Guadagnino	14	$14,319
160	Sharon Barrett	22	$13,962
161	JoAnne Carner	10	$13,344
162	Karen Noble	16	$12,791
163	Heather Drew	14	$12,529
164	Sue Thomas	25	$12,411
165	Robin Hood	20	$12,307
166	Carolyn Hill	10	$12,053
167	Annette DeLuca	20	$11,716
168	Jean Zedlitz	16	$11,704
169	Alice Ritzman	16	$11,666
170	Kim Shipman	16	$10,021
171	Janet Anderson	16	$10,006
172	Shelley Hamlin	20	$9,588
173	NataschaFink	10	$9,523
174	Stephanie Farwig	27	$9,355
175	Laura Baugh	8	$8,228
176	JennyMurdock	14	$7,686
177	KristiCoats	25	$7,607
178	Nancy Taylor	14	$5,850
179	Patty Jordan	20	$5,155
180	Karen Davies	26	$5,154
181	Lenore Rittenhouse	21	$4,008
182	Loretta Alderete	14	$3,503
183	Lauri Merten	7	$2,939
184	JulieBrand	20	$2,604
185	Jerilyn Britz	14	$2,474
186	Barb BunkowskyScherbak	16	$2,368
187	LauraBrown	9	$1,952
188	Donna Wilkins	9	$1,915
189	MicheleVinieratos	16	$1,868
190	Caroline Gowan	13	$1,539
191	Ayako Okamoto	1	$1,433
192	CarolineKeggi	12	$1,320
193	MyraBlackwelder	9	$986
194	Cathy Gerring	9	$841
195	HeidiVoorhees	12	$687
196	Kay Cockerill	5	$574
197	Chela Quintana	22	$564
198	Shirley Furlong	25	$557
199	Rhonda Reilly	9	$510

SCORING LEADERS

Through the LPGA Tour Championship
(Nov. 23)

Rank	Player	
1.	Karrie Webb	70
2.	Annika Sorenstam	70.04
3.	Kelly Robbinst	70.35
4.	Juli Inkster	70.64
5.	Nancy Lopez	70.70
6.	Chris Johnson	70.84
7.	Laura Davies	70.86
8.	Donna Andrews	71.01
9.	Tina Barrett	71.23
10.	Tammie Green	71.24

DRIVING ACCURACY

Through the LPGA Tour Championship (Nov. 23)

Rank	Player	%
1.	Stephanie Maynor	.797
2.	Nancy Ramsbottom	.792
3.	Donna Andrews	.791
4.	Amy Fruhwirth	.781
5.	Caroline Pierce	.778
6.	Penny Hammel	.771
7.	Rosie Jones	.770
8.	Joanne Morley	.769
9.	Michele Mackall	.761
10.	Hiromi Kobayashi	.760

DRIVING DISTANCE

Through the LPGA Tour Championship (Nov. 23)

Rank	Player	Distance
1.	Smriti Mehra	263.0
2.	Jane Geddes	261.3
3.	Laura Davies	258.4
4.	Kris Tschetter	257.0
5.	Michelle McGann	256.2
6.	Kelly Robbins	256.0
7.	Karrie Webb	254.6
8.	Wendy Doolan	253.7
9.	Dale Reid	252.2
10.	Juli Inkster	251.6

BIRDIE LEADERS

Through the LPGA Tour Championship (Nov. 23)

Rank	Player	Stat
1	Kelly Robbins	383
2	Chris Johnson	363
2	Karrie Webb	363
4	Betsy King	357
5	Lorie Kane	336
6	Juli Inkster	329
7	Liselotte Neumann	320
8	Donna Andrews	317
8	Annika Sörenstam	317
10	Michelle McGann	311

EAGLE LEADERS

Through the LPGA Tour Championship

Rank	Player	Stat
1	Kelly Robbins	17
2	Chris Johnson	11
2	Karrie Webb	11
4	Vickie Odegard	9
5	Brandie Burton	8
5	Pat Hurst	8
5	Liselotte Neumann	8
8	Five tied with:	7

GREENS IN REGULATION

Through the LPGA Tour Championship

Rank	Player	Stat
1	Kelly Robbins	.787
2	Karrie Webb	.751
3	Annika Sörenstam	.733
4	Nancy Lopez	.730
5	Donna Andrews	.717
6	Dottie Pepper	.714

7	Sherri Steinhauer	.709
8	Barb Mucha	.706
9	Chris Johnson	.704
10	Jane Geddes	.700

PUTTING LEADERS

Through the LPGA Tour Championship

Rank	Player	Stat
1	Barb Bunkowsky-Scherbak	29.26
2	Brandie Burton	29.34
3	Juli Inkster	29.35
4	Liselotte Neumann	29.36
5	Dana Dormann	29.40
6	Caroline Pierce	29.42
6	BarbWhitehead	29.42
8	Luciana Bemvenuti	29.45
9	Kathy Postlewait	29.46
10	Catrin Nilsmark	29.51

SAND SAVES LEADERS

Through the LPGA Tour Championship

Rank	Player	Stat
1	Caroline Pierce	.567
2	NancyRamsbottom.	.533
3	Laurie Brower	.531
4	Sherrin Smyers	.525
5	Vicki Goetze-Ackerman	.523
6	BarbWhitehead	.513
6	Terry-JoMyers	.513
8	Michelle McGann	.510
9	Patty Sheehan	.508
10	Michele Redman	.505

ALL-TIME MONEY LEADERS

Rank	Player	Money
1	Betsy King	$5,510,481.50
2	Pat Bradley	$5,411,808.03
3	Beth Daniel	$5,135,807.80
4	Patty Sheehan	$5,130,937.01
5	Nancy Lopez	$4,538,135.83
6	Dottie Pepper	$3,685,117.00
7	Amy Alcott	$3,242,555.14
8	Laura Davies	$3,143,308.00
9	Jane Geddes	$2,975,192.30
10	Rosie Jones	$2,895,597.97
11	JoAnne Carter	$2,885,707.63
12	Meg Mallon	$2,807,254.00
13	Ayako Okamoto	$2,741,741.85
14	Juli Inkster	$2,525,817.23
15	Jan Stephenson	$2,427,142.00
16	Liselotte Neumann	$2,295,268.00
17	Colleen Walker	$2,281,470.71
18	Tammie Green	$2,208,218.00
19	Hollis Stacy	$2,127,736.99
20	Val Skinner	$2,106,022.75
21	Judy Dickinson	$2,102,048.92
22	Chris Johnson	$1,954,879.50
23	Deb Richard	$1,946,093.00
24	Michelle McGann	$1,940,964.00
25	Dawn Coe-Jones	$1,918,458.57
26	Danielle Ammaccapane	$1,878,974.00
27	Brandie Burton	$1,844,175.00
28	Sherri Steinhauer	$1,783,349.00
29	Kelly Robbins	$1,778,040.00
30	Sally Little	$1,765,027.80
31	Kathy Whitworth	$1,731,770.01
32	Annika Sorenstam	$1,602,295.00

33	Dale Eggeling	$1,593,559.00	71	Jody Anschutz	$865,209.00
34	Cindy Rarick	$1,568,447.50	72	Joan Pitcock	$835,794.00
35	Alice Ritzman	$1,477,351.32	73	Cathy Gerring	$822,818.00
36	Kathy Postlewait	$1,421,244.27	74	Dana Dormann	$822,753.00
37	Elaine Crosby	$1,410,959.00	75	Robin Walton	$816,654.25
38	Donna Caponi	$1,387,919.73	76	Laurie Rinker-Graham	$810,366.29
39	Donna Andrews	$1,369,618.00	77	Trish Johnson	$789,783.00
40	Vicki Fergon	$1,358,819.59	78	Tracy Kerdyk	$784,903.00
41	Sandre Palmer	$1,354,001.86	79	Cathy Morse	$771,694.08
42	Sherri Turner	$1,350,118.78	80	Allison Finney	$766,187.25
43	Helen Alfredsson	$1,349,233.00	81	Barb Whitehead	$750,182.00
44	Kris Tschetter	$1,346,526.00	82	Sandra Post	$746,714.76
45	Debbie Massey	$1,296,507.13	83	Michelle Estill	$728,135.00
46	Jane Blalock	$1,290,943.62	84	Caroline Pierce	$722,542.00
47	Amy Benz	$1,274,696.15	85	Pam Wright	$714,114.00
48	Martha Nause	$1,266,008.96	86	Lisa Walters	$713,159.00
49	Hiromi Kobayashi	$1,250,216.00	87	Caroline Keggi	$698,023.00
50	Lauri Merten	$1,184,378.65	88	Julie Piers	$688,974.00
51	Missie McGeorge	$1,163,514.25	89	Jenny Lidback	$674,521.00
52	Kristi Albers	$1,149,408.00	90	Janet Anderson	$672,226.84
53	Barb Mucha	$1,148,248.00	91	Laura Baugh	$672,169.17
54	Marta Figueras-Dotti	$1,141,070.00	92	Carolyn Hill	$668,608.29
55	Jane Crafter	$1,125,351.30	93	Shirley Furlong	$665,875.00
56	Nancy Scranton	$1,090,285.00	94	Dris Monaghan	$664,291.00
57	Alice Miller	$1,081,917.72	95	Marianne Morris	$657,446.00
58	Patti Rizzo	$1,072,650.75	96	Maggie Will-Halpin	$657,134.00
59	Sandra Haynie	$1,055,874.57	97	Ok Hee Ku	$644,445.00
60	Missie Berteotti	$1,040,798.00	98	Cindy Figg-Currier	$643,752.00
61	Karrie Webb	$1,002,000.00	99	Emilee Klein	$643,596.00
62	Penny Hammel	$995,935.00	100	Jo Ann Washam	$634,055.04
63	Tina Barrett	$995,678.00	101	Myra Blackwelder	$633,535.82
64	Shelley Hamlin	$973,773.02	102	Gail Graham	$631,511.00
65	Lori Garbacz	$911,341.13	103	Janet Coles	$628,282.33
66	Donna White	$908,589.08	104	Nancy Ramsbottom	$621,315.50
67	Muffin Spencer-Devlin	$892,635.85	105	Mitzi Edge	$616,626.00
68	Judy Rankin	$887,858.44	106	Cathy Johnson-Forbes	$579,178.00
69	Mary Beth Zimmerman	$881,715.29	107	Jerilyn Britz	$576,720.51
70	Barb Bunkowsky Scherbak	$880,502.26	108	Sandra Spuzich	$560,878.03

109	Anne Marie Palli	$546,547.33
110	Penny Pulz	$540,401.66
111	Bonnie Lauer	$539,876.27
112	Kathy Guadagnino	$533,438.25
113	Debbie Austin	$532,972.75
114	Lynn Adams	$529,428.79
115	Susan Redman	$520,004.00
116	Jill Briles-Hinton	$515,624.00
117	Becky Pearson	$511,548.01
118	Silvia Bertolaccini	$511,395.46
119	Michele Redman	$510,126.00
120	Carol Mann	$506,666.00
121	Dorothy Germain	$505,704.33
122	Alison Nicholas	$501,070.00
123	Stephanie Farwig	$483,768.20
124	Marlene Hagge	$481,031.92
125	Lenore Rittenhouse	$470,612.56
126	Nanci Bowen	$458,202.00
127	Cindy Schreyer	$452,137.00
128	Cindy Hill	$442,977.05
129	Katie Peterson-Parker	$441,243.00
130	Lynn Connelly	$440,421.00
131	Terry-Jo Myers	$438,648.00
132	Pat Meyers	$397,488.88
133	Kim Shipman	$396,025.00
134	Alicia Dibos	$392,467.00
135	Cathy Marino	$389,898.45
136	Laurel Kean	$379,722.00
137	Pat Hurst	$371,429.00
138	Jo Ann Prentice	$370,292.87
139	Mickey Wright	$368,770.00
140	Deedee Lasker	$364,297.16
141	Beth Solomon	$362,529.06
142	Amy Fruhwirth	$358,619.00
143	Lisa Kiggens	$357,957.00
144	Susan Sanders	$350,163.00
145	Lori West	$348,701.00
146	Kim Williams	$343,393.00
147	Mary B. Mills	$341,193.00
148	Nina Foust	$339,539.00
149	Florence Descampe	$338,978.00
150	Jennifer Wyatt	$337,674.00
151	Susie M. Berning	$333,160.74
152	Sally Quinlan	$319,559.10
153	Vicki Tabor	$319,139.52
154	Susie McAllister	$317,753.88
155	Cindy Mackey	$313,010.50
156	Sue Ertl	$311,596.10
157	Pearl Sinn	$310,736.00
158	Melissa McNamara	$303,701.00
159	Betsy Rawls	$302,664.00
160	Marlene Floyd	$302,014.87
161	Tracy Hanson	$300,422.00
162	Connie Chillemi	$299,615.00
163	Marci Bozarth	$297,602.00
164	Marilynn Smith	$296,258.03
165	Betty Burtfeindt	$287,742.81
166	Kim Saiki	$286,430.00
167	Martha Faulconer	$284,993.00
168	Clifford Ann Creed	$282,414.49
169	Kathryn Young	$282,397.14
170	Ellie Gibson	$279,194.00
171	Mayume Hirase	$275,772.00
172	Barbara Moxness	$273,361.25
173	Murle Breer	$263,902.37
174	Deborah Vidal	$263,451.00
175	Kathy McMullen	$263,437.49
176	Carin Hj Koch	$258,085.00
177	Heather Drew	$256,569.00
178	Patty Hayes	$254,300.28
179	Stephanie Maynor	$254,131.00
180	M.J. Smith	$253,060.91
181	Pam Higgins	$248,014.92
182	Kathryn Marshall	$242,693.00
183	Robin Hood	$240,764.00
184	Mindy Moore	$240,128.65

185	Janice Gibson	$239,625.00
186	Suzanne Strudwick	$239,358.00
187	Mary Dwyer	$237,075.83
188	Lauren Howe	$236,084.41
189	Gloria Ehret	$235,758.34
190	Vicki Goetze	$234,846.00
191	Beverly Klass	$234,330.88
191	Kathy Cornelius	$228,558.03
293	Kathy Ahern	$222,725.01
194	Nancy Sharff	$213,285.74
195	Cathy Reynolds	$211,806.04
196	Carole Jo Callison Whitted	$207,586.96
197	Catrin Nilsmark	$207,029.00
198	Denise Killeen	$206,016.00
199	Kay Cockerill	$205,664.00
200	Stefania Croce	$205,568.00
201	Sharon Barrett	$203,320.79
202	Karen Davies	$202,191.00
203	Becky Ivereson	$196,979.00
204	Karen Noble	$196,440.00
205	Beth Stone	$195,827.00
206	Tina Tombs	$195,246.00
207	Laurie Brower	$190,924.00
208	Patty Berg	$190,760.00
209	Nancy Harvey	$190,678.00
210	Louise Suggs	$190,475.00
211	Amy Read	$185,769.00
212	Sarah McGuire	$183,901.00
213	Page Dunlap	$183,799.00
214	Judy Kimball Simon	$182,984.96
215	Betsy Cullen	$181,737.74
216	Margaret Ward	$181,699.00
217	Shirley Englehorn	$181,194.32
218	Kathy Hite-James	$178,145.47
219	Mardi Lunn	$177,912.00
220	Sue Thomas	$174,870.00
221	Leta Lindley	$172,634.00
222	Patty Jordan	$172,032.00
223	Heather Farr	$170,038.00
224	Denise Haigh	$169,848.88
225	Barbara Barrow	$165,797.62
226	Nicky Le Roux	$165,281.92
227	Sharon Miller	$164,273.64
228	Jan Ferraris	$164,059.21
229	Angie Ridgeway	$160,308.00
230	Kate Rogerson	$160,147.00
231	Gina Hull	$159,478.00
232	Nancy Brophy	$159,026.00
233	Ruth Jessen	$158,816.00
234	Dianne Dailey	$158,066.90
235	Michelle Mackall	$157,123.00
236	Karen Lunn	$154,183.00
237	Therese Hession	$154,013.83
238	Dina Ammaccapane	$153,878.00
239	Mei-Chi Cheng	$147,287.00
240	Barbara Mizrahie	$145,974.57
241	Carole Charbonnier	$140,834.33
242	Tania Abitbol	$140,000.00
243	LeAnn Cassaday	$139,889.92
244	Bonnie Bryant	$137,293.66
245	Karen Weiss	$136,284.00
246	Gail Toushin	$135,557.39
247	Judy Sams	$134,348.66
248	Leigh Ann Mills	$133,497.00
249	Sherrin Smyers	$133,419.00
250	Caroline Gowan	$130,984.00
251	Mary Murphy	$125,620.00
252	Margie Masters	$122,220.17
253	Sue Roberts	$121,397.91
254	Kristal Parker-Gregory	$118,885.00
255	Helen Dobson	$118,564.00
256	Cathy Mant	$117,022.58
257	Gail Hirata-Chaffin	$116,575.98
258	Cathy Sherk	$115,127.96
259	Catriona Matthew	$114,322.00
260	Gerda Boykin	$114,060.70

261	Nancy Taylor	$113,398.00
262	Jean Zedlitz	$112,465.00
263	Kim Bauer	$111,373.00
264	Debre Steinbach	$111,246.77
265	Mardell Wilkins	$110,726.49
266	Pam Barnett	$110,319.43
267	Louise Parks	$109,264.00
268	Joan Joyce	$107,117.80
269	Beverley Davis	$103,754.88
270	Laura Hurlbut	$103,530.75
271	Jeannette Kohlhaas	$101,112.83
272	Mary Lou Crocker	$100,246.27
273	Charlotte Montgomery	$98,605.97
274	Noelle Daghe	$95,526.00
275	Karolyn Kertzman	$94,224.21
276	Patti Liscio	$93,166.00
277	Linda Hunt	$92,773.36
278	Betty Jameson	$91,740.00
279	Margaret Platt	$91,049.00
280	Catherine Duggan	$90,556.83
281	Mary Lena Faulk	$90,141.50
282	Loretta Alderete	$86,828.00
283	Maria Astrologes Combs	$86,240.63
284	Joan Delk	$83,205.00
285	Shirley G. Spork	$82,720.00
286	Jill McGill	$82,537.00
287	Pam Gietzen	$81,683.75
288	Wendy Ward	$79,461.00
289	Marty Dickerson	$79,295.63
290	Sue Fogleman	$78,826.59
291	Donna Wilkins	$77,386.00
292	Eva Dahllof	$72,541.00
293	Jackie Bertsch	$72,053.28
294	Jocelyn Bourassa	$71,310.00
295	Kate Hughes	$70,713.00
296	Karen Permezel	$70,575.64
297	Michelle Bell	$70,347.00
298	Pamela Allen	$68,992.00
299	Cathy Mockett	$68,432.00
300	Moira Dunn	$67,264.00
301	Julie Cole	$66,567.00
302	Roberta Albers Speer	$66,269.25
303	Michelle Dobek	$66,072.00
304	Amelia Rorer	$65,969.07
305	Sara Anne McGetrick	$65,107.00
306	Marga Stubblefield	$64,246.18
307	Kyle O'Brien Stevens	$64,231.31
308	Renee Heiken	$64,001.00
309	Barbara Romack	$63,663.00
310	Wendy Doolan	$61,985.00
311	Diana Heinicke-Rauch	$61,617.00
312	Lynn Stroney	$59,724.08
313	Nicole Jeray	$59,360.00
314	Karin Mundinger	$59,138.00
315	Terri Luckhurst	$57,066.39
316	Jodi Renner	$54,800.00
317	Kelly Leadbetter	$54,407.00
318	Susan Daniels	$53,292.00
319	Mary Bea Porter-King	$50,253.72
320	Kathy Farrer	$50,034.45
321	Luciana Bemvenuti	$49,739.00
322	Adele Peterson	$49,649.00
323	Kim Cathrein	$47,577.00
324	Kate Golden	$45,433.00
325	Tani Tatum	$45,390.00
326	Alison Munt	$44,272.00
327	Jayne Thoibois	$44,003.00
328	Debbie Skinner	$43,022.57
329	Yuko Moriguchi	$42,137.69
330	Anne Kelly	$42,030.00
331	Susan Beard	$41,962.09
332	Debbie Hall	$41,636.73
333	Rennee Powell	$39,860.36
334	Susan Veasey	$39,405.00
335	Lori Tatum	$36,357.00
336	Peggy Kirsch	$33,921.00

337	Tara Fleming	$33,177.00
338	Sharron Moran	$32,415.00
339	LaRee Pearl Sugg	$30,297.00
340	Lesley Holbert	$28,867.92
341	Janet Le Pera	$28,767.00
342	Lorie Kane	$28,585.00
343	Brenda Goldsmith Hocott	$28,071.98
344	Alice Bauer	$26,156.00
345	Cindy Ferro	$23,893.96
346	Marily Lovander	$23,599.00
347	Carla Glasgow	$23,487.65
348	Sherry Wilder	$21,871.00
349	Denise Philbrick	$21,865.00
350	Leslie Spalding	$21,061.00
351	H.B. Duntz-MacArthur	$19,365.48
352	Jackie Gallagher-Smith	$19,232.00
353	Cindy Scholefield	$18,895.00
354	Cindy Haley	$15,673.00
355	Debbi Koyama	$15,437.00
356	Rebecca Bradley	$15,360.00
357	Ann Walsh	$15,337.00
358	Melissa Whitmire	$14,673.00
359	Patti Berendt	$14,645.00
360	Judi Pavon	$14,518.00
361	Martha Richards	$14,296.00
362	Cynthia S. Anzolut	$14,102.00
363	Laura Brown	$13,722.00
364	Tonya Gill	$13,558.00
365	Pamela Kometani	$13,540.00
366	Shani Waugh	$13,198.00
367	Jean Bartholomew	$12,607.00
368	Tina Paternostro	$12,576.00
369	Joyce Benson	$11,797.34
370	Amaia Arrut	$11,770.00
371	Rhonda Reilly	$11,770.00
372	Michele Ann Thompson	$10,963.00
373	Mary Anne Klinchock	$10,132.00
374	Estefania Knuth	$9,754.00
375	Lia Biehl	$9,038.00
376	Suzy Green	$8,997.00
377	Susan Thielbar	$8,990.00
378	Dale Reid	$8,796.00
379	Gail Davis	$7,440.00
380	Susan Johnson	$7,237.00
381	Kiernan Prechtl	$7,097.00
382	Kelly Holland	$6,963.00
383	Cheryl Stacy	$6,883.00
384	Stephanie Martin-Cobb	$6,648.00
385	Christa Teno	$6,437.00
386	Deborah Lee	$6,255.00
387	Penny Zavichas	$5,771.00
388	Anna Acker-Macosko	$5,625.00
389	Kim Lasken	$5,356.00
390	Mary Bryan	$5,070.00
391	Kristi Coats	$4,920.00
392	Keri Arnold-Cusenza	$4,462.00
393	Michelle Fuller	$4,279.00
394	Terri Thompson	$3,600.00
395	Kerri Clark	$3,591.00
396	Kelly Crawford	$3,291.00
397	Audrey Wooding	$3,228.00
398	Jenny Murdock	$2,675.00
399	Corinne Dibnah	$2,600.00
400	Annette DeLuca	$2,508.00
401	Joal Harding	$2,483.00
402	Jodi Logan Stambaugh	$2,312.00
403	Laura Witvoet	$2,060.00
404	Lisa Marino	$1,729.00
405	Jennifer Graff	$1,570.00
406	Evelyn Orley	$1,499.00
407	Jan Kleiman	$1,403.00
408	Carri Wood	$1,333.00
409	Cameron Seward	$1,114.00
410	Liz Earley	$1,061.00
411	Suzy Whaley	$995.00
412	Kimberly Dirks	$956.00

413	Chris Greatrex	$939.00
414	Linda Galloway	$812.00
415	Liz Rogers	$724.00
416	Heather Cameron	$479.00
417	Jenny Germs	$423.00
418	Becky Larson	$283.00

HALL OF FAME

Year	Player	Induction Method
1995	Betsy King	30 career victories
1994	Dinah Shore	honorary member
1993	Patty Sheehan	32 career victories
1991	Pat Bradley	31 career victories
1987	Nancy Lopez	47 career victories
1982	JoAnne Carner	42 career victories
1977	Carol Mann	38 career victories
1977	Sandra Haynie	42 career victories
1975	Kathy Whitworth	88 career victories
1964	Mickey Wright	82 career victories
1960	Betsy Rawls	55 career victories
1951	Babe Didrikson Zaharias	31 career victories
1951	Louise Suggs	50 career victories
1951	Betty Jameson	10 career victories
1951	Patty Berg	57 career victories

PING LEADERBOARD

Rank	Player	Country	Points
1	Karrie Webb	Australia	463.75
2	Annika Sörenstam	Sweden	454.75
3	Laura Davies	England	346.68
4	Kelly Robbins	US	329.34
5	Liselotte Neumann	Sweden	223.50
6	Chris Johnson	US	206.33
7	Michelle McGann	US	183.48
8	Helen Alfredsson	Sweden	175.61
9	LisaHackney	England	169.08
10	Dottie Pepper	US	168.03
11	Alison Nicholas	England	165.83
12	Juli Inkster	US	164.99
13	Nancy Lopez	US	158.98
14	Tammie Green	US	158.91
15	Jane Geddes	US	156.47
16	MarieLauredeLorenzi	France	150.43
17	AkikoFukushima	Japan	148.58
18	Trish Johnson	England	139.26
19	Rosie Jones	US	132.23
20	Meg Mallon	US	129.00
21	Brandie Burton	US	122.41
22	Hiromi Kobayashi	Japan	120.35
23	Betsy King	US	117.83
24	Donna Andrews	US	116.23
25	Emilee Klein	US	110.96
26	Barb Mucha	US	105.47
27	Pat Hurst	US	99.75
28	Lorie Kane	Canada	95.16
29	Terry-Jo Myers	US	94.58
30	Tina Barrett	US	94.45
31	Kris Tschetter	US	92.45
32	Patty Sheehan	US	89.27
33	JoanneMorley	England	89.02
34	KaoriHarada	Japan	87.14
35	KaoriHigo	Japan	83.99
36	MarnieMcGuire	NewZealand	82.20
37	Deb Richard	US	80.08
38	Karen Lunn	Australia	79.10
39	Kathryn Marshall	Scotland	76.64
40	PatriciaMeunier	France	76.41
41	IkuyoShiotani	Japan	75.72
42	Amy Fruhwirth	US	75.00
43	Kim Saiki	US	74.25

44	Penny Hammel	US	73.75
45	Cindy Figg-Currier	US	73.60
46	Colleen Walker	US	73.42
47	AkiTakamura	Japan	73.25
48	Shani Waugh	Australia	70.25
49	MayumiMurai	Japan	69.63
50	Michele Redman	US	69.43
51	Woo-SoonKo	SKorea	67.38
52	Gail Graham	Canada	65.58
53	CharlottaSorenstam	Sweden	65.10
54	Val Skinner	US	65.09
55	NatsukoNoro	Japan	61.22
56	SuzukoMaeda	Japan	59.93
57	Anne-MarieKnight	Australia	58.92
58	Nanci Bowen	US	57.50
59	Wendy Doolan	Australia	56.75
60	Catriona Matthew	Scotland	56.60
61	JoanneMills	US	56.00
62	Sherri Steinhauer	US	55.70
63	LoraFairclough	England	55.25
64	KarinaOrum	Denmark	55.25
65	LeeYoung-Me	Korea	54.75
66	Beth Daniel	US	54.75
67	LauraNavarro	Spain	54.25
68	Catrin Nilsmark	Sweden	53.33
69	PernillaSterner	US	52.55
70	YukoInoue	Japan	51.75
71	MariaHjorth	US	51.40
72	LoraineLambert	Australia	51.13
73	Ok-HeeKu	Korea	50.98
74	Mayumi Hirase	Japan	50.85
75	Nancy Harvey	Canada	50.50
76	Carin HjKoch	Sweden	50.45
77	FumikoMuraguchi	US	50.25
78	Cindy Schreyer	US	48.76
79	Karen Weiss	US	48.56
80	Corinne Dibnah	Australia	48.50
81	Pat Bradley	US	48.18
82	Jane Crafter	Australia	47.50
83	Marianne Morris	US	47.15
84	MichikoHattori	Japan	46.64
85	MiyukiShimabukuro	Japan	46.50
86	ChiekoNishida	Japan	46.39
87	Dawn Coe-Jones	Canada	46.25
88	SophieGustafson	Sweden	45.88
89	AnnaCJohannson	Sweden	45.55
90	Alicia Dibos	Peru	45.33
91	Ayako Okamoto	Japan	45.13
92	KumikoHiyoshi	Japan	44.88
93	RachelHetherington	Australia	44.67
94	AkaneOhshiro	Japan	44.55
95	Dale Eggeling	US	42.98
96	HelenWadsworth	Wales	42.67
97	Danielle Ammaccapane	US	42.25
98	TinaFischer	Germany	42.17
99	KyokoOno	Japan	42.05
100	Dale Reid	Scotland	41.86

ROUNDS UNDER PAR LEADERS

Through the LPGA Tour Championship

Rank	Player	Rounds	Pct.
1	Karrie Webb	66/95	.695
2	Juli Inkster	60/89	.674
3	Nancy Lopez	35/54	.648
4	Annika Sörenstam	50/78	.641
5	Kelly Robbins	61/96	.635
6	Donna Andrews	54/91	.593
7	Chris Johnson	61/104	.587
8	Laura Davies	40/72	.556
9	Dottie Pepper	46/86	.535
10	Lorie Kane	56/105	.533

TOP TEN FINISH LEADERS

Through the LPGA Tour Championship

Rank	Player	Rounds	Pct.
1	Karrie Webb	21/25	.840
2	Annika Sörenstam	16/22	.727
3	Kelly Robbins	18/28	.643
4	Nancy Lopez	9/16	.563
5	Chris Johnson	15/29	.517
6	Juli Inkster	10/24	.417
7	Donna Andrews	10/26	.385
8	Lisa Hackney	8/22	.364
9	Laura Davies	7/21	.333
10	Two tied with:	8/25	.320

1997 LPGA PLAYER OF THE YEAR

Rank	Player	Stat
1	Annika Sörenstam	313.50
2	Karrie Webb	221.99
3	Kelly Robbins	199.86
4	Chris Johnson	152.70
5	Tammie Green	107.58
6	Betsy King	106.25
7	Colleen Walker	99.50
8	Liselotte Neumann	99.25
9	Juli Inkster	91.50
9	Nancy Lopez	91.50

INDEX OF PLAYERS